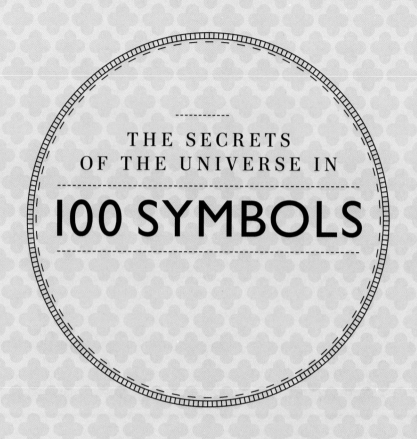

THE SECRETS
OF THE UNIVERSE IN

100 SYMBOLS

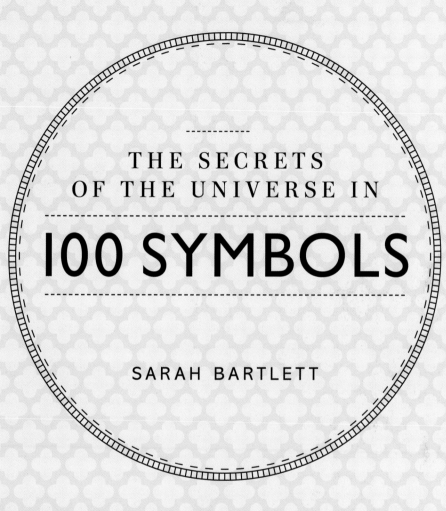

THE SECRETS
OF THE UNIVERSE IN

100 SYMBOLS

SARAH BARTLETT

Fair Winds Press
100 Cummings Center, Suite 406L
Beverly, MA 01915

fairwindspress.com • bodymindbeautyhealth.com

CONTENTS

First published in the USA in 2015 by
Fair Winds Press, a member of
Quarto Publishing Group USA Inc.
100 Cummings Center
Suite 406-L
Beverly, MA 01915-6101
www.fairwindspress.com

19 18 17 16 15   1 2 3 4 5

ISBN: 978-1-59233-676-0

Digital edition published in 2015
eISBN: 978-1-62788-296-5

This book was designed and produced by
Quintessence Editions Ltd.
The Old Brewery, 6 Blundell Street, London, N7 9BH

Project Editor   Becky Gee
Designer   Rod Teasdale
Editorial Assistant   Zoë Smith
Editorial Director   Jane Laing
Publisher   Mark Fletcher

Printed and bound in China

10 9 8 7 6 5 4 3 2 1

SIGNS AND SYSTEMS 124

THE MYSTIC WORLD 186

INTRODUCTION

"A symbol is indeed the only possible expression of some invisible essence, a transparent lamp about a spiritual flame..."

William Butler Yeats

This panel from the Gundestrup Cauldron depicts the horned god Cernunnos, generally thought to be of Celtic origin and described as "lord of the animals."

Humankind has always had an innate urge to express core experiences, such as childhood, virility, fertility, death, sacrifice, and love, through myths and legends, art and architecture, and belief systems. And every culture from every part of the world and every era has used symbols to express those experiences in a universal language that transcends all.

The word "symbol" derives from the Greek *symballein,* meaning "throwing together," as in a moment of sychronicity. The use of an easy-to-recognize symbol connects the strange or mysterious with the familiar to bring immediate illumination and understanding.

In the early twentieth century, Swiss psychologist and psychiatrist Carl Jung wrote: "Every psychological expression is a symbol if we assume that it states or signifies something more and other than itself which eludes our present knowledge." This is why it is empowered with such mystery and fascination. In a flash, the intuitive mind or memory "sees," "understands," or "recalls" a cosmic or secret truth. Jung believed that all human beings are connected to one another through the collective unconscious—a storehouse of knowledge to which every mind has access. He held that every individual inherits all knowledge that has been acquired before, in much the same way that they inherit physical characteristics.

The Secrets of the Universe in 100 Symbols is a beautifully illustrated guide to the origins, application, meaning, and purpose of 100 carefully selected arcane objects, emblems, icons, and motifs that provide insight into and understanding of the mysteries of the universe, as perceived by a wide variety of cultures during every period of history. From the Aztec calendar stone and the spear of destiny to sacred medicine wheels, Egyptian hieroglyphs, and Navaho sandpaintings, each relic, representation, and code is presented and analyzed in detail to reveal the beliefs and practices of past civilizations from all around the globe.

The meaning of a few artifacts featured in this book sadly remains unclear. Historians, cryptographers, linguists, and interpreters continue to strive to understand the Voynich manuscript, discovered in Italy in the fifteenth century. And the seventeenth-century Porta Alchemica, also located in Italy, is decorated with curious sigils, which, according to legend, reveal the formula for turning lead into gold. However, they are yet to be deciphered.

Divided into four chapters, this fascinating volume first takes you through the world of nature. Animals, plants, and the landscape provided the inspiration for the very first ancient symbols, from the phoenix and the serpent to the rainbow and the lotus flower. The various incarnations of such symbols are shown and their original and subsequent evolved meanings revealed and explored. The second chapter introduces you to the world

The Voynich manuscript was hand written in an unidentified language, in cipher, perhaps based on Roman minuscule characters.

The rainbow serpent rock painting at Ubirr Rock, Kakadu National Park, Australia, is a powerful motif of the creation of the universe.

of the divine, in which gods and goddesses have bequeathed their own epithets, motifs, and associations to mortals, from the crescent moon and halo to the all-seeing eye and the cross. As trade between countries developed, symbols traveled, too. For example, the curious horned god Cernunnos, which appears on the Gundestrop Cauldron found in a Scandinavian bog in the second century BCE, is also depicted on the Pashupati Seal (2500–2400 BCE), an ancient image of the Vedic god, Rudra, discovered thousands of miles away in the Indus Valley.

The third chapter explores signs and codified systems: mystical numbers, sacred geometry, mandalas, mantras, and patterns in nature. Early writing systems, such as Sumerian cuneiform,

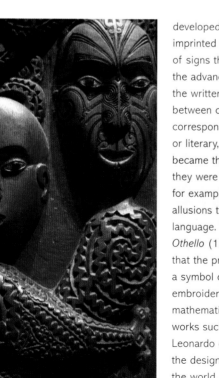

developed from crude marks and pictographs imprinted in clay to an easy-to-use inventory of signs that influenced later alphabets. With the advancement of both mathematics and the written word, ideas were transmitted between cultures. Every letter had a divine correspondence, and whether philosophical or literary, symbolic layers of meaning became threaded within written works as they were within art. Shakespeare's writing, for example, is brimming with symbolic allusions through the characters, plot, and language. This is illustrated in the tragedy of *Othello* (1565), in which the handkerchief that the protagonist gives to Desdemona is a symbol of his love, and the strawberries embroidered on it, a symbol of chastity. In mathematics, the geometric ratios seen in works such as *Vitruvian Man* (1490) by Leonardo da Vinci can also be recognized in the design of ancient buildings throughout the world, in Egypt and Greece, for example.

The Aztec Calendar Stone has the face of Tonatiuh, the Aztec solar god, at its center, surrounded by detailed glyphs.

This nineteenth-century Maori carving depicts Rangi and Papa—sky father and earth mother—in Polynesian mythology.

Opposite: Leonardo da Vinci's *Vitruvian Man* (1490) is a perfect example of the artist's deep understanding of proportion.

Norse gods are closely associated with the magical powers of rune stones, and this twelfth-century tapestry depicts Odin, Thor, and Freyr.

Rosicrucians and Freemasons, cherish an exclusive language that limits the dissemination of rituals and beliefs. The desire to keep secrets and to discover other people's secrets has often led to power plays among emperors and kings. Catherine de' Medici and Elizabeth I of England patronized the most important Renaissance magi of the time. According to some sources, English mathematician and occultist John Dee used an obsidian mirror to reveal the future of the nation to Elizabeth I, while French physician and seer Nostradamus divulged spiritually inspired prophecies to Catherine at the Louvre in Paris.

Throughout the book, in every chapter, you will discover a number of illustrated catalogue pages. Each one displays images of a group of twelve major signs or symbols from a specific culture, whether from the natural, divine, mathematical, or mystic worlds, and explains their meanings. For example, depictions of the twelve Greek gods, including Zeus and his thunderbolt, Poseidon and his trident, and Artemis with her bow and arrow, are presented and their attributes explained. There are also visual catalogues of—among others—twelve American Indian animal emblems, common birds and flowers, the Hindu deities, alchemy symbols, protective amulets, the twelve signs of the zodiac, and the major arcana of the tarot deck. The meanings of each are explored in terms of their historical, cultural, mythological, and religious significance.

Chapter four uncovers the symbolic language of the mystic world, found in astronomy, the zodiac, the tarot, and prophecy. Secret knowledge is a very powerful thing, and such practices have caused great controversy and provided much fascination through the ages. In 1633, at the same time as the great Italian mathematician and astronomer Galileo Galilei was accused of heresy for his theory that the Earth orbited the sun, English astrologer William Lily published his first almanac of zodiac predictions. Both men were considered radical and condemned for their beliefs. Mystical symbols have also been used to invoke gods and spirits, and this chapter features many mysterious objects, such as Chinese oracle bones and the ancient Greek Petelia Tablet, used as tools for such purposes.

Throughout history humankind has shared an innate desire to speak a language that some understand and others do not: to keep our secrets to ourselves or among our brethren or clan. Some secret societies, such as the

In his poem *Auguries of Innocence* (c. 1803), William Blake wrote:

"To see a World in a Grain of Sand
And a Heaven in a Wild Flower,
Hold Infinity in the palm of your hand
And Eternity in an hour."

These words sum up the power of symbols and how they not only evoke emotions and inspiration in each of us as individuals, but also invoke the sense of the divine, and the knowledge that we all share the same experiences and memories.

Opposite: *The Ancient of Days* by William Blake originally appeared as a frontispiece in *Europe a Prophecy* (1794).

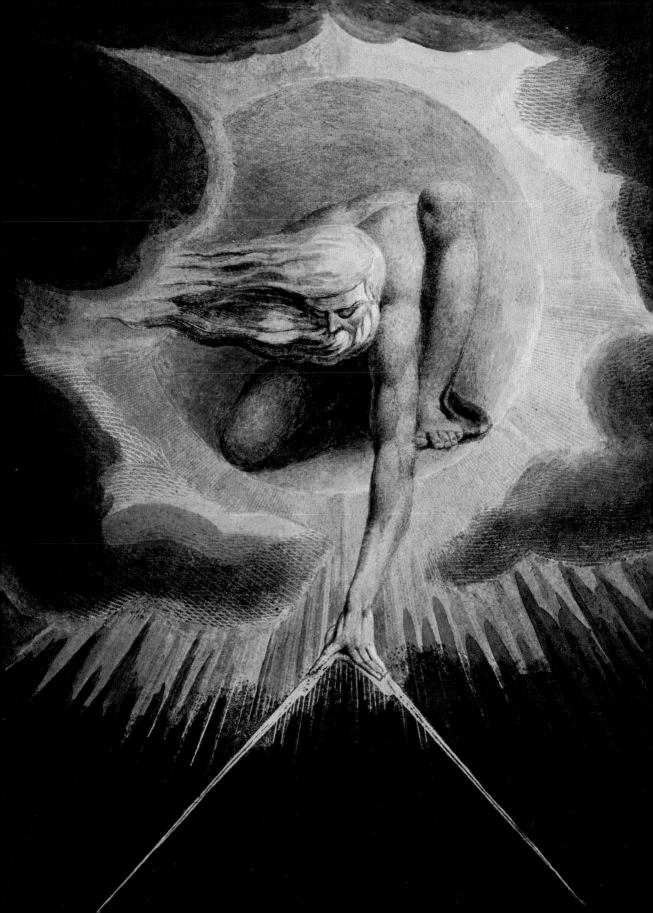

The galactic butterfly is thought to represent all consciousness that has ever existed in the universe. It is the symbol of Hunab Ku, the ultimate Maya creator god.

THE NATURAL WORLD

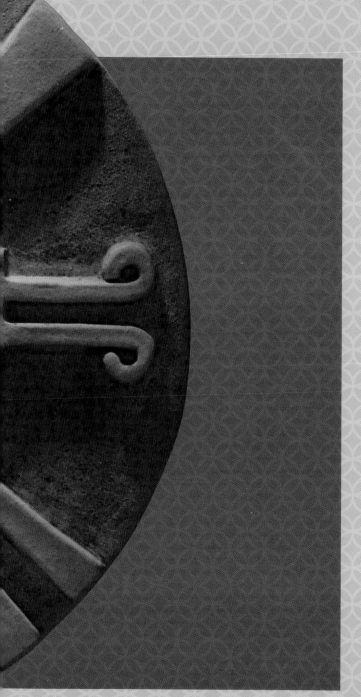

Since the earliest civilizations, humans have developed their communicative powers not only through speech, but also via the early markings and imagery that have been found in caves and in the landscape. Nature was humankind's first inspiration for the language of symbols, and everything in nature—from a bird to a flower to an insect—was identified with particular spirits or numinous beings. Recorded in symbolic form, these deities were often associated with specific aspects of fauna or flora. The Hindu god Ganesha was honored with the head of an elephant; Maya god Camazotz was worshipped as the bat god of the underworld; and the owl was associated with Greek goddess Athena. The influence of Mesopotamian and Greek civilizations and their respect for the natural world can also be seen in the identification of many of the constellations and most of the zodiac signs with animals. Today, nature's archetypal symbols still inhabit our collective unconscious, such as the dove as a symbol of peace, the phallus for virility, and the ubiquitous serpent, which represents the cycle of life.

VENUS PAINTING
CHAUVET-PONT-D'ARC CAVE, ARDÈCHE, FRANCE *c.* 30,000 BCE

Early cave art depicting the vulva, perhaps the first fertility symbol

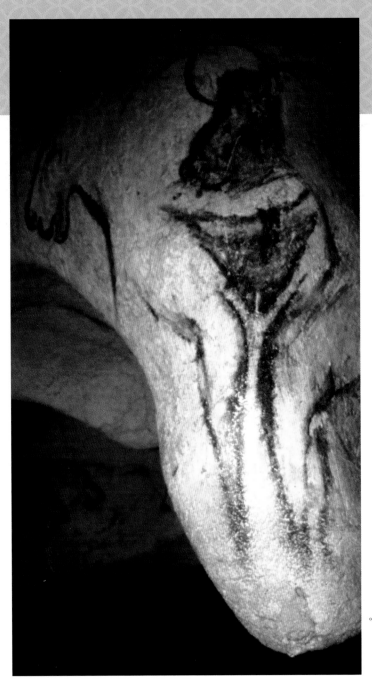

This exaggerated drawing of a female vulva, or Venus, may have been one of the earliest fertility symbols yet discovered.

Tens of thousands of years before the Egyptians had even begun to develop their hieroglyphic language, ancient hunter-gatherers were already leaving their own recorded legacy in the caves of Europe. Hidden among the deep limestone gorges and cliffs of the Ardèche region of France is an extraordinary cave site, unearthed in 1994 and believed to date back more than 30,000 years. Among the earliest discovered cave paintings and drawings to date is, perhaps, the first depiction of a fertility symbol, which went on to become widespread among ancient peoples.

The Chauvet-Pont-d'Arc cave was hidden for thousands of years after an overhanging cliff began to collapse about 29,000 years ago, finally sealing the entrance some 8,000 years later. Inside the many chambers is a collection of elegant, artistic, and spectacular images. These include drawings of red deer, bison, musk-oxen, bears, panthers, horses, lions, and hyenas, all leaping to life in panels across the cave walls. Among the diverse creatures is a bizarre drawing of a minotaur-like beast, painted above the lower body and exaggerated pubic triangle of a female body. There is also a collection of ocher outlines of hands and a series of patterned dots among an array of predatory animals, as well as a claviform symbol: a club-shaped motif similar to a distorted "P." The claviform symbol's meaning is not only much disputed by scholars but also open to subjective interpretation. Some say it represents the female upper body as seen from the side; others that it could be an early phallic symbol.

ABSTRACT MARKINGS

Abstract markings, such as lines and dots—plus two images that could be butterfly or bird shapes—are found throughout the Chauvet-Pont-d'Arc cave. This combination of subjects has led some experts in prehistoric art to conclude that there was a ritualistic aspect to the paintings. It is believed that the various series of red dots in the cave are a kind of signpost from shaman to people, not unlike the way that flashing neon lights currently might indicate where to find a restaurant or bar. Elsewhere, red ocher hand prints and stencil panels were made by spitting pigment over hands, which were then pressed against the cave surface. They were, perhaps, the calling cards of those who came to the cave for shelter or ritual practices. From what is known of Higher Paleolithic cultures, these people formed their own rituals and beliefs where animal, man, and fertility were sacred. Undoubtedly, the cave art and its symbolic embellishments bring to life the distant past and give meaning to a little known culture.

One of the most important images found in the Chauvet-Pont-d'Arc cave is called "Venus and the Sorcerer," and it is located in the deepest of the chambers, the Salle du Fond. Hanging from the ceiling of the 23-foot-high (7 m) cave is a vertical cone of limestone, which ends in a point 3½ feet (1.10 m) from the floor. On this hanging outcrop, "Venus and the Sorcerer" is drawn in black charcoal pigment.

VENUS AND THE SORCERER

The pubic triangle of Venus is at eye level, in the center of the composition, and it is now known to date back several thousand years earlier than her companion, the Sorcerer or man-bison. "The Sorcerer" is a term often used by archaeologists to describe anthropomorphic images that are thought to represent shamans. Chauvet's sorcerer resembles the later Greek mythical animal, the minotaur, his ferocious pagan power looming large. The Venus image dates from the first period of the decoration of the Chauvet cave, during the Aurignacian period of Upper Paleolithic culture. Also seen in the later Venus figurines of Central and

Eastern Europe, such as the Venus of Laussel (c. 25,000 BCE) in the Dordogne region of France, the exaggerated female vulva was an iconic symbol of the power to give life, and may have its origins in the cave rituals of this period. The Aurignacian culture existed from 37,000 to 27,000 years ago and is characterized by the use of bone tools and blade flint technology. The Venus image confirms that the Chauvet cave paintings are, to date, the oldest ever discovered.

With an impressive array of animal characters, the cave exhibits a true gallery of Paleolithic art, relating through images and symbols the culture's way of life and its belief system. In one chamber, a superb portrait of an owl watches over a bear skull placed on a rock. This was believed to be a form of sacred ritual involving ferocious cave bears that were both hunted and venerated. Bears, panthers, lions, and horses were as sacred as the spirits or forces of thunder, rain, and sun, and these are probably the earliest symbols found to reveal a belief in animism: that some divine force flows through everything, whether animal, thunder, or the sun.

The dots and patterns found in cave art are thought to be the earliest form of writing, long before the development of hieroglyphs.

RAINBOW SERPENT
KAKADU NATIONAL PARK, AUSTRALIA *c.* 25,000–20,000 BCE

Powerful Aboriginal creation motif

The rainbow serpent at Nourlangie Rock is a much more ferocious depiction than that at Ubirr Rock, with two rows of long pointed teeth.

At Ubirr Rock in Kakadu National Park, Australia, there is a sacred site known as the Rainbow Serpent Gallery. Here, a simple but vivid Aboriginal rock painting depicts a snake slithering across a solitary rock face. Although the serpent is not literally rainbow colored, it is a powerful motif of the time of the creation of the universe, known to the Aboriginal peoples as the "Dreaming." The painting is one of the oldest known images in Aboriginal art, and the rainbow serpent continues to be a cultural influence today among the indigenous peoples of Australia.

Some accounts of the rainbow serpent claim that the snake emerged from a water hole or came down from the sky during the Dreaming, creating life, water, and fertility. As it slithered across the continent, its movement created the valleys, mountains, and waterways that formed the sacred ancestral landscape.

As the rainbow serpent crossed the land, it "sang" the rocks, plants, animals, and people into existence. Known as song lines or dreaming tracks, the paths it followed became sacred invisible pathways that meander all across Australia. In various local mythologies, the serpent can be female, male, or even androgynous, and it is known by different names, including Julunggul, Kunmanggur, Ungar, or Yurlunggar.

Some scholars have suggested that the link between snake and rainbow was a powerful symbol of the cycle of the seasons and the importance of water in human life. When a rainbow is seen in the sky, it is said that the rainbow serpent is moving from one water hole to another, replenishing the stores of water, and forming gullies and deep channels as she slithers across the landscape, which explains why some water holes never dry up during a drought. Without serpent power, no rain would fall and the earth would dry up. The rainbow serpent is also identified with the halo around the moon that can be regarded as a sign of rain and has divine healing power. Quartz crystal and seashells are associated with the serpent and are used in rituals to invoke its power. It is said, even today, by the indigenous people of Arnhem Land, Australia, that the snake can be seen as a rainbow in the sky, as the colors in mother-of-pearl, or as the spectrum of light across a water hole.

The rainbow serpent is also associated with human blood, especially the menstrual cycle, and blood rituals were once performed in honor of the Aboriginal mother goddess, Kunapipi, who followed the rainbow serpent down to Earth and created people, plants, animals, and insects. Traditionally, the female menstrual cycle is considered sacred to the rainbow serpent, and the most common Aboriginal rainbow serpent myth is the story of the Wawalag sisters. According to legend, the sisters and their offspring were traveling across the land when the older sister gave birth, and her blood flowed to a water hole where the rainbow serpent lived. Tracing the scent back to the sisters who were sleeping in their hut, the snake slithered through the doorway and devoured the women and their children. After being bitten by an ant, the serpent regurgitated the sisters, thus creating Arnhem Land. The shelter is still considered a women-only site, although the rule is relaxed for tourists.

AFRICAN MYTHOLOGY

The rainbow serpent appears as an important part of creation in several African mythologies, such as in Benin, Nigeria, and the Congo, but also features in Haiti, Polynesia, and Papua New Guinea. If, as is believed, indigenous Australians migrated from Africa and arrived in Australia around 50,000 years ago, it is likely that they carried the archetypal image of the rainbow serpent with them, whether through oral narratives or their collective unconscious. Gradually dispersing across the Australian continent over time, these ancient peoples expanded and differentiated into hundreds of distinct groups, each with its own language and culture.

In Africa, the Fon people of Benin believed that the rainbow snake, known as Ayida-Weddo, served the androgynous creator deity Nana Buluku by holding up the heavens. Another West African myth relates how an enormous serpent formed 7,000 coils beneath the earth, protecting it from falling into the Abysmal Sea. It scattered stars in the firmament, shot thunderbolts to Earth, and released the sacred waters to fill the planet with life. As the first rains fell, a rainbow appeared in the sky and mated with the serpent. The spiritual nectar that they created became the milk of women and the semen of men. The serpent and the rainbow taught humankind the link between blood and life—menstruation and birth—and the voodoo sacrament of blood rituals.

Today, the rainbow serpent is still revered by indigenous Australian and African peoples. Aboriginal peoples re-create the story of the rainbow serpent eating the Wawalag sisters during the Dreaming through song, music, and dance. The Rainbow Serpent Festival is an annual Australian music festival, and Aboriginal artists continue to be inspired by the ancient myths and images in their artwork.

The orange rainbow serpent is said to have stopped at Ubirr Rock as she "sang" everything into existence. The site has been sacred to women ever since.

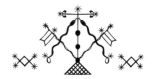

Ayida-Weddo's *veve* is always combined with that of her husband, the sky god Damballa.

SERPENTS

MUCALINDA

Mucalinda was king of the Nagas, a snakelike race of deities. When Buddha was seeking enlightenment under the bodhi tree, the heavens darkened. Mucalinda rose from the earth and protected Buddha from the storm with his cobra's hood. When the rains had gone, the serpent bowed before Buddha and returned to his palace.

JÖRMUNGANDR

The offspring of the giantess Angrboða and the trickster god Loki, Jörmungandr became a sea serpent when Odin tossed him into the ocean. He grew so large that he was able to surround the Earth and grasp his own tail. As a result, he became known as the world serpent. When he lets go of his tail, the world will end.

SHESHA

According to the *Mahabharata*, Shesha was a prince of the Nagas. Brahma was impressed by him and entrusted him with the duty of carrying the world. With this news, Shesha entered a hole in the Earth and slithered all the way to bottom, where he then pulled the Earth over his head to become the serpent upon whom Krishna slept.

NEHEBKAU

A benevolent Egyptian snake god, Nehebkau was one of the original primeval gods. He was linked to the sun god, swimming around in the chaotic waters before creation, and was bound to the sun god when time began. He was also a god who protected the pharaoh, both in life and in the afterlife. Nehebkau is often depicted with two heads.

PYTHON

In pre-Olympian Greece, Python was an earth dragon who lived at Delphi and was originally the oracle for Gaia, Mother Earth. Later, Python became the enemy of Apollo, who eventually destroyed him. Apollo made Delphi his own oracle, and the priestess, Pythia, drew her power from the rotting corpse of the dead snake.

SERPENS

Serpens is part of the constellation of Ophiuchus, and is depicted as either winding around Ophiuchus in the night sky or simply passing through him. Ophiuchus was identified with Laocoön, the priest who warned his fellow Trojans about the Trojan horse. Laocoön was later slain by a pair of sea serpents, one of which was Serpens, sent by Poseidon to punish him.

WADJET

Protector of kings and of women in childbirth, Wadjet is associated with the land and is depicted as a snake-headed woman, or as a deadly Egyptian cobra. She is identified as a goddess, and her oracle is renowned in the temple at Per-Wadjet. This oracle was probably the source for the oracular tradition that spread to Greece from Egypt.

COATLICUE

The Aztec goddess who gave birth to the moon, the stars, and the sun, Coatlicue is known as "the lady of the serpents." She was sacrificed at the beginning of creation, when two serpent heads sprang from her decapitated body. She represents the devouring earth mother in whom both the womb and the grave exist.

THE SERPENT IN THE GARDEN OF EDEN

In the Garden of Eden, although God had warned Adam not to eat from the Tree of Knowledge, the serpent tempted Eve to eat the fruit, which she then gave to Adam. When God found out, he banished Adam and Eve. The snake was punished by being made to crawl on its belly in the dust forever.

NAGA

The nagas were a race of serpent deities who were in constant battle with the great eagle king Garuda. Their epic tales are recounted in the *Mahabharata*. One of the eight great serpent kings, Vasuki, known as Shiva's serpent, helped the gods to recover the elixir of immortality from the depths of the Ocean of Milk.

BASILISK

In medieval Europe, the basilisk was a legendary reptile alleged to be hatched by a cockerel from the egg of a serpent or toad. Much feared in medieval bestiaries, it was said to have the power to cause death with a single glance. According to some legends, basilisks could be killed if they heard the crow of a rooster or gazed at themselves in a mirror.

AVANYU

A Tewa deity, the serpent Avanyu is the guardian of water. Represented variously as a horned or plumed serpent, its many depictions suggest flowing water or the zigzag pattern of lightning. Potrayals of Avanyu appear on the walls of caves located high above canyon rivers in the American Southwest and New Mexico.

HAND PRINT

CUEVAS DE LAS MANOS, PATAGONIA, ARGENTINA *c.* 7000 BCE

Prints and stencils of hands in hunter-gatherer communities

Hundreds of hand prints across cave walls in a remote Patagonian river valley suggest an ancient nomadic people used the caves as a stopover while hunting their prey.

Cuevas de las Manos (Cave of Hands) is a rock art site that not only documents the stories of hunters and the animals that they hunted, but also includes an extraordinary display of hand prints and stencils. Many scholars believe that each hand print is a personal signature of each person's visit—like a calling card, snapshot, or self-portrait—left as reminders for future generations of hunters. However, other scholars believe that the stenciled or painted hand prints, many the size of teenage boys' hands, could be part of an initiation ritual or rite of passage ceremony to celebrate manhood. These peoples were probably the ancestors of the historic hunter-

gatherer communities of Patagonia, discovered by European settlers in the nineteenth century and known as the Tehuelche.

The cave takes its name from the numerous drawings and stencils of hands that can be found across the cave walls. The caves are considered by the international scientific community to be one of the most important sites of the earliest hunter-gatherer groups in South America, dating back to around 7000 BCE.

They lie in a remote river canyon in the middle of the desert northwest of Santa Cruz, with the nearest town, Perito Moreno, some 101 miles (163 km) away. This whole area, which includes the Perito Moreno National Park, is a rich archaeological and paleontological site. The river valley's only sounds are those of the murmuring Patagonian wind and the myriad cries of birds, while a few shrubby trees straggle across the canyon floor to add a welcome dash of green to the barren mountains rising above. Nine thousand years ago, an entire community of primitive hunter-gatherers passed through the river valley and stayed in the Cuevas de las Manos as they followed their prey across Patagonia.

The caves were last inhabited around 700 CE, and the paintings show scenes in which proud displays of guile were more important in the hunt than the kill itself. In one tableau, a crack in the rock represents a ravine into which the hunters chased their prey. Some animals are surrounded by men; others are trapped in ambushes. A number of animals are attacked by hunters using throwing weapons known as "bolas." These were made from large stones with weights on the ends of interconnected cords, designed to capture animals by entangling their legs.

THREE CULTURES

The cave paintings belong to three distinct cultures, and the artistic sequence of cave art began as early as 7300 BCE. However, within the rock shelter itself there are five concentrations of rock art. Frequently, later figures and motifs were superimposed upon those from earlier periods. The first human group comprised long-distance hunters whose main prey was the guanaco (a llama-like animal and a main source of food.) Around 7000 BCE a second cultural level can be identified, distinguished by the many hand stencils, and this culture lasted until around 3300 BCE, when the art became more stylized and included a number of zoomorphic and anthropomorphic figures.

The final culture began around 1300 BCE. The pigments used were of a much brighter red, and the designs concentrated on abstract geometric figures and stylized representations of animals and humans. These paintings are believed to

have been the work of the historic Tehuelche hunter-gatherers who inhabited the vast area of Patagonia up until the first Spanish traders and settlers arrived. The Tehuelche were essentially nomadic people, who lived during the winter on the lowlands, catching fish and shellfish. During spring they migrated to the central highlands of Patagonia and to the Andes, where they spent the summer and hunted game.

It was not until the nineteenth century that the development of enormous cattle ranches in many parts of Patagonia put an end to their nomadic way of life. The Tehuelche community no longer exists, but this remarkable display of red hands is a lasting testament of a people who lived according to the seasons, and who hunted and revered animals such as the guanaco, which symbolized the daily survival of an ancient people.

Rock art depictions in Cuevas de las Manos also include geometric shapes, zigzag patterns, red dots, representations of the sun, lizards and spiders, pregnant animals, baby animals, and evil spirits. Dots on the roof have been thought by some archaeologists to represent the stars in the sky, or a game in which children would throw painted balls into the air to hit the ceiling. The ancient residents of Cuevas de las Manos are some of the earliest narrators of history in which art became a meaningful representation of early beliefs and lifestyle.

Although some hand prints date back to about 1300 BCE, these were placed over even earlier prints dating as far back as 7000 BCE.

Ancient cave hand prints are considered to be personal signatures of individual hunters.

JUDACULLA PETROGLYPH
JACKSON COUNTY, NORTH CAROLINA, USA *c.* 3000–1000 BCE

Sacred site where Cherokee American Indians contact the spirit world

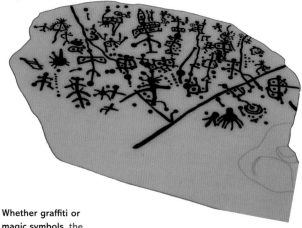

Whether graffiti or magic symbols, the origins of these strange markings have mystified archaeologists for many years.

The Judaculla petroglyph is covered in a strange combination of signs and symbols, and the quest to discover who was responsible for these markings has been a controversial one, shrouded in mystery for many hundreds of years. Made of soapstone and thought to date from thousands of years ago, this large boulder has been recently under the scrutiny of archaeologists in North Carolina. Currently, they believe that the inscriptions were made before the arrival of the Cherokee and probably date from 3000 to 1000 BCE. They believe that over a period of thousands of years, various native peoples came to the Judaculla rock to carve bowls, pipes, and ritual implements, and it may even have been a sacred place where rituals and ceremonies were held. The smaller petroglyphs on the rock could be marks of "graffiti" left by visitors to the rock or magic symbols carved by American Indian shamans.

Other archaeologists believe that the stone is in fact a large map of the area, showing various rivers as routes and markers for trade and travel. These include Little Tennessee River and the Nantahala River. The locations of the rivers are similar to accurate maps today.

There are several petroglyphs in the southeast United States, but the Judaculla rock is one of the largest in Jackson County, North Carolina. The large rock is so densely covered with petroglyphs that distinguishing individual symbols is difficult. However, no other rock in the area has similar markings, and these include abstract lines, humans, animals, and bar and dot glyphs, as well as celestial shapes and geometric figures. Several of these symbols or glyphs correspond to the Mexican Chontal Maya people's pictographs, such as the image of the Great Sun. The Chontal Maya's mythology is filled with supernatural water and mangrove beasts and creatures, as seen in several images depicted on the rock, and it is also probable that they traded far and wide. Could they have traveled this far from home?

According to more recent legends of the American Indian Cherokee, the markings were made by a slant-eyed giant named Tsul'kalu', a great hunter who lived in nearby mountains. One day he jumped from his mountaintop home and landed on the soapstone. In the process, he scratched the rock with his seven-fingered hands. Other legends tell of different giants visiting the Cherokee. They were nearly twice as tall as average men, and their eyes slanted in their heads. The Cherokee called them Tsunil'kälû' or the slant-eyed people. These giants lived very far away in the direction in which the sun goes down. The Cherokee received them as friends, and they stayed for some time until they returned to their home in the west.

The Cherokee used highly decorative symbols and were known to decorate everything from their horses and bodies to their homes. Many of these symbols were spiritual in nature, connecting the Cherokee to the spirits of their ancestors, or were secret messages to

communicate between clans. It is also possible that the symbols scrawled on the rock are messages or map directions left for various tribes or clans, providing routes between rivers and landscape.

On the Judaculla rock is a series of patterns made up of seven points or spokes and also of circles and crosses. The numbers four and seven repeatedly occur in Cherokee myths, stories, and ceremonies. The number four represents earth, wind, fire, and air, and the four cardinal directions: east, west, north, and south. The number seven represents the seven clans of the Cherokee. In addition to the four cardinal directions, three others exist, adding up to the seven spokes. These are up (the Upper World), down (the Lower World), and center (where we live now).

The legendary figure of Tsul'kalu', or the slant-eyed giant, was known as the great lord of the game, and was invoked in Cherokee hunting rites and rituals.

SPHINX

GIZA, EGPYT *c.* 3000–2500 BCE

Potent symbol of the pharoah as sun and lion king

The sphinx is one of the best-known symbols worldwide, but its true origins are still a controversial subject among scholars today.

The sphinx is an ancient symbol associated with the sun in Near Eastern civilizations. For the dynastic pharaohs, it became a tradition to replicate the king's face and head carved on top of a lion's body at their tomb complex. This affinity of pharaoh and lion demonstrated that the king was united with the powerful solar deity Sekhmet, daughter of the sun god Ra, who is depicted herself with the head of a lioness. As a solar symbol, the sphinx was also associated with Harmakhis, Lord of the Two Horizons, who represents the rising and setting sun identified with rebirth and resurrection. The sphinx's dual nature later came to reflect the dual nature of Christ, who was both human and divine. Like other solar symbols, the sphinx was placed in or near early Christian graves to represent the divine Light of the World.

Most scholars conclude that the Great Sphinx of Giza in Egypt was constructed around 2500 BCE by the Old Kingdom pharaoh Khafre. However, others believe that it may well have been the focus of solar worship between 3000 and 2700 BCE, long before the Giza Plateau became a necropolis.

The Egyptian sphinx became a powerful symbol of the pharaoh as sun and lion king. Animal and pharaoh merged into one super being, who was not only the symbolic guardian of the tomb, but also the divine power and

PREDECESSORS OF THE SPHINX

The Lowenfrau goddess, known also as the lion man, is a 32,000-year-old Aurignacian statue that is the oldest known figure of a human body with a lion's head. However, there is much dispute as to whether the body is male or female. Another likely predecessor of the sphinx is the ancient Assyrian Lamassu, or Shedu (right), first depicted around 3000 BCE. Considered to be a beneficial and protective spirit, the Lamassu was portrayed in works of art as a winged lion or bull with the head of a human male. In Hinduism, Narasimha was a man-lion, thought to be an avatar or incarnation of the Hindu god Vishnu. He had a humanlike torso and lower body, with a lionlike face and claws. Known primarily as the "Great Protector," he defended and protected his devotees in times of need. In Persian myth, a creature called the Manticore had the body of a red lion, a human head with three rows of sharp teeth, sometimes bat wings, and a trumpetlike voice. Occasionally it was horned and winged, and even had a dragon or scorpion's tail. Shooting poisonous spines to paralyze its victims, it devoured them whole.

wisdom with which the pharaoh ruled and protected his people. It later became a symbol of mysteries, truth, and unity. At the Giza site, an inscription on a stele by Thutmose IV in 1400 BCE lists three aspects of Ra, known as Khepera-Re-Atum, a more complex solar deity worshipped during that later period.

GREEK SPHINX

Based on a mythological beast with a lion's body and a woman's head, the Greek sphinx also had the wings of an eagle. Sitting atop the cliffs overlooking the entrance to the Greek city of Thebes, according to the myth of Oedipus, the sphinx asked every traveler a riddle before they could enter the city. If they answered wrongly, the sphinx would strangle and eat them. The riddle—"What has four legs in the morning, two at noon, and three at night"—was solved by Oedipus, who answered: "Man—who crawls on all fours as a baby, walks on two feet as an adult, and then uses a walking stick in old age." When Oedipus replied correctly, the sphinx

threw herself from the high rock to her death. By some accounts there was a second riddle— "There are two sisters: one gives birth to the other and she, in turn, gives birth to the first. Who are the two sisters?" The answer was "day and night" because both words are feminine gender in Greek. Since Greek times, the sphinx has become symbolic of riddles, thresholds, and the transition from life to death.

In European decorative art, the Greek sphinx enjoyed a major revival during the Renaissance and is sometimes thought of as the French sphinx. It was particularly popular in the late Baroque style of art in the early eighteenth century, and in the Romantic and Symbolist art movements of the nineteenth century.

As a guardian of mysteries, the sphinx was adopted as a Masonic emblem and is found as a decorative sculpture in front of Masonic temples, or engraved at the head of Masonic documents. However, it is not an ancient symbol of the order. Its introduction is relatively recent, rather as a generic decoration than as a symbol of a particular belief.

Shedu was one of the early predecessors to the Egyptian sphinx. This strange Mesopotamian creature was made up of a winged bull with a man's head.

The sphinx has been used as a symbol of riddles and as a motif in European art since Roman times.

SCARAB

EGYPT *c.* 2613–2160 BCE

A popular sacred motif associated with rebirth and regeneration

"come into being," and as an aspect of Ra, Khepri was not only the bringer of the dawn, but also of bringing the world into being. But why did Khepri have a scarab beetle head, and how did this image evolve as an amulet?

According to archaeologists and scholars, wise Egyptian scribes recorded their observations of the strange behavior of the scarab. They noticed that the beetle rolled a ball of animal dung along the ground everywhere it went, and after a while tiny larvae hatched from the dung ball. As the young beetles miraculously emerged fully formed, just like the sun as it rises every day above the horizon, they were thought to possess the same magical power as the sun

The heart scarab of Sobekemsaf II (*c.* 1590) has a green jasper scarab set in a hollow-sheet gold plinth. The hieroglyphs, taken from The Book of the Dead, recount a spell to prevent the heart from "opposing the deceased" to enable the soul to reach eternal bliss.

Tutankhamun's gold name pendant, inlaid with colored glass and semiprecious stones, is made up of three symbols: the turquoise basket represents the god Neb, the lapis lazuli scarab represents Khepri, and the sun disk inlaid with carnelian symbolizes Ra.

One of the most popular symbols in ancient Egyptian belief, the great scarab beetle was considered the most sacred of insects. The image of the scarab was originally associated with the solar deity Khepri, who was an aspect of the great sun god Ra. This led to the use of the scarab as an important protective amulet for both royalty and for the deceased. Today it is commonly seen in jewelry design, but some traditional Egyptians still believe that taking dried scarab powder will help boost their virility.

The god Khepri was depicted as a human male with a scarab beetle head, or sometimes as scarab beetle only. He represented the rising sun, itself a deeper symbol of the dawn of mankind and the creation myths of ancient Egypt. The Egyptian word *kheper* means to

god. Therefore, they became a sacred symbol of creative manifestation, and like Khepri, they assured the sun's rebirth each day.

As ancient Egyptian religion was concerned with rebirth and resurrection, the beetle's habits came to symbolize these elements, too, and the insect became associated with the daily journey of the sun across the sky. Similar to the rolling dung ball, Khepri rolled the sun across the sky every day, then took it to the otherworld at night. Sometimes scarab-headed Khepri was depicted in a solar barge making his way along the horizon, transforming not only night to day, and day to night, but also into a psychopomp, taking human souls to the afterlife.

PROTECTIVE AMULETS

Scarab beetle amulets began to appear as protective devices in the Old Kingdom period—approximately 2613 to 2160 BCE. Mainly worn as a protection against the evil eye, they were carved from precious stones and were often personalized and inscribed with seals, and also the names of pharaohs and scribes. They were commonly used for official and political purposes, and later as funerary decoration.

The so-called "heart scarab" was made from black or dark green stone, such as jasper or the darkest carnelian, and typically measured between 1 ½ and 4 ½ inches (4–12 cm) long. The heart scarab was either placed on top of a mummified corpse's heart or hung around the mummy's neck with gold wire, like a pendant. The scarab was inscribed with the name of the deceased, along with one of the most important spells from the Egyptian Book of the Dead. The spell informed the deceased's heart not to give evidence against the dead when being judged by the gods, otherwise the deceased's soul would go to the terrifying underworld and not be sent to the afterlife and eternal peace.

From about 760 BCE onward, large, flat, plain scarabs with holes at each side were sewn onto the chests of mummies, together with a pair of separate outstretched wings. These were usually made from blue faience, a type of pottery, or from blue precious stones, such as lapis lazuli.

Recently, zoologist Emily Baird and her team of researchers at Lund University, Sweden, were intrigued to discover how tiny insects navigate the world. Rolling a dung ball in a perfectly straight line, the dung beetle pushes the ball forward with its back legs, with its head facing backward looking at the ground. Every now and then it stops, climbs to the top of the ball, and does a little dance. Dr. Baird suggested that the beetles climb up to see the sun, and use the sun's rays as a celestial compass. By taking the sun's bearings, they know where they are. Could it be that Egyptian observers also realized that the beetle stopped to make direct contact with the sun? It is not known exactly why the scarab was so sacred, but its continued use as a powerful protective device and its link to the source of all life, the sun, have made it an archetypal symbol that continues to capture the popular imagination today.

Dating to the New Kingdom (1570–1070 BCE), this granite scarab statue of the god Khepri is at the Karnak Temple Complex, near Luxor, Egypt.

ANCIENT EGYPTIAN SYMBOLS

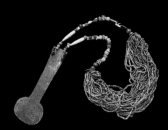

MENAT

Closely connected with the goddess Hathor, the menat is a kind of small, beaded, copper shield, first worn by Hathor's priestesses. It later became a protective amulet worn in the form of a necklace to ensure good fortune and to protect against evil spirits. It was also used for protection in the afterlife and was buried with the dead.

BA

A bird with a human head, Ba represents the personality, one of the five essential components of the soul. The others are Ib (the heart, physically and metaphorically), Sheut (the shadow, which is a reflection of the body and therefore contains some of its essence), Ren (a person's name), and Ka (the spirit that leaves the body when it dies).

DJEW

Djew (meaning "mountain") symbolizes the two peaks between which the Nile River flows and that were said to hold up the sky like a pair of tent poles. The peak on the west bank was Manu; the eastern mountain was Bakhu. Each peak had a guardian lion that protected the sun from interference on its daily journey across the heavens.

MENHED

The menhed is a pallet with black and red pigments alongside a water jar and a pen—the essential tools of the ancient writer's trade. It appears in artistic representations of monarchs and dignitaries to show either that they were themselves literate or that they were the patrons and benefactors of scribes.

NEKHBET

The white vulture that symbolized Upper Egypt is known as Nekhbet. Mystical powers were attributed to vultures because there was no apparent difference between males and females and it was assumed that they reproduced by parthenogenesis (without mating). By analogy, the white vulture was like the state: solitary, inviolable.

KA

Of the five spirits that sustained life (Ba, Ib, Sheut, Ren, and Ka), the ancient Egyptians believed that this one, Ka, was the quintessence. Although Ka left the body at the point of death, it would continue to thrive in the afterlife for as long as it was sustained by food and drink, offerings of which were left in or around the tombs of the deceased.

PSHENT

Pshent is a double crown—often part red, part white—that represents a unified Egypt and, by extension, unity in general. Many depictions of pshent also feature uraeus (a striking cobra), which symbolizes Lower Egypt and its tutelary goddess Wadjet, and a white vulture, the emblem of Upper Egypt and its Nekhbet deity.

REKHYT

The crested lapwing has shackled wings to prevent it from flying. In Egyptian symbolism, rekhyt represents the common man. It appears in many forms of visual art at the feet of the rich and powerful, perhaps to indicate the subjugation of ordinary people. This has led to the conclusion that it is a radical, political symbol.

SA

This symbol—which is taken to represent either the rolled-up shelter of a nomadic herder or a buoyant life preserver of the type used by ancient Egyptian sailors—betokens protection. It frequently appears as an amulet beneath the hoof of Taurt, the hippopotamus goddess of childbirth, as a good luck charm for pregnancy.

BES

The dwarf god of Egypt was the protector god of childbirth, and it was believed that he scared away demons that might harm a newborn child. Bes was the adversary of evil and a frightening deterrent to enemies of Egypt and all evil spirits. His amulet was worn or used in the home, and was said to frighten away snakes and scorpions.

TIET

Alternatively known as the knot of Isis because it is believed to resemble the fastening that secured cloaks at the neck, tiets are made of precious stones or colored glass and are found in many tombs. Their meaning remains a mystery, but Egyptologists speculate that they may symbolize resurrection and eternal life.

USHABTIS

Small, carved, mummylike figures like these were placed in tombs to work for the deceased in the afterlife. Tombs of the highest ranking ancient Egyptians would contain 401 such artifacts: one for every day of the year plus thirty-six foremen. Hierarchy was as strongly maintained in the next world as it was on Earth.

DOVE

MESOPOTAMIA c. 2400–1500 BCE

Widespread symbol of peace and love

In the ancient world, birds were sacred to the all-powerful mother goddess worshipped by the Paleolithic peoples. Doves in particular were associated with her fecundity and life-giving power, not only because of their courtship behavior but also because of their unusual life-long bond as a couple. A number of archaeological discoveries of lifelike bird figures beside figurines of the mother goddess, dating from the Bronze Age (2400–1500 BCE) in Sumerian Mesopotamia, confirms these ancient roots.

Worship of the mother goddess and her bird spread to Crete, where she was depicted with doves on her head, and to Cyprus where images of the birds perching on the temple roof tops can be seen on Roman coins. In Greek religion, Aphrodite was regarded primarily as the goddess of love, to whom offerings were made in exchange for blessings and favors in love affairs, and she was often portrayed with doves. Demeter, the Greek version of the mother goddess, was also associated with the dove symbol.

An ancient Greek myth tells of how two black doves flew from Thebes, one to oak groves at Dodona and one to Libya. In Dodona, the dove spoke aloud declaring that oracles would soon be told there; the second dove changed into the form of Amon, the powerful king of the gods, who was worshipped in Thebes. The doves in the oracular groves at Dodona became sacred to Zeus, and their soft cooing was interpreted by the high priestesses as prophetic messages from Zeus himself.

Another myth, from ancient Syria and dating to around the fourth century BCE, recalls the story of the legendary Queen Semiramis, the mortal daughter of the goddess Derketo. Expressing

A Romantic painter of the nineteenth century, William Bouguereau depicts and idealizes Venus surrounded by her doves.

her shame at giving birth to a mortal, Derketo abandoned the child at birth and flung herself into a lake near Ascalon and drowned. Her body was changed into a fish, and she later became revered as a fish goddess. Doves fed Semiramis until a royal shepherd, Simmas, found the child and raised her. Semiramis later married King Ninus, but after King Ninus conquered Asia, he was fatally wounded by an arrow. Their son was too young to take the throne, so Semiramis ruled as regent, conquering much of Asia herself. The cult temple to the Syrian goddess Atargatis at the ancient city of Mabog was, according to legend, founded by Semiramis, and her temple statue shows her with a golden dove on her head.

In the late nineteenth century the Romantic movement embraced Greek and Roman mythologies, and restored the old stories of gods and goddesses, nymphs, satyrs, and angels to show that mythological images were still as meaningful then as they were thousands of years before. Many of the ancient mother and love goddesses, such as Venus and Aphrodite, were depicted accompanied by doves, as were the earlier Mesopotamian goddesses such as Ishtar, Astarte, and the great mother goddess herself.

Doves frequently appear in stained glass windows of Christian churches, as both a symbol of the Holy Ghost and of divine love.

DOVES IN CHRISTIANITY

Through their writings, Christian fathers assimilated many pagan symbols, deities, and myths into their own religious doctrine while at the same time attempting to convert others to their belief system. These symbolic associations, such as the image of the peace-loving dove deep within the collective unconscious, soon became linked to the Christian message.

One of the earlier and well-known stories from Genesis told of how a dove was released by Noah in order to find land after the flood. When the bird returned, it carried an olive branch in its beak, proving that there was dry land nearby, and therefore hope. To the ancient Greeks and Romans, the olive branch symbolized peace, and the early Christians soon incorporated this imagery with the dove into their own symbol of divine love. The dove became associated with the Holy Ghost, the messenger of the Divine, and at the Annunciation, it was a dove that brought the message from God to Mary. Throughout the medieval era and the Middle Ages, dove images were placed in churches as adornments for pews and as font covers, as well as receptacles for the Holy Sacraments. To the second-century Gnostics, a heretical offshoot of Christianity, the dove became symbolic of the goddess of wisdom, Sophia, whom they considered was the female Holy Spirit.

In Islam, doves are respected because they are believed to have assisted the final prophet of Islam, Muhammad, in distracting his enemies outside the cave of Thaw'r in the great Hijira. Although it originated in the myths and beliefs of the ancient world, the dove is still an archetypal representation of peace, love, and goodness today. The World Peace Congress held in Paris in April 1949 chose Pablo Picasso's lithograph *La Colombe* (*The Dove*, 1949) depicting a traditional dove without an olive branch as an emblem of peace.

The dove has become an iconic symbol of peace worldwide.

BIRDS

HAWK

Usually associated with sun gods, the hawk symbolizes power, the heavens, royalty, and wisdom. In China, seeing more than one hawk signifies war; to the Aztecs, hawks were messengers of the gods. In ancient Egypt, the hawk represented the flight of the soul, and the god of the sky, Horus, was represented by a hieroglyph of a hawk.

CONDOR

In Mesoamerican myth, the eye of the condor was the sun itself, symbolizing the hidden light of the divine. The Andean condor was the augur of the weather, and brought thunder and lightning, wisdom, vision, prophecy, illumination, and creative power. The Californian condor was believed to have supernatural powers.

ALBATROSS

The wandering albatross has long been associated with ocean journeys, and in the West it was believed to embody the soul of a dead sailor. Killing an albatross is said to be unlucky, as highlighted in *The Rime of the Ancient Mariner* (1798) by Samuel Taylor Coleridge. To the Maoris, the bird represents beauty, power, balance, and freedom.

HOOPOE

Long associated with magic and the supernatural, the hoopoe was the bird that told King Solomon secrets about the Queen of Sheba. To the Arabs, the hoopoe was a divine healer that could cure any disease. Its blood was used to write magic spells and its innards dried and worn around the neck as an amulet against the evil eye.

FALCON

Symbolic of masculine power and solar energy to American Indians, the falcon signifies freedom of spirit and is also thought to be a messenger from ancestors. Used by medieval and later nobility for hunting, it became associated with royalty and aristocracy. In ancient Egypt, the falcon was a symbol of divine kingship.

HUMMINGBIRD

The North American Hopi and Zuni nations painted hummingbirds on water jars believing that the birds worked with the gods to bring rain to humankind. In a Cherokee Indian myth, a shaman transformed himself into a hummingbird so that he could find the much-prized tobacco plant. When used as a totem, the tiny bird represents lightness of life and resilience.

OWL

To the ancient Greeks, the owl was associated with the goddess of wisdom, Athena, and was the guardian of the Acropolis. The bird was also the companion of Hecate, the goddess of magic, night, and the underworld. As a nocturnal bird of prey, it became linked to evil by the Romans, but it is still symbolic of wisdom in esoteric circles.

CRANE

In the Far East, the crane symbolizes longevity and faithfulness. The ancient Chinese referred to the birds as "blessed" or "heavenly," and believed they carried legendary sages on their backs as they flew between worlds. In ancient Greece, the crane was a symbol of the sun god Apollo, who disguised himself as the bird whenever visiting Earth.

RAVEN

In Norse mythology, the god Odin had two ravens who flew to Earth to report on humankind. Ravens represent intelligence and wisdom, while early North Americans believed the bird was a symbol of the creator. The raven was also thought to be a shape-shifting witch in European folklore; in Hindu myth it was considered a messenger of death.

VULTURE

As a bird that ate the dead, the vulture was seen by the Maya as capable of converting death to life. The bird was therefore considered a symbol of cleansing and transformation. American Indian traditions believe that the vulture is a symbol of renewal and link it with cyclical themes, such as the rising of

SWALLOW

In ancient Greece, the swallow was associated with Aphrodite, the goddess of love, and was thought to bring good luck and happiness. The ancient Romans believed that swallows embodied the souls of children who had been lost in childbirth. Modern Christians see the swallow as a symbol of sacrifice,

SPARROW

This bird is either a harbinger of good or bad luck. In the West, the sparrow is seen as a sign of God's benevolence, but also as an omen of death. In Indonesia, if a sparrow enters a home, the family believe it is a portent of a wedding, and if a woman spies a sparrow on Valentine's Day, she will find happiness only by

MEDICINE WHEEL

BIGHORN MOUNTAINS, WYOMING, USA *c.* 1500 BCE–500 CE

An American Indian site of contact with the spirit world

In American Indian traditions, medicine wheels such as this one at Bighorn represent the "Great Spirit" known as Wakan-Tanka, the life force that animates everything.

Stone medicine wheels are scattered across the plains of the northern United States and southern Canada. Some are extremely large with a diameter greater then 40 feet (12 m). The superb prehistoric rock structure at Bighorn Mountains is known to be a powerful and sacred cosmological site for American Indians. Originally created by an ancient Aztec-Tanoan culture between 1500 BCE and 500 CE, the medicine wheel was first discovered by Crow Indian hunters nearly 300 years ago. However, they were afraid of its energy, and as the news spread across the plains, other indigenous

native tribes began to fear it, too. To the Crows, the medicine wheel was the place where the first people on Earth emerged as spirits from the underworld through a passage topped by the large central stone cairn. Members of the Crow, who used the medicine wheel for rituals, believed it was created because of a boy named Burnt Face. The boy fell into a fire as a baby and was scarred severely. When Burnt Face reached his teenage years, he went on a vision quest in the mountains, where he fasted and built the medicine wheel. During his quest, he helped drive away an animal that attacked baby eaglets.

In return, he was carried off by an eagle and his face was made smooth again.

According to most American Indian peoples, the circle or wheel represents Wakan-Tanka, the "Great Spirit." The American Indian use of the word "medicine" is not the same as the modern use today. In fact, it refers to the vital power or force that is inherent in nature itself, and to the personal power within oneself that can enable a being to become whole. In American Indian spirituality, the medicine wheel represents connection and harmony and it is a major symbol of peaceful interaction among all living beings on Earth. Scholars believe that the wheels had a ceremonial or ritual purpose, and there is evidence of dancing within some of them. Other wheels were probably used as part of a ritual vision quest.

ASTRONOMY

Twentieth-century U.S. astronomer John A. Eddy put forth the theory that some of the medicine wheels had astronomical significance, and that the longest spoke on a wheel could be pointing to a particular star at a particular time of the year, suggesting that the wheels were a way in which to mark certain days of the year. A series of rocks or large stones was placed on the ground in a circular pattern. Lines of rock, sometimes four or more, were positioned to create spokes, or to delineate segments of the circle. Medicine wheels were also believed to mark the geographical directions and astronomical events of the sun, moon, fixed stars, and planets in relation to Earth's horizon at that location. These rock sites were used for important ceremonies and teachings, and as sacred places to offer thanks to the creator god of the specific culture.

The medicine wheel usually has some significant symbol relating to the four directions, and also to Father Sky, Mother Earth, and Spirit Tree. All of these symbolize dimensions of health and the cycles of life. Typically each of the four directions (east, south, west, and north) is represented by a distinctive color,

such as black, red, yellow, and white. Other symbols of the four directions include the stages of life: birth, youth, adult, elder; seasons of the year: spring, summer, fall, winter; and elements of nature: fire, air water, earth. Animals such as the eagle, bear, wolf, and buffalo are often represented, and ceremonial plants including tobacco, sweet grass, sage, and cedar correspond to the elements, as do weather patterns and human qualities. The medicine wheel can take many different forms, but mostly it is found as artwork, paintings, or drawn on rocks, or discovered as a physical construction on the land such as at Bighorn Mountains.

Today, adherents of American Indian ritual and magic, and those involved in new age, Wiccan, or neopagan communities still use the medicine wheel and its symbolic powers on many different levels. It is a circle that represents natural and personal powers in complete balance, and shows that everything is interconnected and part of one cosmic whole. It is a shamanic map, or philosophical system, that can be employed as a guide to help us find our way and to ground us when we embark on inner journeys. It can be used for finding direction in life, and for people to align with the natural energies that affect their lives.

A new age medicine wheel in Arizona, USA. Although some astronomers believe the wheel may be a form of astral map, it is generally considered to be a symbolic interface between the spirit and tangible worlds.

The four compass directions of the medicine wheel—north, south east, and west—are often represented by animals, colors, or elements of nature.

LOTUS FLOWER
INDIA c. 1400 BCE

Ancient symbol of purity in Buddhism and of divine love in Hinduism

In Hindu art, the great god Vishnu and his wife Lakshmi are always accompanied by an open lotus flower, signifying divine love.

The lotus flower has become an iconic symbol of Hindu religion and dates back to the early Vedic texts of around 1400 BCE. Its most powerful association is with the favorite Hindu gods, Vishnu and his consort Lakshmi. From the depths of a muddy pond, the lotus flower begins its journey to the light and air. With the dawn, it opens its magnificent eight petals a few centimeters above the water's surface. This aquatic perennial, indigenous to the Middle and Far East, is distinguished from the familiar water lily by its circular seedpod sitting neatly in the center of the petals.

For thousands of years the lotus flower has been a powerful symbol of purity in Buddhist belief, and of divine love in Hinduism. Because of the way it grows, from the dark waters and up into the light, the lotus has over the centuries become a popular symbol for overcoming the odds and getting through difficult times, as well as a symbol of the renaissance of the spirit, soul, or self.

In Hinduism, many of the gods and goddesses are assigned or depicted with a lotus, either seated on a fully open bloom or holding a flower in their hand. Vishnu is described as the "Lotus Eyed One" and is often portrayed with a pink lotus alongside Lakshmi, goddess of prosperity. Likewise Brahma, god of creation, is depicted as emerging from a lotus in Vishnu's navel.

In ancient Egypt the lotus came to symbolize the sun and creation. In many hieroglyphic works the lotus is depicted as emerging from the primeval water, also known as the god Nun who gave birth to the sun god Ra. The lotus was also symbolic of rebirth, and the Egyptian Book of the Dead included spells to transform a person into a lotus, thus enabling their resurrection. The lotus was used in the hieroglyphics and art of the kingdom of Upper Egypt, while the papyrus plant was favored in Lower Egypt. Eventually, in later dynastic Egyptian art, pictures of lotus and papyrus become intertwined as a symbol of the merger of the two kingdoms.

BUDDHIST TRADITION

Signifying purity in Buddhist religion, the lotus flower is considered to represent a wise and spiritually enlightened quality in a person. The phrase "om mane padme om," used as a mantra during meditation, means "hail to the jewel of the lotus." Among contemporary spiritual circles, the unopened bud is representative of a prenascent soul, which has the potential to unfold and open itself up to the divine truth. According to legend, the Buddha Siddhartha Gautama left a trail of white lotus flowers wherever he went, signifying spiritual awakening and enlightenment. In most Buddhist traditions, the red lotus is symbolic of love and heartfelt passion.

The rare blue lotus, a form of water lily and not a true lotus, was scattered on the tomb of Tutankhamun by priests. This precious blue lotus can be found in ancient Egyptian imagery, for example in stylized friezes on temple and palace walls. Containing a soporific substance known

as an apomorphine, it induced a trancelike, drugged state and symbolized sacred power. In smaller doses the plant was also used by the ancient Egyptians as an aphrodisiac.

In Greek mythology, the lotus was referred to in the story of Odysseus, when one of his ships was lost and landed on an island where the so-called lotus eaters lived. The sailors began to eat lotus flowers, probably the blue lotus, and drifted off into a deep sleep. This tale inspired Alfred Tennyson to write the poem "The Song of the Lotus Eaters" (1832), thus immortalizing the lotus as a symbol of spiritual awakening and as having a narcotic nature.

The lotus flower's eight petals are said to represent the eight cardinal points—north, south, east, west, northeast, northwest, southeast, southwest—as the rulers of the eight quarters of the universe, known in Hinduism as Ashtadikpalas. The lotus is also a symbol of the chakra system used in yoga, each petal relating to the functions of each chakra's energy center as it spirals invisibly from and within the body. Although there are only seven chakras, the eighth petal represents the merger of the crown chakra with the divine, attainable only by those who have reached the highest state of enlightenment. As the lotus petals unfurl, so too does the mind develop and awaken to the spiritual or transcendent realm.

At the seventh-century CE **Kapaleeshwarar Temple in Chennai, India, the triad of Vishnu, Brahma, and Shiva gives blessings seated upon a lotus flower.**

The petals of the lotus are equated to the chakra system as a symbol of spiritual awakening.

FLEUR-DE-LIS
EGYPT AND MESOPOTAMIA c. 900–300 BCE

Popular decorative motif of purity

The fleur-de-lis has long been identified with French kings, but decorative imagery of the flower, thought to be a stylized version of an iris, has been found on ancient Mesopotamian and Egyptian pottery, as well as on the Babylonian Ishtar Gate built in the sixth century BCE. Indian and Egyptian cultures also used the flower in art to symbolize life and resurrection.

The French fleur-de-lis probably derives from a species of yellow and white iris that grows by rivers, marshes, and in damp shady places. According to some scholars, before the ancient Franks entered Gaul they lived in the Netherlands near a river named Luts. This river was bordered with wild irises, and it is likely that the Frankish kings chose an image from their surroundings as a symbol of their power. However, other historians suggest that the fleur-de-lis derives from the German name for the flower, *Lieschblume*.

Most scholars concur that the association of the fleur-de-lis with French kings started with the crowning of Clovis I in 496 CE; when he converted to Christianity, iris oil was allegedly used in his baptism. Legend tells how an angel descended with a vial of fleur-de-lis oil to anoint the king, and since then it has always been considered a symbol of divine purity. Later "anointed" kings of France, such as the

A tiled wall plaque from the Renaissance Villa d'Este in Rome reveals that the family's emblems included the fleur-de-lis.

eighth-century ruler Charlemagne, believed, like Clovis, that they were given divine authority directly from God. A ninth-century mosaic, from San Giovanni church in Rome, shows St. Peter handing the imperial banner, known as the "oriflamme," to the conquering Charlemagne. The finial of the oriflamme is clearly a spearhead, but it also closely resembles the fleur-de-lis icon. Perhaps it is because of the oriflamme's association with Charlemagne that the fleur-de-lis became a symbol of French royalty. Since then, the fleur-de-lis has been a popular religious, political, dynastic, emblematic, and symbolic icon in French heraldry.

GODDESS OF THE RAINBOW

Long before the iris became associated with the French kings, it was considered a symbol of power by the ancient Egyptians, who placed an image of the iris on the brow of a sphinx for example, and on scepters of their kings. In 1479 BCE, to commemorate his victory in Syria, the Egyptian pharaoh Thutmose III had pictures of irises drawn on the walls of his temple.

The iris flower got its name from the Greek goddess Iris, the goddess of the rainbow, the bridge between heaven and Earth, mortality and immortality. Iris was a messenger on Mount Olympus, but she also led mortal souls to the Elysian Fields. In ancient Greece, men would often plant an iris on the grave of their beloved as a tribute to the goddess, in the hope that Iris would take the deceased across the dangerous landscape of the underworld and lead them to eternal bliss. As a sacred flower, the iris was credited with healing powers and was used in ancient Greek medicine. By the first century CE, the Greek physician Dioscorides recommended iris root drunk with honey, vinegar, or wine for coughs, colds, indigestion, and sciatica.

In Christianity, like the lily, the iris was associated with the Virgin Mary, and by the reign of the thirteenth-century French king Louis IX, three petals of the flower were said to represent faith, wisdom, and chivalry, and to be a sign of divine favor bestowed on France by God. The symbolic trinity later spread to other countries, as French and European settlers set out to colonize the New World. The fleur-de-lis appears on the flag of Quebec, and also on the flags of Montreal and Trois-Rivieres. In the United States, the fleur-de-lis decorates flags and coats of arms for St. Louis, Detroit, New Orleans, and Baton Rouge. Following Hurricane Katrina in 2005, the fleur-de-lis was used in New Orleans as a symbol of grassroot support for the city's recovery.

This iconic symbol remains in our collective psyche as a motif of royalty, wisdom, and faith.

FLOWERS

ROSE

Attributed to ancient goddesses such as Isis and Aphrodite, the rose is a symbol of fertility, beauty, passion, and divine love. White roses were painted on Roman banquet hall ceilings to remind diners that whatever was said at the table was secret. This was the source of the Latin phrase for secrecy *sub rosa*, beneath the rose.

IRIS

In Greek mythology, Iris was the personification of the rainbow, and she represented the power of light, messages, hope, and the promise of love. In China, the iris represents beauty in solitude; in ancient Egypt, resurrection; and for the French the fleur-de-lis—an iris not a lily—represents faith, wisdom, and courage.

CHERRY BLOSSOM

Cherry blossom is the national flower of Japan. When the blossom falls, it does so all at once. To the Samurai, the flower symbolized the ephemeral nature of life and the spirit of fearlessness. To the Japanese, the tree also represents ascetic beauty and the honor of graceful acceptance for one's life, however short or long.

DAISY

This flower has always been associated with the sun. A symbol of modesty, simplicity, and innocence, it is also symbolic of loyalty in love. In medieval Europe, girls would divine whether their suitor was true or not by plucking the petals one by one, and chanting, "He loves me, he loves me not." The last petal determined the answer.

FORGET-ME-NOT

Associated with remembrance and fidelity, the forget-me-not has many legends surrounding its name. In Christian lore, when God was walking in the Garden of Eden he noticed a small blue flower and asked its name. The flower whispered, "I am afraid I have forgotten, Lord." God answered, "Forget Me not. Yet I will not forget thee."

TULIP

Once an emblem of the Ottoman empire, the tulip was an ancient Persian symbol of love. When introduced to Europe in the sixteenth century, the flowers became a status symbol for the wealthy—the only people who were able to afford them. Red tulips were symbolic of irresistible love, and they were given by suitors as a romantic declaration.

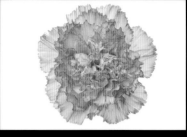

CARNATION

According to a Christian legend, when Mary saw Jesus carrying the cross she began to cry and carnations grew where her tears fell. Plague-stricken Crusaders mixed carnation leaves with wine to subdue their raging fevers. From the Renaissance onward, carnations were considered to symbolize love, fertility, marriage, and motherhood.

HYACINTH

When Apollo's companion Hyacinth was killed, Apollo named a flower that grew from his blood after her. The purple hyacinth symbolized forgiveness, constancy, and prudence. In the nineteenth century it was sent between lovers to say they were sorry for hasty words, while in witchcraft it is used for protection against evil and curses.

CHRYSANTHEMUM

In the Far East, this flower is associated with longevity, wealth, and happiness. European legend tells how Christ, disguised as a beggar, was taken in by a poor family. The next morning two white chrysanthemums were found by the door. In Germany, these flowers are often on display on Christmas Eve to welcome Christ.

LILY

Symbolic of peace and purity in China, the lily is also an emblem of abundance. In ancient Greek mythology, it was associated with the Greek goddess Hera, from whose fallen drops of breast milk the first lilies sprang. In Christian legend, the lily was yellow until the day the Virgin Mary stooped to pick it and it changed to white.

MARIGOLD

Once known as the "herb of the sun," the flower has always been associated with solar power. It is a symbol of vitality, life force, and passion. In China it is a symbol of longevity, and in India it is associated with the god Krishna. Marigold was called "Mary's Gold" by early Christians who placed the flowers around statues of Mary.

VIOLET

The Athenians considered violets to be emblems of their city. The founder of Athens was welcomed by water nymphs, who gave him violets as a sign of good wishes. Violets are used as charms against evil, and symbolize faithfulness. Giving blue violets shows constancy; white violets reveal a desire to take a chance in love.

RAINBOW

GREECE eighth century BCE

Influential symbol often associated with hope

Iris Carrying the Water of the River Styx to Olympus for the Gods to Swear By (c. 1793) by Guy Head shows the goddess as an envoy between heaven and the underworld.

As messenger of the gods, fleet-footed Iris was the goddess of light, while her sisters were the much-feared goddesses of darkness, the Harpies. Iris was at the beck and call of the gods and appears in many myths as a go-between or informant. For example, Zeus sent a message via Iris to Demeter to be reconciled after the rape and abduction of Persephone. And Hera sent Iris to Menelaus in Crete to tell him the tragic news of Helen's elopement with Paris to Troy.

Iris was married to the god of the west wind, Zephyrus, and in the Greek tragedy *Herakles* by Euripides, she appears alongside Lyssa, the spirit of madness, to curse the heroic Herakles with a fit of insanity in which he kills his three sons and his wife, Megara. Iris also appears in Virgil's *Aeneid* as an agent of Juno sent to pluck a lock of hair from the head of dying Queen Dido so that her spirit would be released to the otherworld.

REPRESENTATIONS

In the Sumerian poem *Epic of Gilgamesh*, the rainbow is portrayed as the bejeweled necklace of the great goddess Ishtar, which she lifts into the sky as a reminder that she will never forget the days of the great flood that destroyed all her children. In Norse mythology, the rainbow is described as a burning bridge, Bifrost, that links Asgard, the home of the gods, with Midgard, the Earth. Bifrost can be used only by gods and those who are killed in battle. It is eventually shattered at Ragnarok, the end of time. The rainbow is the rain and thunder god Indra's bow in Hinduism, while in the traditional Shinto belief of Japan rainbows were bridges that ancestral spirits used to descend to Earth.

Throughout most world mythology, the rainbow was seen as a bridge to the heavens: a link between the manifest world and the divine world, and a sign of hope and peace. However, one of the most influential and empowering symbols is that of the rainbow personified as the Greek goddess Iris.

It is not only the rainbow itself that has significance but also its colors. In Tantric Buddhism, the seven colors of the rainbow that make up the clarity of pure light, represent the penultimate meditational state before attaining enlightenment. The colors of the spectrum have deep significance for followers of Islam, too. The different hues are thought to be qualities of the divine being made visible in the material world. In Hinduism, the seven colors represent each of the seven heavens.

Central Asian shamans wore rainbow-colored robes, cloaks, or feathered headwear to aid their journey to the spirit world, whereas in Mesoamerican mythology the Incas believed that the rainbow was the multicolored feathered crown of Illapa, the god of thunder, lightning, and rain. Fearful of the rainbow, the people dared not look at it, and they also covered their mouths with their hands when a rainbow appeared. One word spoken meant that Illapa would bring thunderstorms to their lands.

Many cultures such as the Aboriginal peoples of Australia saw the rainbow as a mother serpent who created the Earth. Rainbows are also identified with serpents in African mythology, as well as in Chinese legend, in

which one of the Eight Immortals is transformed into a rainbow coiled like a sleeping serpent. The Navajo peoples use an image of a rainbow on their flag to symbolize sovereignty and the merger of all the tribes into the Rainbow Nation, whereas the Maori rainbow god, Kahukura, was invoked in war and is a symbol of man's mortality and the pathway to heaven.

In the Bible the rainbow that appears at the end of Noah's journey in the ark symbolized the reunion of God with humankind, and in Genesis 9:12–13, God says to Noah: " . . . I set my bow in the clouds and it shall be a token of the covenant between me and the Earth."

The traditional folk myth that a pot of gold can be found at the end of a rainbow derives from Irish legends of mischievous male fairies known as leprechauns. The leprechauns are rich shoemakers, who store their gold coins in a pot hidden at the end of the rainbow. Of course, the end of the rainbow is impossible to reach, and the symbolic "pot of gold" is never attainable.

Throughout mythology, art, and literature, the rainbow has been cherished as a symbol of divine presence, illumination, and peace. Also a sign of clearing storms, welcome rains, and a bridge between worlds, its majestic appearance across our skies evokes a sense of positive news, joy, and wonder.

When Noah saw a rainbow in the sky, God told him it was a sign of his promise to reunite with the Earth (engraving of an original watercolor by Jacques Le Moyne de Morgues.)

The seven colors of the rainbow are each symbolic of a divine essence in various religions and mythologies.

This frontispiece from *Book of the Epic* (1916) by H. A. Guerber depicts Bifrost, or the burning bridge, in Norse mythology.

PHOENIX
GREECE *c.* 800–146 BCE

Mythical bird associated with regeneration and resurrection

In Renaissance Europe, the phoenix became a powerful symbol in occult circles, and was also worn as a pendant by Queen Elizabeth I.

The origins of the phoenix date back to the ninth century BCE, when Greek writer Hesiod described this mythical creature as "the brilliant one." However, many scholars have argued that the phoenix originated from the Egyptian myth of the benu bird, also known as the purple heron. During the annual flooding of the River Nile, the heron managed to remain safe, nesting in high rocky plains. As it flew above the flood,

it appeared to resemble the sun moving across the water. Called "the ascending one," the bird was thought to be the soul of the sun god Ra. It was venerated especially in Heliopolis, "city of the sun," so called by the Greeks after Alexander the Great conquered Egypt in 332 BCE. According to one myth, the benu created itself from a fire that had burned on a holy tree in one of the sacred precincts of the Temple of Ra. The benu had alighted on a pillar known as the "bnbn-stone" and had remained there for its first 1,000-year cycle. The priests showed this pillar to visitors, who considered it the most holy place on Earth. In another myth, the bird was associated with the god Osiris, springing from the god's heart after his resurrection.

In Greek mythology, many legends recalled the phoenix, which either by rising from the ashes of its predecessor or by regenerating itself was believed to be a real-life bird. Hesiod

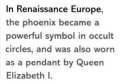

MYTHOLOGICAL BIRDS

GARUDA

The garuda is a large mythical bird that appears in both Buddhist and Hindu mythologies. It is often depicted as having the golden body of a man with a white face, red wings, and an eagle's beak. This ancient deity was said to be large enough to block out the sun, and was the eternal enemy of the deadly serpent race known as the Naga.

FENG HUANG

A Chinese mythological bird, the feng huang is often described as a composite of many birds. It represents the six celestial bodies: head—sky, eyes—sun, back—moon, wings—wind, feet—earth, and tail—planets.

SIMURGH

Depicted in Iranian art as a winged creature in the shape of a bird, the simurgh is big enough to carry off an elephant or a whale. It appears as a peacock often with the head of a dog and the claws of a lion, and sometimes with a human face. Iranian legends consider the bird so old that it has seen the destruction of the world three times over.

believed that the bird lived for a cycle of 100,000 years before it burned to ashes so that a new one could be born from the old. The phoenix was subsequently adopted in early Christian iconography as a symbol of Jesus's sacrifice and resurrection.

In medieval artwork and literature, the phoenix was depicted with a nimbus or sunlike halo of seven rays, emphasizing its connection with the sun god Helios in Greek mythology, who was always depicted with a solar halo. The first-century CE Roman writer and historian Pliny described the bird as having a crest of feathers on its head, whereas Ezekiel the Dramatist compared it to a rooster. Later, during the Renaissance, the phoenix became associated with royalty and the color purple. In c. 1575 a portrait of Elizabeth I, attributed to Nicholas Hilliard was made. At the time, the idea of Elizabeth I as the "Virgin Queen" had developed

into a mystery cult. Although many of the symbolic elements in several of her portraits were believed to allude to her unmarried status, there was something more enigmatic at work. Painted when the queen was in her early forties, almost halfway through her reign, Hilliard's portrait features an elaborate phoenix pendant, which Elizabeth I chose, it is believed, as an ostensible reassurance to her courtiers that she intended to regenerate the dynasty, virgin or not.

On a more esoteric level, Elizabeth I was closely advised by alchemist Sir Philip Sidney and astrologer John Dee. Both men were very aware that in Renaissance alchemy the phoenix, and also the pelican, was a secret symbol of the final stages of the transcendence of the human soul toward immortality. The mythical phoenix, therefore, was a perfect emblem for the long-living and seemingly immortal English queen.

A symbol of regeneration in Christian iconography, the phoenix also represents the Resurrection.

DRAGON
CHINA c. 475–221 BCE

Symbol of auspicious powers including knowledge, strength, and good fortune

This third-century CE painting on silk symbolizes a wealthy man's happy ascension to the spiritual world as he rides upon an auspicious dragon.

A legendary creature in Chinese mythology, the dragon traditionally symbolizes auspicious powers and, historically, it has been used as the primary symbol of the emperor of China. According to legend, the mythical founder of China, Emperor Yu, was a dragon being, and all subsequent emperors are said to be Yu's incarnation. Various dragons were assigned different qualities during the Zhou dynasty (c. 1046–256 BCE). The most important was the five-clawed blue-green dragon, which symbolized celestial and imperial power, the sun, joy, fertility, and knowledge.

In folklore Chinese dragons are traditionally associated with their control over water, rainfall, hurricane, and floods. They are believed to be the rulers of moving bodies of water, such as waterfalls, rivers, or seas. They can show themselves as water spouts, tornados, whirlpools, and angry seas. As the ruler of water and weather, the dragon is often personified as a king wearing a water-inspired headdress made from seaweed, rolling surf, or wild waves. There are four major dragons representing each of the Four Seas: the East Sea Dragon, corresponding to the East China Sea; the South Sea Dragon, corresponding to the South China Sea; the West Sea Dragon, representing Qinghai Lake; and the North Sea Dragon usually referring to Lake Baikal.

Today in Chinese culture, the dragon is still considered a symbol of power, strength, and good luck, and it is used as an important beneficial image in the art of feng shui. Where dragons are seen to move across the countryside, they bind together all the energy in nature and can be the source of both benevolent and disastrous weather. According to the art of feng shui, dragons also determine the form of the landscape, and buildings and furniture are placed in accordance with "dragon lines," the powerful currents of dragon energy running through the earth.

In Chinese astrology, the dragon is associated with the number nine, a highly auspicious number in feng shui. A wall, known as the

Nine-Dragon Wall, can be found throughout imperial Chinese palaces and gardens, such as those in Beijing, Datong, and Hong Kong. The walls feature a series of nine dragons, all bringing wealth, power, and success to the city. Of the twelve animals in the Chinese zodiac calendar, the year of the dragon, which occurs once every twelve years, is considered the most auspicious in which to be born. Dragon people are supposedly strong-willed and arrogant, but usually successful and enterprising, too.

Historically, worldwide, the dragon is likely to have developed from myths involving ancient serpents, and many myths exist in which monstrous beasts are overcome by mortal or semi-divine heroes. For example, in the ancient Near East are myths such as that of Huwawa, the fire-breathing, dragon-fanged beast first described in the Epic of Gilgamesh. In Indian mythology, the monster dragon Vrtra is slain by Indra, as recounted in the *Rigveda*. In medieval legend and folklore, dragon slayers such as Beowulf, Sigurd, and Tristan abound. But here, far from being auspicious, the dragon is considered to be evil.

According to Revelation 12, the leader of the heavenly angels, Michael, defeated a seven-headed dragon that was the embodiment of Satan. The seven heads symbolized the seven deadly sins, and in most Western traditions, dragon blood symbolizes deadly poison. From medieval times onward, in Western art and literature, one of the best-known motifs is that of a hero overcoming a dragon. Perhaps the best-known example is St. George, who saves a Libyan princess from the terrible fate of being devoured by the dragon, eventually killing the terrifying monster with his sword.

St. George and the Dragon (c. 1470) by Paolo Uccello depicts the legend of St. George, a metaphor for how Christianity, in the guise of St. George, overcame all evil, represented by the dragon.

The dragon symbol can be seen as either beneficial or malevolent.

MYTHOLOGICAL BEASTS

BEHEMOTH

Behemoth was a beast first mentioned in the biblical book of Job. Various identities have been given to it, from a mythological creature to an elephant, hippopotamus, rhinoceros, or crocodile. It is also thought to be a monster destroyed by a creator deity. The name is today used as a metaphor for any extremely large or powerful entity.

CENTAUR

With the head, arms, and upper torso of a man, and the legs and main body of a horse, the Greek mythological centaur is thought to symbolize two natures: the untamed and the civilized aspects of man. The best-known centaur was Chiron, a respected healer, who ironically could not heal himself and was placed in the sky as the constellation Centaurus.

CHIMERA

This monstrous fire-breathing creature from ancient Asia Minor was composed of the parts of three animals—lion, goat, and snake—and was usually depicted as a lion with the head of a goat and a tail that ends in a snake's head. He was the offspring of Typhon and Echidna, and his siblings were all monsters, such as the three-headed dog of the underworld Cerberus.

SATYR

Companions of Dionysus, satyrs were usually depicted with horselike features, including a tail and ears, and sometimes a phallus. Satyrs acquired their goatlike aspect in Roman times and were described in Latin literature as having the upper half of a man and the lower half of a goat, with a goat's tail in place of the horse's tail.

GORGON

The gorgon was a dangerous female monster mentioned in the earliest examples of Greek literature. It was commonly referred to as any of the three sisters who had hair made of living, venomous snakes. The gorgons had horrifying faces that turned those who beheld them to stone. The best known is Medusa, who was killed by Perseus..

HYDRA

An ancient Greek water monster, the hydra possessed endless heads, and for each head cut off it grew two more. It had poisonous breath and venomous blood so virulent that even its tracks were deadly. Heracles managed to kill the hydra of Lerna by cutting off one head and dipping his sword in its venom, which he then used to cauterize the head so it could not grow back.

GRIFFIN

The griffin was an ancient Greek mythical beast, with the body, tail, and back legs of a lion, and the head, wings and talons of an eagle. The lion was considered to be the king of the beasts and the eagle the king of birds. Consequently, the griffin was thought to be an especially powerful and majestic creature, a symbol of divine power and protection.

INCUBUS

An incubus was an ancient demon who appeared in male form and, according to various mythological and legendary traditions, silently appeared in the dark of night to have sex with sleeping women. Its female counterpart is known as the succubus. The legendary wizard Merlin was thought to have been born from the mating of a mortal woman with an incubus.

MINOTAUR

With the head of a bull and the body of a man, the minotaur dwelled at the center of the labyrinth at Knossos, Crete. The labyrinth had been designed by the architect Daedalus on the command of King Minos to house the terrible creature. The offspring of a sacrificial bull and Minos's wife, the minotaur was eventually killed by the Athenian hero Theseus.

MAKARA

A sea monster in Hindu mythology, the Makara was depicted as an elephant, crocodile, stag, or deer at its front part, and as an aquatic animal, in the form of a fish, seal, or peacock tail in the hind part. Makara was also the vessel used by the goddess of the Ganges, Ganga, and the god of the oceans, Varuna, to move freely among the waters.

TENGU

The tengu took the form of a bird of prey in Japanese Shinto tradition, and was depicted with human and bird characteristics. The earliest tengu were pictured with beaks, which eventually became humanized into an unnaturally long nose. In Buddhist tradition tengu were associated with troublesome or spiteful ghosts and spirits.

THUNDERBIRD

A legendary creature in North American traditions, the thunderbird was a supernatural bird of power and strength. It was believed that the beating of its enormous wings caused thunder and stirred the wind. Sheet lightning was made by the light flashing from its eyes, and individual lightning bolts by glowing snakes slithering to the ground.

VISION SERPENT
MEXICO *c.* 400 BCE

The vision serpent served as a gateway to the spirit world

In Lintel 15, Lady Wak Tuun is seen holding bloodletting paraphernalia and communing with the waterlily serpent, an aspect of the lightning deity K'awiil, whom she called up from the otherworld.

Vision serpents were an important part of bloodletting, a common practice in Maya life from around 400 BCE and an essential part of rulership and public rituals. The rituals were enacted on the summits of pyramids or in open courtyards where the populace could congregate and view the bloodletting. The Maya elite drew blood from various parts of their bodies using lancets made of stingray spine, flint, bone, or obsidian. Serpents symbolized the spirit of life, and in Maya belief sacred ancestors would appear as vision serpents to confirm that the ascending ruler was the right one. During

the bloodletting ritual, parchment or paper was soaked in blood and burned to release the vision serpent, which would manifest as an ancestral spirit in the smoke.

At the Maya site of the ancient city and temple complex of Yaxchilan, Mexico, are various eighth-century narrative stone lintels across temple doorways that portray scenes from Maya life. The part known as Lintel 15 depicts one of the bloodletting rituals under the reign of Bird Jaguar IV. It shows Bird Jaguar IV's wife gazing up at the vision serpent. In her left hand, she holds a bowl containing a stingray spine, an obsidian lancet, and bark paper spattered with blood. During the ritual, the vision serpent rises in smoke-filled flames from the bowl, and from its jaws an ancestral warrior appears as if by magic. Bird Jaguar IV continued to rule after the period of prosperity started by his father B'alam II. However, he was considered not to be the rightful heir to the throne and had to struggle to hold power; this bloodletting ritual was performed to prove that Bird Jaguar IV was the rightful heir.

On Lintel 24, another king, Shield Jaguar, holds a flaming torch. Kneeling in front of him is his queen, Lady Xok, who takes a rope studded with thorns or spines and runs it right through her tongue. Spots of blood fall on the paper in a basket in front of her. Out of her blood emerges another huge, writhing, twisting serpent. And out of its mouth a warrior ancestor appears.

MAYA MYTHOLOGY

The vision serpent originates in the earliest Maya mythology as the center of the spiritual world tree. The myths describe serpents as being the means by which celestial bodies, such as the sun and stars, cross the heavens. The

serpents' shedding of their skin made them a symbol of rebirth and renewal. Indeed, they were so revered that one of the most important Mesoamerican deities, Quetzalcoatl, was represented as a feathered serpent. The name means "beautiful serpent." It was through bloodletting rituals that the king proved his contact with the vision serpent and thus the center of the spiritual world, acting as a doorway between the tangible and spiritual worlds.

In the 1930s, archaeologists noticed that the Q'eqchi Maya in Belize still performed a similar ritual with a vision serpent at the initiation ceremony of a shaman, although bloodletting was no longer involved. It was believed that the initiate, in a trance-induced state, came into direct contact with a giant serpent, Ochan. It was through this experience that he completed his initiation rites and gained the knowledge that was needed to become a shaman.

The Pyramid of the Feathered Serpent (c. 150–200) at Teotihuacan features some of the earliest images of Quetzalcoatl.

The vision serpent was an important symbol in Maya belief and provided a medium between the physical world and deities, and also between the living and the dead.

MAYA DEITIES

ACAN

Acan was the god of intoxication, wine, and the art of brewing a kind of strong mead known as balché. His name means "belch" or "groan," and he is associated with the Maya god of drunkenness Bohr, with whom he was apparently great friends. A bit of a fool, Acan was boisterous and was honored whenever celebrations were held.

BACABS

The Bacabs were the four gods of the winds who held up the four corners of the world: Muluc (east), Kan (south), Ix (north), and Cauac (west). Muluc and Kan generated positive energies while Ix and Cauac brought negative forces. This confluence enabled the early gods to create human beings and the physical and non-physical worlds.

CAMAZOTZ

The bat god of the underworld in Maya mythology, Camazotz fed on the blood of humans who were decapitated or torn to shreds in ritual executions. In the *Popol Vuh*, an epic legend, Camazotz tore off the head of one of the hero twins, Hun Hunahpu, who was then revived by his brother. Camazotz was then defeated and cast out.

HUNAB KU

Invisible and without form, Hunab Ku is identified as an aspect of the god Itzamna, referred to as his son, and also as the husband of Ixazaluoh, the divine mother, associated with water, life, and weaving. Some inscriptions refer to him as "the eyes and ears of the sun," who like the Christian God is ubiquitous and knows all.

HURACAN

Also known as "heart of the sky" and "one-leg," Huracan was a storm god. In the *Popol Vuh* he was the supreme creator of Earth who thought existence into being, participated in the creation of human beings, and sent the great flood to destroy his inferior creations. He is further referred to as lord of the whirlwind.

ITZAMNA

Teacher of literacy, medicine, science, art, and agriculture, Itzamna created and ordered the calendar, instructing humans in the proper cultivation of maize and cacao. He was also a healer and resurrected the dead. Itzamna is associated with the prophet Zamana, who brought the sacred writings to the city of Izamal on the command of the great goddess.

CHAAC

Chaac was the supreme god of storms and rain and also associated with agriculture and fertility. He was known as the lord of the rains and winds and maintained important water sources such as wells and springs. A lord of the sky, he was the sworn enemy of the lords of the underworld, and was thought of as a caring, if unpredictable, deity.

EKCHUAH

Ekchuah was also known as Ek Ahau and, earlier, as "God M." He presided over and protected travelers, merchants, and warriors and was depicted as a dark-skinned male with a large lower lip, carrying a bag over his shoulder and a spear. He was also recognized as the patron and protector of cacao and cacao products.

GUKUMATZ

Known also as Kukulcan and, most famously, as Quetzalcoatl (the plumed serpent or the featherd serpent), Gukumatz was worshipped as early as the first century BCE at the great Mesoamerican city of Teotihuacan. Gukumatz is identified as one of thirteen deities who shaped the world and created human beings.

IXCHEL

Known as the "rainbow goddess," Ixchel was venerated by women who wanted to become pregnant. She was known as the goddess of healing, and her other role was as a goddess of war, thus she was able both to give life and to take it away. She was often depicted in ancient images with claws, surrounded by or adorned with bones.

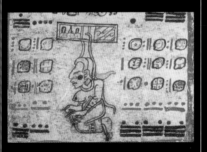

IXTAB

"Rope Woman" Ixtab was the goddess of suicides, particularly those who died by hanging. She was depicted as the rotting corpse of a woman hanging from a noose in the heavens. Self-inflicted death guaranteed people an instant passage escorted by Ixtab to paradise and meant they could bypass the underworld.

KINICH AHAU

The sun god known as the "face of the sun," and sometimes referred to as Kinich Ajaw, was a god of healing and medicine. Hunab Ku is thought to be a later assimilation of Kinich Ahau with the Spanish Catholic, one and only God. In some early myths, Kinich Ahau is the consort of the divine mother Ixazaluoh.

BUTTERFLY
TEOTIHUACAN, MEXICO *c.* 200 BCE

Worldwide symbol of transformation

Itzpapalotl is depicted in Aztec art as a skeletal figure with jaguar claws and butterfly wings with knives on the tips. She is best known as representing the darker aspects of the earth mother figures.

The galactic butterfly is a symbol of all that has been thought into being in the universe.

In the ancient city of Teotihuacan, built around 200 BCE, the image of the butterfly was carved into temples, buildings, stones, lintels, and walls. Sometimes the butterfly was depicted with the jaws of a jaguar, whereas other species were considered to be the reincarnations of the souls of dead warriors. The brightly colored quetzal bird was revered in ancient Mesoamerica, and many images depict the bird with the wings of a butterfly, a creature that became known as the Quetzalpapalotl. Other jaguar-butterfly and bird-butterfly images have been found among the Zapotec and Maya civilizations as symbols of warfare and death. To the Aztecs, Itzpapalotl (meaning obsidian or clawed butterfly) was a fierce warrior goddess of the night.

The ancient Greeks and Romans also revered butterflies, but for different reasons. The Greek goddess Psyche was goddess of the soul, and she was depicted in ancient mosaics as a butterfly-winged goddess in the company of her husband Eros. The word "psyche" means "soul" and "butterfly," so it was easy to see how the symbolic link between a butterfly and the soul developed in European traditions.

The Celts believed that butterflies were human souls in search of their mothers, and in Japan one butterfly is a symbol of vanity, whereas two butterflies are considered to represent marriage and love. One Japanese superstition says that if a butterfly enters your room and perches behind the bamboo screen, the person whom you most love is coming to visit you.

To the ancient Chinese, the butterfly was the Taoist symbol of change and transformation. According to one Taoist legend, the philosopher Zhuangzi was sleeping beside a river when he dreamed of being a butterfly. As he awoke, it was unclear to him whether he was actually awake or still dreaming. He wondered whether

A carving in the Palace of
Quetzalpapalotl, Teotihuacan,
depicts the mythical bird
butterfly god Quetzal Mariposa.

he was Zhuangzi dreaming of being a butterfly, or a butterfly dreaming of being Zhuangzi?

In American Indian traditions, the butterfly is a symbol of joy, change, and transformation. Among the Hopi peoples, virgin girls braided their hair in the shape of butterfly wings to show that they were single or free to marry.

From egg to larvae to pupa, the butterfly has an extraordinary metamorphosis, and then from the cocoon the butterfly emerges in all its winged glory. As one of nature's most perfect examples of change and growth, it is hardly surprising that the butterfly has become a worldwide symbol of transformation, and is often considered an intermediary between the spiritual and apparent real world.

CREATURE SYMBOLS

BEE
Bees found in ancient Near East and Aegean cultures were thought to bridge the upperworld and the underworld. They appeared in funerary decorations, and Mycenean tombs were even shaped as beehives. Bee symbols are also found in Mesoamerican civilization, such as Ah-Muzen-Cab, the Maya bee god. Honey bees, signifying immortality and resurrection, were royal symbols for the Merovingians, the seventh-century dynasty of French kings.

BEETLE
The scarab beetle of ancient Egypt is known for its symbolism of rebirth and renewal, but the beetle was considered by many European folk traditions to represent change and the flow of life. For example, the stag beetle was devoted to the Norse god Thor, and was reputed to bring changing weather, such as lightning and thunder.

SCORPION
In Greek mythology the scorpion was symbolic of death, treachery, and transition when Artemis used the scorpion to sting Orion's foot, causing his death. Afterward, Zeus made the scorpion a zodiac sign among the stars. There are some species in which the venom is actually the antidote for the sting. In Egypt and Tibet this is seen as a good omen, so scorpions are often depicted in amulets that signify protection and ward off evil.

SPIDER
Along with its web, the spider has been a worldwide symbol of mystery, power, and destiny since ancient times. In ancient Egypt, the spider was associated with the goddess Neith in her aspect as spinner and weaver of destiny. In Greek mythology, the goddess Athena, an expert in crafts, challenged the nymph Arachne to a weaving contest. When Arachne won, the goddess spared her but turned her into a spider to continue weaving.

HALLEY'S COMET
BABYLON, MESOPOTAMIA *c.* 164 BCE

A portent of both good and evil

The first recorded appearance of Halley's Comet may have been as early as 467 BCE, when a comet was recorded in ancient Greece; its timing, location, duration, and associated meteor shower all suggest it was Halley. However, the only surviving record is of the 164 BCE apparition, and this is found on two fragmentary Babylonian tablets held in the British Museum, London. A later apparition of 87 BCE was also recorded on Babylonian tablets, and these state that the comet was seen "day beyond day" for a month. This was the first time that the comet seems to have been associated with an event or have had some powerful influence. The event was used as a power symbol for the Armenian king Tigranes the Great, and it was depicted on coins with a crown that features a star with a curved tail. This may well have heralded the New Era of the King of Kings. Halley's appearance in 12 BCE, only a few years after the conventionally assigned date of Jesus Christ's birth, has led many astronomers and theologians to believe that the comet may explain the story of the Star of Bethlehem.

Halley's Comet completes its eccentric orbit within a period of 200 years or less, and it is the only comet visible to the naked eye. Its approximate seventy-six-year cycle means that it is the only comet that most people can hope to see at least once, if not twice, during their lifetime. Because of this uniqueness and its often dazzling appearance, it has gained a reputation for being a harbinger of not only doom, but also an auspicious future.

Strange happenings in the sky have always been signs of something good or bad about to happen to different civilizations throughout history. This includes meteor showers, lunar and solar eclipses, comets, the Northern Lights, hurricanes, tornados, and two planets appearing in conjunction—side by side in the heavens. To the ancients, comets were "hairy stars" because they appeared to be unpredictable in the sky. The most well-known comet is Halley's Comet, notorious for its portent of doom, gloom, and marvel. Like eclipses, the appearance of a comet is a spectacular event, marking an important time for rulers, leaders, kings, and prophets. Consequently, the comet itself became a symbol or a sign of things to come, whether for good or bad.

During the Dark Ages little recorded evidence exists, but the biggest change in its symbol as an omen came in 1066 when Halley's appearance was thought to be an omen of

Ancient Babylonian tablets record the passing of Halley's Comet a hundred years or so before the birth of Jesus Christ.

disaster. In the same year, Harold II of England was defeated and died at the Battle of Hastings. However, the comet proved to be a good omen for the man who defeated him, William the Conqueror. In the Bayeux Tapestry the comet is shown as a fiery star, and extant accounts of its appearance described it as being four times the size of Venus and shining with a light equal to a quarter of that of the moon.

Halley's return in 1222 was, according to astrologers and seers, responsible for a more startling event. Genghis Khan is said to have considered the comet his personal star, and its westward trajectory inspired him to head west himself, launching an invasion of southeastern Europe that would leave a path of destruction behind him. It is likely, however, that Genghis Khan had little concern for celestial signs and was intent on conquering most of the civilized world whatever was happening in the sky.

In 1456, Halley's apparition was witnessed in Kashmir and depicted in great detail by Srivara, a Sanskrit poet and biographer to the sultans of Kashmir. He saw the apparition as a portent of doom foreshadowing the imminent fall of Sultan Zayn al-Abidin. In the same year, Emperor Zara Yaqob, ruler of Ethiopia from 1434 to

1468, after witnessing a bright light in the sky that most historians have identified as Halley's Comet, founded the City of Light and made it his capital for the remainder of his reign.

The first realization that comets were cyclical was made by Sir Edmond Halley, who utilized Newton's laws of gravity and Kepler's laws of planetary motion to predict the return of Halley's Comet in 1758. The appearance of Halley in 1910 was preceded by an unexpected appearance of a totally different comet in January the same year. Due to media hype, this became a sign of the imminent end of the world. This double whammy of comet doom and gloom led to the announcement of comet parties in Parisian suburbs to celebrate Halley's passing and the end of the world. Some feared that its tail was filled with deadly poisonous gases that would wipe out the world. One bright and bemused journalist suggested wise and wealthy Parisians should hire a submarine for a few days and submerge themselves in the North Sea while the comet passed over.

Comets and other celestial activity have always been symbolic of portents, and even today eclipses are thought to be highly important signs of forthcoming events.

The Bayeux Tapestry records the sighting of Halley's comet in 1066, which was considered by English astrologers as a bad omen for King Harold.

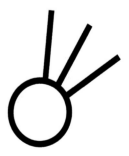

Comets were not only considered symbols of forthcoming doom and bad luck, but also of auspicious events.

HORNED GOD
DENMARK 152–150 BCE

Associated with fertility, growth, nature, and rebirth

This richly decorated silver vessel from the second century BCE was found in a peat bog in Denmark and its imagery is believed to have Thracian, Celtic, or even Hindu associations.

The mysterious figure of a horned god, beaten out of the superb silver vessel known as the Gundestrup Cauldron, is Cernunnos, god of Celtic and pagan polytheism. Cernunnos is often portrayed with animals such as the stag, and sometimes appears with the ram-horned serpent, as well as with bulls, dogs, and rats. Because of his association with creatures, Cernunnos is often described by scholars as the "lord of the animals" or "god of wild things," but he is also known as a peaceful god of nature and fruitfulness.

Various scholars have speculated that the Cernunnos figure may have been a deity of particular importance to a magic tradition common across Eurasia and still surviving in Tantric yoga and Siberian shamanism. Interestingly, there is a similar horned god on the Pashupati Seal (2500–2400 BCE), found in Mohenjodaro in the Indus Valley. The image is thought to be either one of the earliest depictions of the Hindu god Shiva, in his epithet Pashupati, or of the Vedic deity Rudra, god of the hunt and wild animals.

The name Cernunnos first appears inscribed in Latin on the Pillar of the Boatmen, a square-section limestone bas-relief that features depictions of several deities, both Gaulish and Roman. The Gallic-Roman monument dates to the early first century CE and originally stood in a temple in Lutetia, or the Roman-Gaul Paris. The Cernunnos depiction refers to a god seated cross-legged with stag's antlers in their early stage of annual growth. Both antlers have torques or stiff metal neck rings hanging from them.

The main dedication on the stone is to the god Jupiter. The remaining dedications accompany the depictions of the other gods, although they are not all clear or complete. These are, in order after Jupiter: Tarvos Trigaranus, Volcanus, Esus, Cernunnos, Castor, Smertrios, and Fortuna. It is thought that Cernunnos would originally have been in a cross-legged seated position.

EGYPTIAN ORIGINS

The horned god may also have origins in Egyptian deities such as Hathor, the cow goddess, and her predecessor, Bat, the goddess of late Paleolithic cattle herding in predynastic Egypt. In dynastic Egypt, a cult developed around the god Amon-Ra, who was depicted with ram horns. Rams were symbols of virility because of their violent rutting behavior. The horns of Amon also represented the directions east and west, or the rising and setting of the sun, which the Egyptians believed was the sun god Ra traveling across the sky.

Alexander the Great was depicted with the horns of Amon as a result of his conquest of Egypt in 332 BCE. The priests of Amon received Alexander as the son of Amon, and the god was later identified with Zeus. This new combined deity, Zeus-Amon, became a distinctive god in his own right with a bearded face and striking rams horns, as well as his own cult following.

From the early Middle Ages, the Christian Church was intent on stamping out any kind of pagan worship throughout Europe. Ancient cults surrounding gods such as the Greek Dionysus were effectively suppressed, and the horned god Cernunnos was demonized by the Church. His worshippers were subsequently accused of witchcraft and of forming pacts with the devil.

As a symbol of fertility, growth, nature, and rebirth, horned gods, including Cernunnos, from various cultures are still revered in Wicca and other forms of neopaganism. For these belief systems, the horned god symbolizes the seasons of the year in an annual cycle of life, death, and rebirth. Cernunnos is also associated with nature, wilderness, sexuality, hunting, and the cycle of life. Although depictions of the deity vary, he is always shown with either horns or antlers, and sometimes as having a beast's head.

Other horned gods include the ancient Greek god Pan, whose homeland was in rustic Arcadia. With the hindquarters, legs, and horns of a goat, Pan is associated with nature, mountains, hunting, and rustic music. Like other horned gods, he was a fertility symbol and god of the spring season.

This first-century CE Roman cast terra-cotta sculpture depicts the bearded, ram-horned Jupiter-Amon.

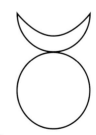

The astrological symbol for Taurus represents a bull's head and horns, associated with many ancient gods.

ALGOL, OR DEMON STAR

c. second century CE

A foreboding fixed star associated with bloody violence

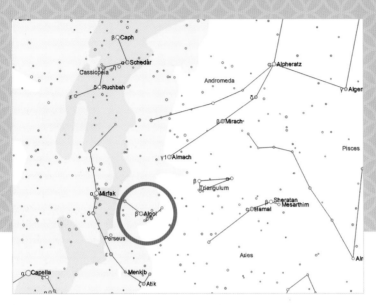

In astrology, the infamous Algol fixed star lies in the astronomical constellation Perseus. Algol was regarded by the ancients as the most evil star in the heavens.

Algol, or the Demon Star, is one of fifteen fixed stars that were used in astrological talismanic magic throughout medieval and Renaissance Europe and in the Arab world. It is best known for having mythological associations with the serpent-headed monster, Medusa, and takes its name from an Arabic word meaning "the demon's head." The star is said to depict the terrifying snake head of the Medusa monster due to it unpredictable behavior in the sky. The Alexandrian astronomer Ptolemy referred to Algol in his second-century text as the Gorgon of Perseus, and since then in literature and art it has been symbolic of death by decapitation.

In Greek mythology, Medusa was originally a temple virgin to Athena. Beautiful, charming, and wise, she was admired for her glorious hair. Overcome by lust, Poseidon ravished the virgin in the temple. Athena was not amused so she cursed Medusa for defiling her sacred ground. Out of jealousy, she turned Medusa

into a hideous serpent-headed gorgon with a petrifying stare. Perseus was sent to slay the gorgon and managed to decapitate Medusa while looking at her reflection in the mirrored shield he had received from Athena. When Perseus beheaded Medusa, Pegasus, a winged horse, and Chrysaor, a golden, sword-wielding giant, sprang from her body. Drops of blood from Medusa's head turned into the monster Amphisbaena, a serpent with a head at each end. This creature symbolized duality, disunity, and the unpredictable because it was able to attack from either end at will. Perseus used Medusa's head to turn enemies to stone and later gave it to Athena, who placed it on her shield, the Aegis. In recent feminist and psychological circles, Medusa's horrific decapitated head is considered a symbol of female rage.

Historically, the Algol star has been symbolic of bloody violence across a wide variety of cultures. In Hebrew, this triple star system, with its binary eclipsing star, is called Rosh ha Satan: the head of Satan. In Arabic, the star is called Ra's al Ghul, the demon's head, and in Chinese, it is called the Fifth Star of Mausoleum. In astrology, Algol is considered one of the most foreboding and evil fixed stars in the sky, and was listed as one of the fifteen Behenian stars in Early Renaissance magic and astrology.

The Behenian fixed stars are symbols used in talismanic magic. Their name derives from the Arabic word *bahman*, meaning "root." Each was considered the source of a specific power when in alignment with one or more of the planets. Each star corresponds to both a gemstone and a plant, and when used together in ritual magic would draw down the star's influence into the talisman. When a planet was within six degrees of the fixed star, this was a particularly potent influence and indicated that it was time to perform the ritual.

In the sixteenth century, magician and astrologer Cornelius Agrippa discussed the fifteen stars in his *Three Books of Occult Philosophy*, describing their magical workings and listing their esoteric symbols. He listed all fifteen stars, and gave beneficial times for performing the magical ritual and associated plant, gemstone, and planetary configuration. Although the true origin of these workings remains unknown, the early twentieth century Egyptologist Sir Wallis Budge believed that they derived from an ancient Sumerian source.

INTERPRETING THE STARS

When the moon was in conjunction with the rising Plaeides (considered a group of fixed stars by the ancients), it was time to summon demons—at the time demons were nature spirits rather than anything sinister—and spirits of the dead, and to call on the winds, reveal secrets, and admit things that were lost.

The fixed star Aldebaran, when rising and conjunct the moon, was thought to increase riches and honor. However Algol, with its ancient association with bad luck, was described as "granting vengeance over anyone one wished" and as bringing "hatred to any man." The method was simply to take the appropriate gemstone, plus the herb or plant extract, and make a ring out of the metal corresponding to the star, then fasten it to the stone. Next the magician would place the herb beneath the ring, adding important inscriptions and secret symbols as described. For example, in order for Algol's magic to work, one would mix black hellebore juice with an equal amount of wormwood and place it under a diamond.

Early stargazers would have watched this strange, almost winking star in a sky full of steadily shining ones. It was hardly surprising that Algol had a bad reputation because it stood out as being different, and anything that was unusual, variable, and uncertain to the ancients was worthy of superstition and fear.

Algol is now known as a variable star, which waxes and wanes in brightness. It brightens and dims with clockwork regularity, completing one cycle in two days, twenty hours, and forty-nine minutes, and its entire cycle is visible to the naked eye. This is because it is an eclipsing binary star. In other words, it is composed of two stars, with each star revolving around the other. From Earth, we can see the orbital plane of this binary star almost exactly edge-on. Therefore, when the dimmer of the two stars swings in front of the brighter star, we see Algol at minimum brightness. To the observer it looks like a winking, evil eye in the sky.

The hero Perseus was able to slay Medusa by using a mirrored shield, and it was believed her slain head became the terrifying winking Algol star.

The sigil for Algol was reputed to bring hatred to any man.

PHALLUS
CERNE ABBAS, DORSET, ENGLAND *c.* 183–1650

Powerful symbol of fertility and virility

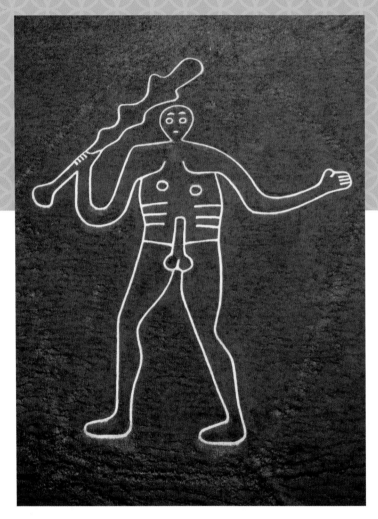

This mysterious giant with his huge erect phallus may have been cut into the grass when Britain was ruled by the Romans.

is one of the most well-known and provocative phallic symbols in Europe. Situated not far from the quaint village of Cerne Abbas in Dorset, England, it is a spectacular cut figure carved into a west-facing hill. For centuries there have been numerous legends about the giant and why and how he came to be on the hillside. Some say he was a real giant, Danish in origin, who terrorized the locals and ate their sheep. While the giant slept on the hill one night, the people of Cerne Abbas killed him and then dug an outline around his body, marking him forever on the hillside. Some locals now claim that the giant figure comes alive at night and makes his way down to the nearby stream to drink.

In the medieval times, locals would put up a maypole on the earthwork area above the area of his head. Childless couples would dance around the maypole in the hope of promoting fertility. Infertility was also thought to be cured by having sex on top of the figure, and legend tells of how infertile women were able to conceive after sleeping for a night on the ground near the giant's phallus. Other stories abound about how young women were able to keep their lovers faithful by walking three times around the giant's figure.

GREEK AND ROMAN MYTHS

With his huge erect phallus and testicles, the Cerne Abbas giant is believed to be a pagan symbol of fertility. Although no one really knows at what date the figure was carved, since medieval times the site has been used for popular fertility rites and ceremonies.

Standing an impressive 180 feet (55 m) high, the mighty Cerne Abbas giant was formed by a trench carved into the chalky turf and it

Historians believe that the Cerne Abbas giant could also be an image of the Greek-Roman god Hercules, who had been amalgamated with a local god of pagan worship between 180 and 192 CE. At the time, Roman Emperor Commodus, who ruled this part of Britain, believed himself to be a reincarnation of Hercules and may well have developed the cult in England as a form of personal self-aggrandizement.

This engraving of an ancient Greek decorative vase, in the Collection of the Comte de Lamberg (1813–1824), depicts the gods (from left to right) Hermes, Dionysus, and Priapus.

However, other scholars have linked the giant to the ancient Greek myth of Priapus, the ugly god who was cast out of Mount Olympus and thrown down to Earth and left on a hillside. Priapus was cursed with impotence and foul-mindedness by Hera while he was still in Aphrodite's womb, in revenge for the hero, Paris, having the gall to judge Aphrodite more beautiful than Hera. After being thrown down to Earth, Priapus joined Pan and the satyrs as a fertility spirit. Eternally frustrated by his impotence, he was finally sexually aroused by the goddess Hestia visiting the meadow nymphs on Earth. As she lay sleeping, he attempted to rape her, but at the critical moment, a braying ass caused him to lose his erection and wake Hestia. The episode gave him a lasting hatred of asses, and later in Roman culture the animals were often destroyed in his honor.

In Greece, the phallus was thought to have a mind of its own, animal-like and separate from the mind of man. Represented in its erect form, the phallus was present in almost every aspect of daily life, and statues of a hugely erect Priapus were believed to avert the evil eye. In order to appease Priapus, travelers would stroke the statue's penis as they passed by. The Athenians merged Priapus with Hermes, the god of boundaries, and depicted a hybrid deity with a winged helmet, winged sandals, and a huge erection.

As far back as ancient Egypt, the phallus played an important role in the cult of Osiris, and the Egyptian fertility god Min was usually depicted with an erect penis. The phallus was a familiar symbol in ancient Roman culture, too, and protective phallic charms called "fascinum" were popular forms of jewelry. Equally popular were garden statues of Priapus, who guarded and promoted fertility in the household. Young Roman boys also wore the bulla, an amulet containing a phallic charm, until they formally came of age. Priapus and his lustful nature were not only depicted comically by the Romans in their erotic literature and art, but also became an important symbol of virility and power among ordinary folk.

The phallus has throughout history been considered a symbol of male virility and power.

This third-century fascinum amulet would have been worn as a pendant.

NAZCA LINES
NAZCA DESERT, PERU *c.* 500

Zoomorphic and geometric geoglyphs etched into the desert

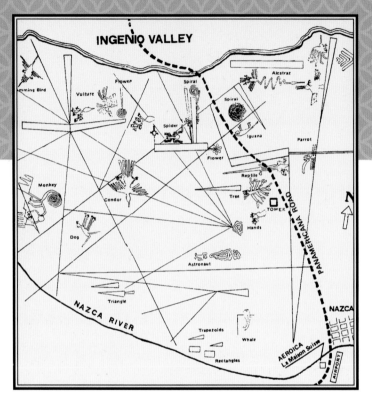

The Nazca lines are a series of vast, mostly zoomorphic symbols—monkey, condor, heron, spider, for example—the meaning of which still puzzles archaeologists.

Two thousand years ago, the city of Cahuachi was built as a sacred site of ceremony and ritual in the hot, dusty Nazca desert. Here, geometric lines and shapes of animals, birds, and strange figures, known as the Nazca lines, were etched in the dry stone of the desert. But for what reason?

Once a lush oasis, two natural disasters in the fourth century devastated Cahuachi. First a huge flood cut off the city's natural water supplies, then a massive earthquake split the temples apart. This led to the fall of Cahuachi's religious power. Believing that the mountains, sky, rivers, floods, and earthquakes were all ruled by the gods, the Nazca people assumed that the deities had caused these natural disasters to show their displeasure and so abandoned the once sacred center for ceremonial rituals.

In Cahuachi, elite priests were apparently more like shamans or sorcerers. One legend tells of how these priests could fly through the air directing workers to make the Nazca lines. Across the pampas from Cahuachi lay the huge city of Ventilla, and many believe that the lines were sacred walkways linking the cities and their vital water source.

The mysterious lines, seen most clearly from the air, are also thought to have an astrological or astronomical significance. Others believe that they were the work of ancient UFOs. It is commonly thought that the lines were a form of worship to the sky and mountain gods, and mostly they were used for rituals and ceremonies to invoke the nature gods and their need for water.

ZOOMORPHIC SYMBOLS

Animal symbolism is common throughout the Andes, and the Nazca lines include a wide range of zoomorphic symbols, such as the monkey, spider, dog, hummingbird, condor, heron, whale, and pelican. For the ancient Andean peoples, seeing a spider crawl out of a hole was believed to be a sign of rain. Respected for its weaving and ambivalent nature—some species were poisonous, whereas others were useful killers of dangerous insects—the spider became a symbol of silent power. In some indigenous peoples of Mesoamerica, the spider was often revered as a god, such as the Great Weaver of the Maya who spins the web of life.

To the Nazca people, the hummingbird was thought to be a messenger from the gods because it was the only bird able to fly

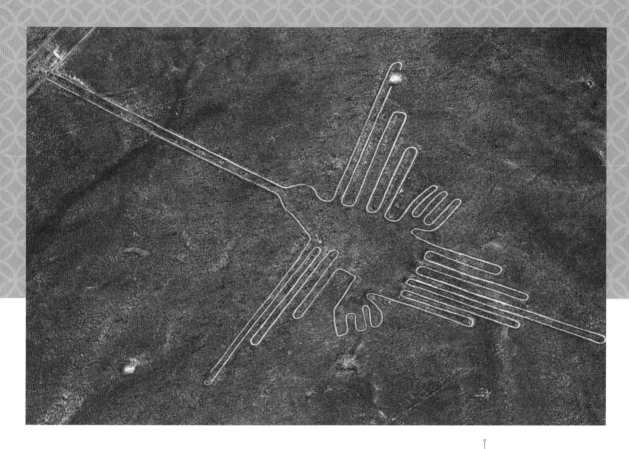

backward, as if from the divine world to the real world. The hummingbird has a powerful spiritual significance throughout the Andes where it is also a symbol of resurrection. From legend, it appears to die on cold nights, but comes back to life again at sunrise.

Monkeys were abundant in the Amazon region and invoked the heavy rainfall of that area. However, in many cultures the monkey was a symbol of humanlike characteristics such as mimicry, cunning, duplicity, and greed. Monkeys are often shape-shifters, and far across the oceans from South America, the popular monkey god in Indian Hinduism, Hanuman, was a brave, yet cunning shape-shifter who helped the divine hero Rama defeat Ravana, the evil king.

To the Nazcas, the pelican and heron were symbols of water places, and their propitiation and worship invoked rain or made rivers swell. The condor is one of the largest geoglyphs at the site, and like other eagles, the bird soared high and had powerful eyesight; it was considered to be the lord of the sky. The condor also looked down upon the land, and its flight path could lead to rivers and fertile plains.

Nowadays, the coastal region of southern Peru and northern Chile is one of the driest places on Earth. In the small, protected basin where the Nazca culture arose, ten rivers descend from the Andes to the east, most of them dry for part of the year. These ten ribbons of fertile water were the perfect place for the emergence of an early civilization. But it seems likely, due to dramatic climate change, that these precious rivers eventually dried up.

Almost all of the iconic Nazca animal figures, such as the spider and the hummingbird, were single-line drawings with open pathways. This has suggested to archaeologists that at some point the lines evolved from mere images to ritual walkways and ceremonial processions for invoking the power of these animals, perhaps for the need for water, in an attempt to retain the fertility of the lands.

In many Andean cultures, the hummingbird was thought to be able to fly between worlds, taking messages from the gods to humankind.

The hummingbird loses body heat while sleeping. Its body heat is restored with the rising sun, and it is thus considered a symbol of resurrection.

SKULL

MESOAMERICA *c.* 600–1250

A symbol of death in numerous civilizations throughout the world

The Aztecs displayed the skulls of the conquered on racks, such as this tzompantli at Templo Mayor, Tenochtitlan, Mexico, to show off their warring powers.

The skull is a symbol of death throughout many civilizations and religions. Among the Mesoamerican civilizations, large numbers of skulls were exhibited on a tzompanti, or skull rack, which was used for public displays of human skulls, commonly of war or sacrificial victims. It was made up of a scaffoldlike construction of wooden poles, and heads and skulls were placed on the tzompanti after holes had been drilled through the skull. Most skull racks date from around 600 to 1250.

The Aztecs were particularly proud of displaying trophies of their enemies: either warriors or the elite, who were sacrificed to the gods on capture. The heart would usually be torn from the victim's chest while still alive, and the corpse pushed or thrown down the steps of the temple. At the bottom of the temple, attendants were responsible for severing the limbs and head from the torso, and the warrior who brought the captive would be given the limbs as property; sometimes the skull would be skinned. The limbs were often eaten as a sign of respect and also of empowerment. The skulls or heads were then placed on the poles and mounted on the rack.

In the mythological and religious account known as the Popol Vuh (Book of the People), the story of the hero twins, Hunahpú and Xbalanqué, describes their descent to the underworld to find their murdered father. When Hunahpú was killed by the lords of the

The Mexican Day of the Dead is celebrated with totem skeletons and skulls, and offerings are made to family ancestors.

underworld, his head was hung in a gourd tree next to a ball court. The court was where the twins found the entrance to the underworld, and gourd trees became symbolic depictions of death, used throughout Mesoamerican decorative art.

The symbol of the skull still appears in many forms on the Day of the Dead, a Mexican celebration. The holiday focuses on gatherings of family and friends to pray for and remember those who have died. Skull masks and skeletons are popular, as are confections such as sugar or chocolate skulls, which are inscribed with the name of the recipient on the forehead. Sugar skulls can be given as gifts to both the living and the dead. In Hinduism, the goddess of death, Kali, is often depicted wearing a garland of skulls. One Hindu myth relates how she leaped out of Durga's forehead carrying a skull-topped staff, decorated with a necklace of skulls, and clad in a tiger's skin. She soon devoured the clones of the demon Raktabija, sucked the blood from the leader, then danced on the field of battle, stepping on the corpses of the slain. In twentieth-century Germany, the Nazi SS incorporated the skull into the uniforms of its concentration camp guards.

A more positive symbol can be found in the thousands of skulls and bones of monks located in an ossuary in Rome, the Capuchin Crypt. This strange display of skulls and bones, collected between 1528 and 1870, decorates the walls of the crypt in dramatic Baroque and Rococo style. The collection is more positive than it first appears because it reminds the people who visit of their own mortality. However, the skulls also emphasize that we must take each moment as it comes and get on with living. Similarly, the symbol of a skull crowned by a wreath of roses is referred to as a "carpe diem"—a reference to the Latin phrase in a poem by Horace—which translates as "seize the day."

The skull and crossbones symbol was placed on bottles of poison as a visual reminder of danger. Also commonly associated with pirates, the skull and crossbones was probably the most unwelcome flag to be seen on the high seas.

The skull and crossbones is a familiar symbol of danger and death on the ocean, and is still used by pirates today.

TOTEM POLE

NORTH AMERICA *c.* 1500

American Indian celebratory wooden monolith

Totem poles such as this one in the Rocky Mountains, British Columbia, Canada, are carved with depictions of spirit symbols and iconic legends.

The word "totem" most probably derives from an Algonquian word *odoodem* meaning "kinship group." Totem poles are physical manifestations of a spiritual idea or belief that belongs to the people who made it. American Indian beliefs are essentially animistic; in other words, people believe that everything in the natural world is infused with spirit, either of its own or of some immanent force, or both. As varied as the cultures that have carved them, totem poles usually recount familiar legends and myths, clan lineages, notable ancestors or events, and spirit symbols. Some poles celebrate cultural beliefs, while others are mostly artistic. Certain types of totem poles are often part of funerary structures and incorporate coffins

KACHINA

For the Hopi and Pueblo peoples, the kachina is the life bringer. Kachinas are spirits or personifications of things in the real world. A kachina can represent anything in the natural world, from a revered ancestor to a location, quality, natural phenomenon, or concept.

MANITOU

The manitou is the spiritual and fundamental life force of the Algonquian indigenous peoples. The Meskwaki peoples of the Great Lakes region believed that the manitou lived in the stones of the sweat lodge. When the stove was alight, the heat of the fire forced the manitou to leave the stones and to energize the human body.

WAKAN TANKA

Wakan Tanka, or the Great Spirit, is believed by the Sioux peoples, for example, to be personal and close to the people, and to permeate the fabric of the material world.

hero, warrior, or even animal with supernatural powers. The myths and symbols associated with these people and animals meant that the people would learn about their own civilization, culture, and creation through their identification with the totem, and it is the animal ancestors who are often the most common form of depiction on a totem pole. Elaborate animal symbols are carved into the totem pole not only to signify the community's very essence of that animal, but also to give that community meaning and belief. For example, a thunderbird symbolizes power, a frog represents a sign of prosperity, and a bear is symbolic of strength and protection. Totem animals are sacred to the clan, and killing one is taboo. The carving of human faces, particularly common on Alaskan totem poles and often known as wild men and women of the woods, was linked to ancestor spirits, either those who had been lost in the forests or perished from drowning in rivers or the sea.

Worldwide, notable indigenous peoples with similar totem polelike objects include the Jilin of northeast China, the Ainu indigenous people of north Japan, the Maori of New Zealand, and the Madia Gond of India. In Maori culture, "pou whenuas" are decorative wooden posts that mark territorial boundaries or places of sacred significance. They are generally artistically and elaborately carved and can be found throughout New Zealand. Like totem poles, pou whenuas tell a story that is significant to the Maori civilization. Specifically, they reflect the relationship between the ancestors, the environment, and the reputation or standing of the indigenous Maori people. In India, decorative pillars are also indicators of reputation. Madia Gond bridegrooms, once they become engaged to be married, carve a one-piece pillar known as a Mundha and keep it in front of the community dormitory until the marriage ceremony, as a sign of their loyalty and fertility.

with carved supporting poles or recessed areas for funerary relics. Poles also illustrate stories that are symbolic of shamanic powers or demonstrate the success of various clans and families. It is believed by some historians that totem poles originated from the Haida people, whose territories span the boundary between Alaska and British Columbia.

Among the indigenous peoples of the Pacific Northwest, monumental sculptures carved from the trunks of large trees dot the landscape. Most of the poles are carved from the western or giant red cedar. However, the wood quickly decays in the damp climate of the region, which is why, although early poles originated around 1500, few carved before 1900 exist today.

Many American Indian cultures have specific hero or warrior figures in their mythology who influenced some aspect of that society and its culture. This may be an ancestral figure,

The Star House Pole is a frontal house pole commissioned in the nineteenth century by Anetlas, chief of the K'ouwas eagle clan, for an adoption ceremony.

AMERICAN INDIAN ANIMAL SPIRITS

FOX

By living between light and darkness, the fox sees into both worlds. It is physically and mentally quick and extremely agile, teaching us to respond quickly to situations by using the power of inner instincts and knowing. The Hopi, Cherokee, and other tribes believe that fox medicine brings great healing power.

HORSE

To the American Indian, the horse symbolizes freedom and the power that comes with being free. For those who seek the spirit of the horse, the idea of freedom is a predominant theme. The horse brought ease of movement to indigenous people, who quickly learned they could hunt and move into new territories as never before.

OTTER

Otters are free-spirited and playful, and they symbolize universal love not personal love. They remind us to love one another and share in the joy of living. Otter spirit teaches us how to swim through problems and emotional upheavals of life. It represents letting go of negative emotions such as anger, jealousy, and fear.

COYOTE

Coyote is the subject of many American Indian legends, songs, and ceremonies, and it is often referred to as the trickster. Coyotes can adapt to almost any environment, but prefer the prairies and low foothills. Coyote's medicine is that of the teacher: we must remember wisdom is the true use of knowledge.

RAVEN

The raven is often referred to by some indigenous tribes as the "secret keeper." Its ebony black color is sometimes associated with darkness. A magical bird that carries messages and prayers to the spirits, the raven comes only to those whom it can trust with its secrets. It is also a shape-shifter, and its medicine is one of change.

COUGAR

The cougar is agile, unhesitating, and powerful. Cougar medicine is about not rushing in too fast and being stealthy, wise, and patient. His lesson is one of being a balanced leader. However, when someone is ready to act they must throw themselves one hundred percent into the goal, just as the cougar does when he finally sets off after his prey.

BEAVER

The beaver is well equipped to defend its home and family. Its message is: to keep active and busy; to be resourceful and practical; to be open to change when necessary; to use team effort when working toward your goals and objectives; to be alert to alternative solutions; and to make use of available resources whenever possible.

BUFFALO

The smaller woodland buffalo and its bigger cousin the plains buffalo were revered and honored in ceremony and everyday life. To the plains Indian, the buffalo meant sacred life and the abundance of the creator's blessing on Mother Earth. The buffalo is a powerful symbol of sacrifice and service to the community.

BEAR

In North America, native peoples believed the Great Mystery lived in the spirit of bear. Many American Indian tribes have bear clans and bear ceremonies, and the bear represents the west side of the medicine wheel. The west is the place of intuition, transformation, inner knowing, shamanic journeying, dreams, and visions.

CROW

Crow is the guardian of ceremonial magic and healing and the sacred keeper of the law. Crow medicine signifies a firsthand knowledge of a higher order of right and wrong than that indicated by the laws created in human culture. Crow medicine people are masters of illusion and bring messages from the spirit world.

EAGLE

American Indians see the eagle as a sacred messenger that carries prayers to the creator and returns with gifts and visions. In many cultures it as a symbol of courage, vision, strength, and endurance. Eagles need isolation in the wild to prosper. This teaches us that we have a singular walk in life and must face life on its terms.

SPIDER

In American Indian traditions, the first dream catcher was made by Grandmother Spider to catch the bad dreams of children. Grandmother spider is a wise old teacher and weaver of many stories. Her unique tapestry of life offers many paths to the center of oneself and creation. Her medicine speaks of connections and unity of spirit.

At the UNESCO site of Lara Jonggrang Temple, Java, the wise Hindu god, Ganesha surveys all who pass by.

THE DIVINE WORLD

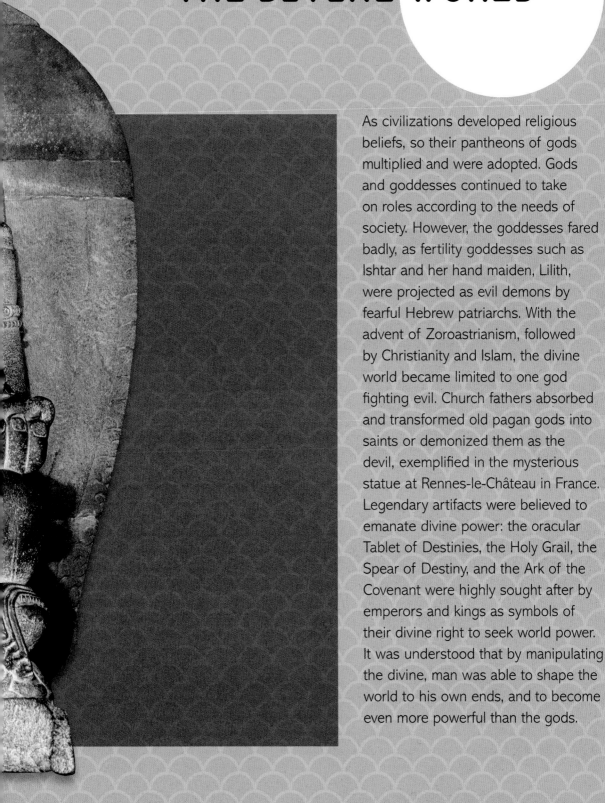

As civilizations developed religious beliefs, so their pantheons of gods multiplied and were adopted. Gods and goddesses continued to take on roles according to the needs of society. However, the goddesses fared badly, as fertility goddesses such as Ishtar and her hand maiden, Lilith, were projected as evil demons by fearful Hebrew patriarchs. With the advent of Zoroastrianism, followed by Christianity and Islam, the divine world became limited to one god fighting evil. Church fathers absorbed and transformed old pagan gods into saints or demonized them as the devil, exemplified in the mysterious statue at Rennes-le-Château in France. Legendary artifacts were believed to emanate divine power: the oracular Tablet of Destinies, the Holy Grail, the Spear of Destiny, and the Ark of the Covenant were highly sought after by emperors and kings as symbols of their divine right to seek world power. It was understood that by manipulating the divine, man was able to shape the world to his own ends, and to become even more powerful than the gods.

CRESCENT MOON

VÉZÈRE VALLEY, FRANCE c. 22,000–18,000 BCE

One of the earliest goddess figurines holds a crescent moon

The Goddess of Laussel holds a crescent moon, both a symbol of female fertility and of the importance of the lunar cycles for hunting.

civilizations developed their pantheons of gods. The shelter, hidden under an overhanging cliff, looks over a valley and is thought to have been an ancient ceremonial center. Believed to originate from the Upper Paleolithic period of around 22,000 BCE, the carvings include a woman with her head apparently covered with a net; a younger, slimmer, female figure; and a plump Venus figure.

The most impressive of the carvings is the Goddess of Laussel: a 1½-foot-high (0.45 m) sculpture of a woman with large breasts, belly, and thighs, and well-defined genitalia, holding in her right hand what looks like a large horn. Curiously, the object has thirteen vertical lines carved into it. Many scholars believe that these represent the thirteen-day cycle of either the waxing or waning moon, or simply the thirteenth lunar month. In fact, the object is thought to be not a horn but the crescent moon or first quarter moon of the lunar cycle. Whether the figure is a fertility goddess or a lunar one, the etched crescent moon has been interpreted as referring to the number of menstrual cycles in one year of a woman's life.

These ancient civilizations were essentially moon worshippers, and time was divided into lunar cycles. The waxing crescent moon—that is, up until the full moon—marked a time of growth and renewal; the waning moon, with its diminishing crescent moon, was a sign of closing down, rest, and dormancy. A crescent moon was also a symbol of the mother goddess in Vedic literature, in which it is said that worshippers "bow to the mother who holds the moon." In Sumeria and Mesopotamia, the mother goddess evolved to become

An early depiction of a crescent moon was discovered in 1911 on a bas-relief carved into a limestone rock shelter in the Dordogne region of France, with three other ancient carvings. It reveals evidence of ancient goddess worship by prehistoric civilizations, and depicts a goddess who was a personification of the Earth, moon, and sky, long before patriarchal

ISHTAR

Worshipped in Mesopotamia, Ishtar was the goddess of love, war, fertility, and sexuality. Her symbol is the eight-pointed star, and when she was assimilated into the Babylonian pantheon she became the divine personification of the planet Venus.

CYBELE

Cybele is believed to have evolved from an Anatolian mother goddess, and is similar to a stone carving of a seated woman giving birth on her throne, found at Catalhoyuk (in modern day Turkey) dating to 6,000 BCE. In Greece, a cult developed around her as both a mother goddess and as mistress of the animals, usually shown attended by hawks and lions.

ADITI

In the Indian Vedas texts of around 1700 BCE, Aditi is the mother of all the gods. She is a cosmic matrix who gave birth to all the heavenly bodies. As celestial mother of every existing form and being—the synthesis of all things—she is associated with space and with mystical wisdom.

The eight-pointed star was used by early Babylonian skywatchers to represent the planet Venus, or Ishtar, as the morning star.

identified with fertility and love goddesses such as Ishtar and Inanna; farther west, she was associated with the worship of Cybele and Anahita, as well as Aditi in India, Isis in Egypt, and Aphrodite in Greece.

MATRIARCHY

Other theories have been put forward about the figurine's meaning. Some historians say that the moon is a "a horn of plenty," representing fertility, whereas others believe that it is a musical instrument, symbolizing the power of shamanistic worship through music and chanting. Yet during this ancient period, there is substantial evidence to show that the worship of the great goddess was common and linked to the Earth, fertility, the moon, and the stars. Many other Venus figurines have been found throughout Europe, so it seems likely that these are traces of a matriarchal society found in the Paleolithic period. This lunar mother symbolism and its associations with the Earth prospered throughout ancient civilizations. Interestingly, names such as Ashtar and Ishtar are rooted in the Sanskrit words for "female" and "star," and the primary goddess was often known as the "female of the stars."

With the moon as time keeper, secret rituals to venerate the goddess and to ensure a successful hunt or gathering of fruit were performed at the most auspicious times according to the lunar phases. These lunar cycles later became interwoven with the cycles of the planets and the sun. It was during these rituals that secret wisdom was supposed to be discovered by initiates in dark caves, such as at Laussel. It was a wisdom that was believed to be given by the goddess, her symbol carved in rock as a reminder of her immanent power.

This is a waning crescent moon symbol, indicating a time to bring events to an end, to rest, and to take time to reflect.

Diana (1898) by Albert Edelfelt depicts the Roman goddess Diana, one of the most well-known deities associated with the moon.

LIBATION

EGYPT *c.* 3500–1500 BCE

Ritual pouring of liquid to honor the gods

The Egyptian offerings table of Nakht dates to around 1800 BCE and is decorated with a relief of bread, other offerings, and a libation scene.

The ritual pouring of a liquid as an offering to the gods, or in memory of those who have died, is known as libation. Common in many ancient religions, the practice still occurs in various cultures today. The most common substances used for libations in Greco-Roman culture were wine and olive oil, and in India, ghee, a type of clarified butter. The libation was often poured onto the earth, altar, or stone from a shallow metal or ceramic bowl known as a "patera."

It appears that libation originated as part of ancient Egyptian culture, in which it was simply a drink taken to honor and please the various gods, sacred ancestors, and the fertility of the lands. However, by the third millennium BCE, libation rituals had become a central and vital aspect of ancient Greek daily life. Those who worshipped the gods performed libations to begin meals, to start the day, and to end the day, as well as to thank the spirits of the dead for their protection.

One form of libation known as *sponde* was the ritualized pouring of wine from a jug or bowl. After wine was poured from the phial, the remainder of the contents was drunk by the offerer. As early as Homer's epic tales, the tradition of serving wine was accompanied by a libation made to Zeus and the other Olympian gods. Sometimes heroes were offered a libation as was the spirit of the vineyards. Libations poured onto the earth were meant for the dead or for the underworld gods. In the *Odyssey*, Odysseus digs an offering pit to the gods, around which he pours honey, wine, and water. Libations poured onto altars or tables that were carved with various figures or symbols activated the symbols, and thus activated the power of the gods.

In Roman culture, Liber Pater, or Father Liber, was the god of libations. In Roman art, the libation is shown performed at an altar or a special table. The introductory rite before performing an animal sacrifice included a wine libation, poured onto a burning altar. Emperors and gods are frequently depicted on coins, pouring libations.

From Hinduism to Siberian shamanism, the custom of libation is a traditional and valued part of all forms of worship. This symbol of offering liquids to the gods, or to the earth itself, was a deep-rooted connection and a sign of giving something back to the universe and to the gods to whom we owe our existence. It remains a symbol of offering, giving, and respect for what we have received and will receive. For example, among the Quechua and

Aymara cultures of South America, it is still common to pour a small amount of liquid on the ground before taking a drink, as an offering to the earth goddess Pachamama. In Japanese Shinto religion, the sake or rice wine used in libation rituals is often called Miki "the liquor of the gods." The practice of libation was also common in the ancient Jewish religion, mentioned in Genesis: "Jacob set up a pillar in the place where he had spoken with [God], a pillar of stone, and he poured out a drink offering on it, and poured oil on it."

In many West African traditions, libations are the offerings that are made to the spirits of the ancestor who are invited to attend any ceremonies, rituals, or particularly public festivities. Prayers are made by the elders, and libations of palm wine or water are performed. In Eastern Europe and Russia, one old tradition involved pouring vodka onto the grave of the ancestor, whereas in Chinese traditions, rice wine or tea is poured in front of an altar or tombstone, horizontally from right to left with both hands. In this way, it is both in honor of the dead, but also serves as an offering to the gods. In Hindu temples, Vishnu and other deities are offered libations of water, but these are often embellished with other substances such as milk, ghee, honey, or sugar.

The painted wooden Pitsa Tablet (*c.* 540 BCE) **from Corinthia, Greece, depicts a sacrificial procession to the libation altar.**

This detail from a fresco (*c.* 60–50 BCE) **at the Villa of Mysteries, Pompeii, Italy, depicts Dionysus performing an initiation ceremony.**

QUEEN OF THE NIGHT

IRAQ c. 1800–1750 BCE

Ancient depiction of a winged goddess with divine symbols, the rod and ring

The mysterious goddess depicted on the Queen of the Night relief (nineteenth-century BCE) became identified in Jewish scriptures with all that was demonic.

Lilith was a symbol of all things dark and feminine and remains a symbol of evil even today.

The Sumerian terra-cotta plaque known originally as the Burney relief is now called the Queen of the Night relief. There has been an ongoing debate not only about whom it represents, but also its real significance. The striking, magnificent winged goddess with taloned feet, accompanied by lions and two owls, is thought to be either Lilith (the demonic first wife of Adam, debased in Hebrew

mythology) or Inanna, the earlier version of Ishtar. Inanna and Ishtar were both aspects of the great goddess. The Sumerian Inanna was the first to be worshipped, at Uruk in 4000 BCE, and Ishtar was her later Assyrian counterpart. Lilith was also known to be Inanna's hand maiden, or possibly an aspect of Inanna.

Various metaphors in the imagery of the carving link the owl, lions, and talons with the worship of Inanna, and a similar motif appears on what is known as the Ishtar Vase, held in the Louvre, Paris. Other scholars believe the relief to be the only extant depiction of a Sumerian female demon called Lilitu. From the early Uruk culture of around 3450 BCE to the arrival of the first Semitic peoples near Byblos in Lebanon in 3200 BCE, the female demon Lilitu was particularly feared. Yet according to more recent scholarly research at the British Museum, the figure is neither Lilith nor Inanna/Ishtar, but Inanna's sister, Ereshkigal, the goddess of the underworld.

In the story of Inanna's descent to the underworld, Ereshkigal traps her sister in her kingdom, and Inanna is only able to leave it by sacrificing her husband, Dumuzi, in exchange for herself. During her stay in the underworld, Ereshkigal takes away Inanna's divine symbols, the rod and ring, shown on the Queen of the Night relief. It may be that the relief is a symbolic depiction of the demonic act in which Ereshkigal takes all of Inanna's power for herself.

The belief that the Queen of the Night figure is a demonic one, or an underworld figure at the very least, is based on the fact that the wings are not outspread and that the background of the relief was painted black originally. If this is the correct identification, it would make the relief the only known figurative representation of Ereshkigal, or a female demon.

However, there are many lingering myths surrounding the figure of Lilith, depicting her as the symbol of all that was considered by patriarchal societies as dark, evil, and feminine. She first appeared in the Hebrew Bible in Isaiah 34:14, where her name translated to "night hag," "screech owl," or "night monster." In the Songs of the Sage from the Dead Sea Scrolls, her name also occurs on a list of monsters. By the sixth century CE, in magical inscriptions on bowls and amulets, Lilith was identified and depicted as a terrifying female demon. Bowls were buried upside down in houses to trap the demon, and almost every Jewish house in Nippur was found to have such protective pottery buried in the ground. Amulets were worn

In *Lilith* (1892) Romantic painter John Collier not only idealizes Lilith, but also reveals the dark sexuality that she symbolizes.

to protect pregnant women, children, and young men from the terrors of Lilith, who invoked lust and caused men to be led astray. She was also apparently a child-killing witch who strangled helpless babies and murdered unborn babies in the womb.

At some point in Jewish mythology, between the eighth and tenth centuries CE, Lilith became the first wife of Adam, but then left him after she refused to become subservient to him and mated instead with the archangel Samael. In other accounts, Lilith was Asmodeus, the demon king's wife and lover. Her origins and the intended meaning of the Queen of the Night relief may never be confirmed, but the symbol of Lilith as demonic has continued to be a lasting influence in art, literature, and filmmaking to this today.

MESOPOTAMIAN DEITIES

ADAD

Adad was the god of storms.
He was usually shown carrying
a lightning fork to represent his
power over the storm forces
of nature. This Babylonian and
Assyrian god was known to
the Sumerians as Ishkur, and is
often shown with a lion-dragon
or bull. Adad's wife was the
goddess Shala.

ENLIL

God of breath, wind, height, and
distance, Enlil helped to create
humans. However, he soon tired of
their noise and tried to kill them
by sending a devastating flood.
A mortal known as Utnapishtim
survived the flood through the help
of another god, Ea. Utnapishtim
was made immortal by Enlil after his
fury had subsided.

ANU

The sky god, also known as the
king of gods, spirits, and demons,
Anu dwelled in the highest heavenly
regions. It was believed he had
the power to judge those who
had committed crimes, and that
he created the stars as soldiers to
destroy the wicked. His attendant
and minister of state was the god,
Illabrat.

MARDUK

Marduk, once a legendary mortal
who went on an epic journey
in search of immortality, was
renowned as the patron deity of
Babylon. When the city became a
political center in the eighteenth
century BCE, Marduk gradually rose
to become head of the Babylonian
gods and resided in the temple
Esagila.

NABU

Nabu was the Mesopotamian
god of writing and scribes and
he was also the keeper of the
Tablet of Destinies, on which the
fate of humankind was recorded.
He was also sometimes worshipped
as a fertility god and as a god of
water. His symbols are the clay
writing tablet and accompanying
stylus.

NERGAL

God of plague, war, and the sun in
its destructive capacity, Nergal was
assigned the role of husband of
the underworld goddess Ereshkigal.
Portrayed as a god of war and
pestilence, Nergal represented the
high summer: the dead season in
the Mesopotamian annual cycle. He
was also the head deity assigned to
the government of the dead.

ENKI

Enki was keeper of the divine powers called "Me," and his symbol was of two entwined snakes. He was often shown with the horned crown of divinity dressed in the skin of a carp. Considered the master shaper of the world, and god of wisdom and all magic, Enki was also the lord of freshwater seas, lakes, and underground waters.

BAU

Bau, also known as Nintinugga, was originally the goddess of the dog and later became the goddess of healing. Dogs were often seen accompanying her in healing rituals. It was believed that dogs' saliva could heal wounds, and parts of dogs were used in magic healing spells. After the Great Flood, Bau breathed life back into humankind.

ISHTAR

Ishtar was the goddess of love, war, fertility, and sexuality, and was worshipped throughout northern Mesopotamia, with important temples in many Assyrian cities. On Ishtar's Gate in Babylon, her symbols included a lion and an eight-pointed star. In the Babylonian pantheon, she was the divine personification of the planet Venus.

NINLIL

Goddess of the wind, Ninlil was ravaged by her husband, Enlil, who impregnated her with water and she gave birth to the future moon god. As punishment Enlil was dispatched to the underworld where Ninlil joined him. Enlil impregnated her again, disguised as the gatekeeper, and she gave birth to their son, Nergal, the god of death.

SHAMASH

God of law, justice, and salvation, Shamash was one of the three powers symbolizing the forces of nature: the moon, the sun, and the life-giving Earth. Just as the sun dispersed darkness, so Shamash brought wrongs and injustice to light. He was regarded as the god who released sufferers from the grasp of the demons.

SIN

Sin, the moon god, was regarded as the head of the pantheon. At the time, the moon and its phases were central to all aspects of civilization, whether for agriculture, seasons, or astrological portents. Sin was father of the gods and creator of all things, and his wisdom was important in the development of Babylonian astronomical observation.

ALL-SEEING EYE

EGYPT c. 1450 BCE

Decorative motif from ancient Egypt asociated with protection and healing

This faience amulet, from the British Museum in London, England, depicts the left eye of Horus that was stabbed out by Seth.

The human eye has been used as a magical symbol and religious motif for thousands of years. Considered an all-seeing power, it evokes solar energy, vitality, protection, and healing. The earliest all-seeing eye symbols date to ancient Egypt when the eye of Horus and the eye of Ra were powerful talismans or amulets associated with the myths of these two gods. The "wadjet" eye from earliest Egyptian times symbolized the power of the goddess Wadjet as protectress, warrior, and sorceress. In later Egyptian dynasties, wadjet or wedjat refers to the lunar or left eye of Horus and became a generic magical eye of destiny.

The creator god Atum gave birth to a daughter, Wadjet. As his all-seeing eye, she was sent to search the universe for his lost sons, Tefnut and Shu. When she found them, Atum cried with happiness and all his tears became humans. As a reward, Atum placed

Wadjet on his head as a cobra crown, known as the uraeus, where she was both feared and respected by all gods and men. Depicted as an Egyptian cobra, or a snake with a woman's head, Wadjet is renowned for her oracle at Per-Wadjet Temple. The city was dedicated to her worship and was probably the source of the oracular tradition that spread throughout Egypt and Greece.

Wadjet was the personification of the eye of Horus, the Egyptian sky god. There were in fact two gods called Horus. Blind Horus was killed by the god of chaos, Seth, and later reincarnated as the son of Isis and Osiris as Horus. At one point in the earlier ongoing struggle with Seth for the throne, Seth tore out Horus's eye, which was healed by Hathor, Horus's consort. Consequently the eye of Horus became associated with healing and restoration. Horus was also a hawk-headed warrior and Osiris's representative in the upper world after Osiris became ruler of the underworld. Horus was rather like Hermes in that he was able to mediate between the two worlds, guiding the souls of the dead to be judged by Osiris.

EYES FOR THE DEAD

From the Middle Kingdom dynasty period, two eyes were shown on coffins, and this practice remained popular into the Greco-Roman period. The dead were laid to rest facing to the left. Twin eyes on the left side of coffins were thought to allow the dead person to see back to the world from which they had departed, and into the world in which they were about to live forever. By the New Kingdom, the eye was frequently shown in vignettes accompanying chapters of the Book of the Dead, the funerary guide to the otherworld that accompanied the deceased. In the scribe Ani's version of the book, the eye is depicted as a funerary and magical protection amulet. Egyptian eye amulets were usually small pieces of crystal, gems, or precious stones that were used for protection. Most amulets were associated with specific spells and chosen for their particular magical properties. Although some elaborate amulets were placed with mummified bodies in elite tombs, many more were used by ordinary people, often just drawn on linen, papyrus, or skin.

Funerary amulets were often made in the shape of the eye of Horus. They were placed with the corpse for protection and to ensure a good journey to the afterlife. The Wadjet eye can be found as a central icon on gold, carnelian, and lapis lazuli bracelets

discovered on the mummy of the well-loved pharaoh Shoshenq II.

The eye was sometimes used to calculate fractions for purposes of medicinal prescription and measuring grain. Each section of the eye represented a proportion by which the components could be measured. The iris of the eye, for example, represented a quarter, whereas the eyebrow represented one-eighth.

More recently, the eye of Horus has been used by occultists such as the Thelemists, who consider the date 1904 to be the start of the age of Horus. Thelemic thought belongs to a religious cult developed by English occultist Aleister Crowley in the early twentieth century, in which "do what thou wilt" was a key philosophy. The Illuminati, who some believe to be the secret power behind many businesses and governments today, also use the eye as a symbol of control of knowledge, illusion, manipulation, and power. The eye is often depicted within a triangle as a symbol of magical power, and it appears that the all-seeing eye is one of the most potent symbols of the power of divine knowledge.

This ancient Egyptian symbol denotes royal power, protection, and good health.

A fragment of a bronze statue depicts Horus wearing the double crown of upper and lower Egypt, (305–30 BCE).

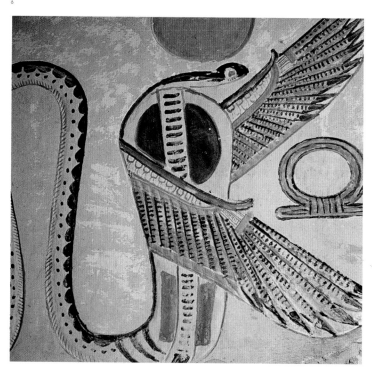

Wadjet is depicted as a striking cobra with halo in this detail from a wall painting in the Valley of the Queens, Thebes, Egypt.

CHARIOT OF THE SUN
TRUNDHOLM, DENMARK *c.* 1400 BCE

A Norse symbol of the solar cycle and new beginnings

The bronze chariot found on a moor in Denmark has been interpreted as a depiction of the sun being pulled across the sky by a mare.

The spectacular statue of a horse drawing the sun in a chariot is a symbol not only of growth, light, life, and new beginnings, but also of the solar cycle and the movement of the daily rising and setting of the sun. This remarkable bronze chariot was discovered in 1902 in the Trundholm moor near Nykøbing Sjælland, Denmark. A depiction of a horse-drawn vehicle on spoked wheels in Northern Europe at such an early date is unusual, and it is the earliest known such style of chariot recorded. The disk is gilded only on the right-hand side. Thought to be symbolic of the sun being drawn across the heavens from east to west during the day, the gilding represents its bright side; the sun's journey from west to east during the night is symbolized by its dark, ungilded side.

In ancient Egyptian times, the solar barge, or "sun barque," was a popular mythological representation of the sun god Ra riding in a boat. The Khufu ship, a life-size 142-foot (43.5-m) vessel, was sealed into a pit at the foot of the Great Pyramid of Giza around 2500 BCE. In other cultures, the Greek sun god Helios rides a chariot, as does the Vedic sun god Surya, who rides in a chariot drawn by seven horses. The myth of Phaethon, son of Helios, recounts how the young god was teased by the other gods to prove that his father was in fact the sun god. When Helios promised to grant him whatever he wanted, Phaethon insisted on being allowed to drive the sun chariot for a day. Placed in charge of the chariot, he was unable to control the horses. The earth was in danger of being burned up and, to prevent this terrible disaster, Zeus killed Phaethon with a thunderbolt.

Norse myths were preserved orally, and it was not until the Middle Ages that they were written down as texts. In one Norse myth, Sol was the personified goddess of the sun. Every day she rode through the sky on her chariot pulled by two horses, Arvak and Alsvid. It is believed that the bronze chariot and its solar disk discovered in Trundholm may indeed represent Sol. In the medieval Norse texts known as the Eddas, Sol is described as the sister of the moon god Mani.

Scholars have several theories about the development of the goddess from Indo-European roots. According to stories of ancient solar deities of central Asia, such as the Hindu Surya, it appears that Sol may have traveled, not necessarily in her chariot, across the Steppes and plains of central Asia. In Slavic mythology, the sun god Dazbog had two daughters both known as Zorya: the morning star who opened the palaces gates at dawn for the sun chariot to pass by, and the evening star who opened the gates each night for the chariot's return.

Western arts tend to regard the symbolic deity for the sun as male, but sun goddesses are found all around the world. They include Al-Lat in Arabia, Bila and Walo in Australia, and Pattini in Sri Lanka. Among the Hittites the goddess is Wurusemu and the Babylonians worship Shapash; in Native America, among the Cherokee is Unelanuhi, the Inuit refer to Malina, and the Miwok indigenous peoples worship Hekoolas.

This second-century CE Greek silver *didrachm* from Rhodes depicts Helios, the sun god.

Used in ancient Egyptian iconography, the winged sun disk was a symbol of life and destruction.

BREASTPLATE OF AARON

ISRAEL c. 1400–1300 BCE

Oracle worn by ancient Hebrew priests

Aaron the High Priest
(nineteenth century)
by William Etty depicts
Aaron wearing his priest's
robes and ceremonial
breastplate, set with
twelve jewels.

Aaron was the brother of Moses and became the leader of the priestly tribe of Israel. The Book of Exodus records God's directions concerning a mystical breastplate that was to be worn by Aaron and subsequent leaders. It was to be made of gold, blue, and scarlet linen, folded double, and mounted with four rows of precious stones, each jewel to be framed in gold. The breastplate is referred to as a hoshen, a term that appears to be connected either to its function or to its appearance. Some scholars think that the name originated from the Hebrew word *hasuna*, meaning "beautiful," but it could also derive from *sinus*, meaning "a fold for containing something."

The breastplate was attached to the ephod—an apronlike sacred vestment—using gold chains tied to gold rings on the ephod's shoulder straps, and with blue ribbon tied to the gold rings at the lower parts of the ephod. The breastplate was similar to a backless waistcoat, with a pouch inside to contain the Urim and Thummim, used for divination. Curiously, no one really knows what the Urim and Thummim are. Scholars believe that they may have been objects that were put into some sort of pouch, then one of them was selected by touch and withdrawn or thrown out of the pouch as a divination device. Presumably the Urim and Thummim were fairly small and flat, to fit inside a pouch, and were possibly tablets of wood or bone. According to most experts, Urim means guilty and Thummim means innocent. This would imply that the purpose of the Urim and Thummim was a test to confirm or deny suspected guilt; if the Urim was selected it meant guilt, while selection of the Thummim would mean innocence.

According to Islamic sources, there was a similar form of divination in ancient Arabian and Persian culture. Two arrow shafts were kept in a container (without heads or feathers). On one was written a command to act, and the other a prohibition. These were stored in the Kaaba, an ancient sacred building, at Mecca. Whenever someone wished to know whether to get married, go on a journey, or to make some other similar decision, one of the Kaaba's priests would randomly pull one of the arrow shafts out of the container. The word written upon it was said to indicate the will of the specific god concerning the matter in question.

The **Kaaba** at the center of Islam's mosque in Mecca, Saudi Arabia, is the most sacred point in Islam. When in prayer, Muslims are expected to face the Kaaba from wherever they are in the world.

Sometimes a third, blank, arrow shaft would be used to represent the refusal of the deity to give an answer. This practice is called rhabdomancy, after the Greek roots *rhabd*—"rod"—and *mancy*—"divination." The twelve jewels in the breastplate were, according to the biblical description, made from twelve different stones. Each of them represented a specific tribe of Israel, whose name was then inscribed on the stone.

Founder of the Latter Day Saint Movement, Joseph Smith apparently used similar objects to interpret and translate the *Book of Mormon* from the legendary golden plates found on a hill in New York. Similar in appearance to a pair of stone spectacles, the plates were also fastened to a breastplate, and Smith later referred to the device as the Urim and Thummim. Smith's mother described the Urim and Thummim as being like "two smooth three-cornered diamonds." Smith also said that he used the Urim and Thummim to assist him in receiving other divine revelations. Latter Day Saints followers believe that Smith's Urim and Thummim were identical in function to the biblical version, but there is no evidence that the latter was ever used to translate unknown texts. Smith believed that Urim and Thummim could be translated as "light and truth."

IMPORTANT BREASTPLATE GEMS

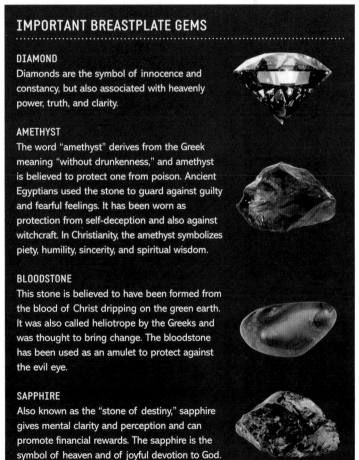

DIAMOND
Diamonds are the symbol of innocence and constancy, but also associated with heavenly power, truth, and clarity.

AMETHYST
The word "amethyst" derives from the Greek meaning "without drunkenness," and amethyst is believed to protect one from poison. Ancient Egyptians used the stone to guard against guilty and fearful feelings. It has been worn as protection from self-deception and also against witchcraft. In Christianity, the amethyst symbolizes piety, humility, sincerity, and spiritual wisdom.

BLOODSTONE
This stone is believed to have been formed from the blood of Christ dripping on the green earth. It was also called heliotrope by the Greeks and was thought to bring change. The bloodstone has been used as an amulet to protect against the evil eye.

SAPPHIRE
Also known as the "stone of destiny," sapphire gives mental clarity and perception and can promote financial rewards. The sapphire is the symbol of heaven and of joyful devotion to God.

HERM

GREECE c. 1300 BCE

Stone placed by the wayside that embodied the power of the god Hermes

This second-century CE copy of a fifth-century BCE milestone by Alkamenes depicts Hermes, the ancient Greek god of trade and communication.

A herm is a quadrangular stone sculpture, usually positioned outdoors, that serves as a boundary marker, signpost, milestone, or memorial. It always features a bearded man's head and has either stunted arms or no arms; the square slab also often displays an erect phallus. According to many historians, such as the ancient Greek writer Pausanius, the early Greeks worshipped stones and rocks, and it was only in classical Greece that the stones were transformed into more formal statues representing the gods.

The name "herm" is related to Hermes, the Greek god of trade and communication. However, Hermes was also derived from a more ancient god associated with boundaries and fertility, and as a countryside deity he protected flocks and their pastures. As a symbol of fertility, Hermes was associated with Dionysus, Pan, and Priapus: the phallic gods. It is probable that the stylized embodiment of this bearded god originally developed out of stone and wooden sculptures found dotted in the countryside. These were meant to embody the god of the mystic marriage, Dionysus. In ancient Greek religions, secret "brides" were initiated into the Dionysian Mysteries—a liberation ritual involving intoxicants—and led to sacred temples to become priestesses or temple prostitutes. These temples were hidden within the woods and groves, and the small wooden statues of Dionysus that surrounded the groves were used as protective and empowering devices.

With the classical Athenian development of art and architecture, the rustic herm no longer appeared. Instead herms were placed beside doorways and along roadsides to draw on the power of Hermes, who was assigned new roles as the god of transitions, trade, roadsides, and travel, and as a symbol of phallic power.

When Hermes was eventually honored with the title of god of the crossroads, he joined an

Herms were often used as decorative items, particularly in the gardens and villas of wealthy Romans, as seen in the fresco *Garden with Herms and Fountain* at Casa del Bracciale d'Oro, Pompeii, Italy.

earlier crossroads deity. Predating Hermes, the chthonic Greek goddess of the underworld Hecate orginally ruled the waysides and crossings. The Greeks often placed offerings of "Hecate cakes" at the junction of ways. The cakes were sometimes marked with a single candle so that Hecate could find her way to the offering in the dark. Similarly, the ancient Vedic Indian god Bhairava was said to guard the crossroads at the edge of each village. Stone phalluses and statues were left there to honor him as watcher of the boundaries between worlds. If propitiated correctly, he could bring guidance on one's future choices. In African traditions, the crossroads gods included Eshu, Legba, Ellegua, Ndumba, and Nzila, who showed the way to spiritual power and wisdom.

EARTH AND LANDSCAPE

Stones play an important part in Eastern traditions as a symbol of the earth. Mani stones are stones, rocks, or pebbles that are inscribed with the six-syllable mantra—*Om mani padme hum*—used as a prayer in Tibetan Buddhism. Mani stones are placed along roadsides and by rivers and pathways, as well as sometimes along walls, to form mounds as an offering to the spirits of a particular place. They occur not only in Buddhist traditions, but also in animist cultures such as Celtic, American Indian, and African traditions. Examples of Mani stones resembling tablets carved out of the sides of rock formations are found in the Himalayas.

Among many American Indian peoples, rock represents the bones of Mother Earth, while in Australia, the Aboriginal peoples consider all rock outcrops, landscapes, and mountains, such as Ayers Rock in the Northern Territory, to be sacred Dreamtime places, each imbued with their own spirit. To the Chinese, a valley is symbolic of fertility, shelter, and feminine. It represents the yin aspect in Taoism, but in some religions, such as Judaism and Christianity, valleys can be associated with death.

In Christian and Islamic traditions, the desert represents retreat and enlightenment. However, in most pagan belief systems, the desert is a symbol of survival, desolation, emptiness, and the battle for survival. Among the American Indian peoples, caves represent the womb and rebirth, and lead to the center of the universe. In other traditions, such as in Greek mythology, they are associated with the entrance to the underworld, or are portals to hell.

The Roman god, Mercury, the equivalent of Hermes, was usually depicted with a winged helmet.

GREEK DEITIES

ZEUS

Ruler of Olympus, Zeus grew up in Crete and when he was old enough, his sister, Metis, told Zeus how to rescue his other siblings who had been eaten by his father, Kronos. Disguised as a cupbearer, Zeus gave his father a drink of deadly nectar. Kronos vomited up all the other gods who then joined Zeus in overthrowing his father.

HERMES

Known as the winged messenger, Hermes ran errands between heaven and Earth and was a psychopomp, guiding souls to the underworld. As a trickster god of cunning, thieves, boundaries, writing, travelers, and commerce, Hermes appeared in the *Iliad*, the *Odyssey*, and the myths of Perseus and Prometheus.

EROS

Predating Zeus, Eros eventually became identified with the Roman god Cupid. A much maligned and misrepresented god, he was an ancient symbol of potent life force and was a primal, phallic deity in pre–Hellenic Greece. He was later manifested in the Olympic pantheon as the offspring of Aphrodite and either Zeus, Ares, or Hermes.

POSEIDON

Poseidon (drink giver) was as dangerous with his trident as Zeus was with his thunderbolts. The cyclops made him the trident for the battle against the Titans, and he could fork up mountain ridges, underwater shelves, islands, and even continents. After the war the trident became his most powerful instrument.

ATHENE

Athene sprang from Zeus's head and proved to be a loyal supporter of Zeus. She became known first for her patriotic warrior spirit and was later worshipped for her protection of the state. She was admired for possessing right-brain intellect, but was rarely valued for her female wisdom. She was the inspiration behind the Trojan horse.

DIONYSUS

The son of Zeus and the mortal Semele, Dionysus was brought up by mountain nymphs in safety away from Zeus's jealous wife, Hera. Spending most of his time wandering around the world with satyrs and the wild Maenads, Dionysus was the god of the moment of choice as well as of the moment before surrendering to irrational desire, or resisting it.

APHRODITE

Aphrodite was the goddess of desire, love, beauty, and fertility and evolved from earlier goddesses such as Inanna and Ishtar. She was the wife of Hephaistos, and her role as goddess of sexual love was consistent with her appetite for men and gods alike. Her name means "foam born" after the method of her birth.

HADES

Hades became the ruler of the underworld after the Titans were overthrown, and he was often known as Plouton, ruler of precious stones, metals, and the hidden wealth buried in the earth. Hades visited the upper world only when overcome by lust. He abducted Persephone, then later fell for a nymph called Minthe.

DEMETER

Demeter was known as a bringer of fertility, and was the goddess of agriculture and the harvest. She was part of a long tradition of earth goddesses and was best known for her part in the story of the abduction of her daughter, Persephone, by Hades, which underpinned the Greek philosophy of the cycles of the seasons.

APOLLO

The god of light, archery, and the arts, Apollo was also the god of oracles. Apollo promised the gift of prophecy to the mortal Cassandra if she allowed him to seduce her. But after their first encounter she rejected him. In revenge he gave her the gift of prophecy, anyway, but it was cursed: whatever she said would never be believed.

HERA

Hera epitomized the ideal wife, and her marriage to Zeus became the prototype for monogamy. She became the protector of wives. She later became symbolic of pathological jealousy—fueled by her resentment at being left out of the initial division of the universe, and by her endless revenge on Zeus's many lovers.

ARTEMIS

The twin sister of Apollo, Artemis was the Hellenic goddess of the hunt—the equivalent to the Roman goddess Diana. As goddess of wild animals, childbirth, and young girls and women, Artemis was depicted as a huntress carrying a bow and arrows. The deer, the bear, the hawk and the cypress were all sacred to her.

ARK OF THE COVENANT
JERUSALEM, ISRAEL *c.* 970 BCE

Contains the tablets of stone on which the Ten Commandments were inscribed

This detail is from Lorenzo Ghiberti's bronze relief *Israelites Carrying the Ark of the Covenant, from the Gates of Paradise* (1425–1452).

The Ark of the Covenant is said to contain the tablets of stone on which the Ten Commandments were inscribed. The biblical account relates that about a year after the Israelites' exodus from Egypt, the ark was created according to a design given to Moses by God on Mount Sinai. When carried, the ark was hidden under a large veil made of skins and blue cloth, always carefully concealed, even from the eyes of the priests and the Levites who carried it.

The Ark of the Covenant was not only a fabulous shrine containing the tablets of the Ten Commandments, but it also contained Aaron's Rod and a pot of Manna: an edible substance that the children of Israel lived on during their time in the wilderness. According to the Bible, the ark was made of acacia wood overlaid with gold. Carried by two long bars of gold-plated wood, the ark was guarded by figures of cherubim and angels. These messengers of God have remained important guardians and protective symbols in Western art and religion, and are still popular today in modern culture.

The biblical account of the ark states that the Israelites carried it with them wherever they went. It possessed divine power, and if stolen it would prove fatal to those who tried to claim it for themselves. When the Temple of Jerusalem was built, the ark was enshrined there and could be approached only by the high priest. However, at some point, the ark disappeared, and the whereabouts of the sacred artifact continued to fascinate archaeologists, historians, and believers alike. Theories as to its current location include a tunnel in Jerusalem and the top of Mount Nebo in Jordan.

According to the Ethiopian royal chronicles, the ark left Jerusalem in the days of King Solomon and was brought to Ethiopia by Menelik, the son of Solomon and Makeda, Queen of Sheba. Kept there for 800 years by a Judaic sect, it was seized by the Knights Templar, who thought that it was the Holy Grail. The Knights converted the Jews, who then hid the ark in the church. In the 1960s, the Old Church of St. Mary of Zion at Axum was constructed to house the ark, and today it is apparently enshrined in the small treasury building next door to the church.

Cherubim and seraphim were popular in Western art; in this engraving they are seen guarding the ark.

CHERUBIM AND SERAPHIM

Angels and cherubim guard not only the ark but also people, and appear throughout Western art from ancient Byzantine winged figures to the elaborate angels of nineteenth-century Romantic art. Regarded as messengers of God by Jews, Christians, and Muslims, they embody heavenly purity and benevolence and are considered to have a hierarchy: each rank is allocated different duties and has its own symbolism. The fifth-century scholar Dionysius the Aeropagite describes the angels as belonging to three choirs: the first includes the seraphim, cherubim, and thrones; the second choir comprises dominations, virtues, and powers; and the third principalities, archangels, and angels.

The seraphim are closest to God; they fly above God's throne singing his praises and symbolize light and love. The cherubim were responsible for the expulsion of Adam and Eve from the Garden of Eden and symbolize God's will. The seven archangels are the only named angels in the Bible: they represent God's will on Earth and relay important messages to

people. They include Gabriel, usually depicted with a trumpet, who announced Jesus's coming birth to Mary, and in Islam revealed the Koran to Muhammad. Raphael symbolizes healing and judgment, whereas Michael is considered the protector of Israel but was also able to rid heaven of Satan. Not to be confused with the cherubim are the so-called cherubs, or "putti." Introduced as an artistic device, these classical images of male children with wings represent innocence and purity. They first became popular during the Renaissance, and later in the Baroque period, when they appeared on furniture and in architecture, and were highly gilded to reveal their heavenly associations.

Since the end of the twentieth century, there has been a renewed interest and identification with guardian angels, and many books and websites are devoted to angel therapy and healing. A study in 2002 of 350 people revealed that they all believed they had had contact with angels in some form or another. This included visions; a sense of being touched, pushed, or lifted; smelling beautiful fragrances; or hearing voices. In the visual experiences, the angels described appeared in various forms, either with wings or as extraordinarily radiant human beings, and as beings of light.

Carried on bars or poles, the Ark of the Covenant was a symbol of divine power.

TABLET OF DESTINIES

NINEVEH, IRAQ c. seventh century BCE

Stone tablet that bestowed the owner with the great power of the divine

The so-called Tablet of Destinies is thought to be an oracle with magical powers. In the 1840s, in Nineveh, Iraq, British explorers discovered a considerable number of Babylonian stone cuneiform tablets among the ruins of the Library of King Ashurbanipal, named for the last great king of the Assyrian Empire who ruled in the seventh century BCE. Thousands of tablets were taken back to the British Museum in London, and many of the inscriptions were translated during the 1870s. These tablets contain poems, parts of which are known as the Enuma Elish. There are myths of creation, an epic legend of Marduk, and a story of the hero Gilgamesh, as well as the tale of Inanna's descent into the underworld and various flood stories. Included on these tablets are references to the Tablet of Destinies.

In the epic story of the rise to glory of the Babylonian god Marduk, the Tablet of Destinies is first passed on from the primordial sea goddess serpent, Tiamat, to her right-hand man, Kingu. During her battle against Marduk, Tiamat fastened the tablet to Kingu's breast, telling him that whatever he prophesied would come true. Although Kingu's magical power was established, it was not long before Marduk managed to destroy Tiamat and her allies, and steal the Tablet of Destinies from Kingu's breastplate, placing it on his own and thus strengthening his rule among the gods.

In other Mesopotamian myths, the Tablet of Destinies was considered to be a mixture

This tablet is the third in a series of twenty-four that include descriptions of human deformities and how to interpret them.

of oracle and horoscope. The tablet predicted and influenced the future, and owning it meant absolute power. In Akkadian mythology, the tablet is stolen from Enlil, the chief sky god, by the divine storm bird and personification of the wind, Anzu, who believes he will be able to determine the fate of all things. The Tablet of Destinies is also described as the possession of Ashur, the supreme god of Assyrian mythology.

The symbolic quality of this tablet or stone is one of the earliest "oracles." Oracles and horoscopes were a symbol of power to kings, pharaohs, and prophets: not only the power of knowing one's own destiny, but also, more importantly, of knowing someone else's, or even a country's, future. The oracle, both the written form and later the spoken form, was to become one of the most important cultural, political, and warring divination aids given by the gods. Its power continued through other civilizations such as the Greco-Roman world.

GREEK ORACLES

In Greece, the first oracles were devoted to the mother goddess, including Dione at Dodona. Dione was the earlier and feminine form of Dios, the god of the heavens who became known as Zeus. Similarly, Python, whose mother was Gaia the earth goddess, was a serpent creature whose oracular powers were stolen by Apollo at Delphi when Apollo slew the serpent with an arrow. This Greek oracular tradition is most likely to have derived from ancient Egypt, where the goddess Wadjet was first depicted as a snake-headed woman, and her oracle was heard through the high priestesses in the renowned temple in Buto.

The word "oracle" comes from the Latin word *orare* "to speak" and refers to the priest or priestess uttering the prediction. Back in ancient Mesopotamia, this is exactly what Tiamat told Kingu: that by wearing the Tablet of Destinies, whatever he "spoke" would come true. In this sense Tiamat, Kingu, and

Marduk were the first oracles. Oracles were different from seers because seers interpreted signs sent by the gods through bird signs, animal entrails, and other methods. Apollo's oracle at Delphi, the priestess known as Pythia, was said to be infallible. She gave prophecies only on the seventh day of each month, seven being the number most associated with Apollo, and only during the warmer months of the year. In order to avoid the lines at Delphi, and to ensure that they received a good response from the oracle, wealthier individuals made animal sacrifices to please Apollo.

The Delphic oracle exerted considerable influence and was essentially the highest authority, both civilly and religiously, in the male-dominated Hellenic culture. The high priestess who "spoke" for Apollo responded to questions posed by foreigners, kings, and philosophers on issues of politics, war, duty, crime, law, and even personal and family matters. Similar to the Tablet of Destinies, the oracle has since been a symbol of divine power known only to a few.

This red-figure tondo (c. 440 BCE) depicts Aegeus consulting the oracle of Delphi with the help of the seated priestess Themis.

The crown worn by this gold cobra (600 BCE) suggests that it represents the goddess Wadjet.

FUJIIN AND RAIJIN
JAPAN c. 660 BCE

Early Shinto gods of wind and thunder

Early Edo panels by Tawaraya Sotatsu portray Fujiin and Raijin, the wind and thunder gods in the Shinto pantheon.

The Japanese symbol for the wind has an ambivalent influence.

In Shinto mythology, there are thousands of *kami*, or spirits, ranging from higher gods to lesser spirits. Yet Fujiin the wind god and Raijin the thunder god have always been especially important in the divine pantheon due to their association with the earliest creator gods.

It is believed that after the first divine beings, Izanami and Izanagi, created the Earth and Japan, they then created thunder, lightning, wind, and rain. The god of thunder Raijin was also a manifestation of the neverending turmoil between the two creator gods after Izanami was banished to the underworld. In Japanese folklore, children are told to hide their belly buttons during thunderstorms because Raijin not only likes to eat navels but also hides in them. Fujiin carries a large bag over his shoulder filled with thousands of different winds, from gentle breezes to gale force hurricanes. From the bag, he selects the type of wind he wants to blow, and the intensity of the wind depends on how wide the mouth of the bag is opened.

Raijin is a well-known deity and his fame has spawned characters in Japanese popular culture. He appears in role-playing video games such as Final Fantasy VIII (1999), and in the television series *Madan Senki Ryukendo* (Magic Bullet Chronicles, 2006), in which transformed warriors say their names followed by the word "Raijin!" to mean "wake up!" or "stand up!"

OTHER WEATHER GODS

Throughout all polytheistic cultures there have been important wind, thunder, and lightning gods, but most of these personifications of the weather do not have a standard depiction and vary based on meteorological and cultural differences. In Indo-European cultures, the thunder god is often known as the chief of the gods: for example, Zeus in Greece, Thor in Norse mythology, and Indra in Hinduism. In Greek mythology, Zeus is also the god of lightning, law, order, and fate and he was responsible for the creation of Elysium, the resting place for heroic and virtuous souls.

Some thunder gods are female personifications, such as Oya in the Oruba traditions of Africa. She appears in many aspects as a warrior spirit of the wind, fertility, fire, magic, thunder, and lightning. She also creates hurricanes and tornadoes and guards the underworld. She is the spirit of tornadoes (which are said to be her whirling skirts as she dances), lightning, and any kind of destruction. Beyond destruction, Oya is the spirit of change, transition, and chaos. Some myths recount that she lives at the gates of cemeteries (as opposed to the gates to the underworld), which reveals her in her aspect as the god of transition.

Throughout world mythology, wind gods could be either unwelcome, such as Pazuzu the demon Babylonian god of the southwest wind and bringer of drought, or welcome, such as the calming influence of the wind god Shu in Egyptian mythology.

This detail from *Tor's Fight with the Giants* (1872) by Mårten Eskil Winge depicts Thor, the thunder god of Norse mythology, who stormed around the heavens wielding his ax and causing havoc as he fought the giants.

IMPORTANT SHINTO GODS

AMATERASU

Not to be confused with the Italian pudding tiramisu, Amaterasu was the personification of the sun and the purported ancestor of the imperial royalty of Japan. Her full name—Amaterasu Omikami—means "great goddess" or "great spirit who shines in the heavens, " and she is considered to be the primary god of Shinto belief.

UZUME

Uzume is the goddess of the dawn. She may even be an aspect of the sun goddess Amaterasu, who, startled by the behavior of her brother, Susanoo, hid in a cave, thereby plunging the world into darkness until she was willing to emerge. This event represented the moon and its power to block out the sun at night. Uzume is also known as the "great persuader" and the "heavenly alarming female."

HACHIMAN

The god of war and the protector of Japan is known as Hachiman. Originally an agricultural god, he later became the guardian of the eighth- to tenth-century nobility who ruled Japan with the emperor's backing. He is a popular Shinto deity and is usually worshipped alongside his mother, the empress Jingo, and the goddess Hime-gami. His symbolic animal and messenger is the dove.

IZANAGI

Izanagi is the father of the gods. With Izanami he was responsible for the birth of the islands of Japan. Although Izanami died when she gave birth to the fire god Kagutsuchi, Izanagi followed her to the underworld but failed to bring her back to the living world. An eternal marital row between the pair caused the cycle of life and death for all living beings.

SPEAR OF DESTINY

JERUSALEM, ISRAEL first century CE

Used at the Crucifixion to wound the side of Christ

The spear at the Hofburg Palace, Vienna, Austria, has been highly prized by emperors and rulers in the belief that whoever owned it would rule the world.

Alleged to have amazing talismanic power, the spear of destiny, also known as the holy spear, holy lance, lance of Longinus, and spear of Longinus, is the name given to the spear that pierced the side of Jesus as he hung on the cross. The gospel of St. John states that the Romans planned to break Jesus's legs, a practice known as crurifragium and a method of hastening death during a crucifixion. Moments before the soldiers were about to do this, they believed Jesus to be already dead, so a Roman soldier known in legend as Longinus stabbed him in the side, just to be sure.

There are numerous claims as to what became of the true spear of destiny, particularly as legend told that whoever possessed the lance would rule the world. One of the earliest mentions of a preserved holy lance is in the account of the sixth-century pilgrim Antoninus of Piacenza, who, while describing the holy places of Jerusalem, saw in the basilica of Mount Zion "the crown of thorns with which Our Lord was crowned and the lance with which he was struck in the side." Since then, many holy emperors, kings, and rulers have laid claim to possessing the spear.

The ancient artifact in the Imperial Treasury at the Hofburg Palace in Vienna, Austria, appears to have a bit of a history attached to it. It is part of the Imperial Regalia of the Holy Roman emperors and was taken to Vienna for safe-keeping during the French Revolution. Dr. Robert Feather, an English metallurgist and technical engineering writer, tested the lance in Vienna in January 2003. He was given unprecedented permission not only to examine the spear in a laboratory environment, but was also allowed to remove the delicate bands of gold and silver that hold it together. In the opinion of Feather and other academic experts, the likeliest date of the spearhead is seventh century. However an iron pin—long claimed to be a nail from the crucifixion, hammered into the blade and set off by tiny brass crosses—is consistent in length and shape with a first-century Roman nail.

During the Anschluss, when Austria was annexed to Germany in 1938, Adolf Hitler removed the lance from Vienna; it was, however, returned to Austria by General George S. Patton after World War II. More recently, the term "spear of destiny" is the name used in various accounts that attribute mystical powers to the lance. Trevor Ravenscroft's book *The Spear of Destiny* (1973) claims that Hitler began World War II solely in order to steal the spear, such was his obsession with it. According to another legend, losing the spear would result in death, a prophecy that was fulfilled when Hitler committed suicide and Patton died in a car accident in an army camp.

SYMBOLIC WEAPONS

Other weapons were believed to have symbolic meanings. The dagger was used by ancient cultures for ritual sacrifices, both human and animal. It is a powerful symbol of bloodletting as an appeasement to the gods. The Southeast Asian dagger known as the Kris is decorated with inscriptions from the Koran to symbolize absolute truth. Swords have universally been seen as symbols of royal power, military strength, and honor, and even Christian saints were depicted carrying swords. In the medieval

The fresco (c. 1440) by Fra Angelico at the Dominican monastery at San Marco, Florence, depicts Longinus, the soldier who stabbed Jesus with his lance to see if he was actually dead.

courts of Europe, a knight or cavalier was honored by the king or ruler, who would touch the right shoulder of the subject in question as a symbolic ascension of rank and status.

The arrow alone is not only considered a powerful phallic symbol, but also one of male potency, representing the hunt and the chase. The bow represents spiritual energy and discipline, and is often considered in Hindu and other Eastern beliefs to symbolize the feminine ability to "draw" the arrow, or male, into her. For Christians, the piercing arrow is a symbol of the Ecstasy of St. Theresa, well known from Gian Lorenzo Bernini's sculpture of 1645–1652 at the Cornaro Chapel in Santa Maria della Vittoria in Rome. St. Theresa's vision of Jesus thrusting and drawing an arrow from her heart also held an underlying sexual symbolism in Renaissance art.

THOR'S HAMMER

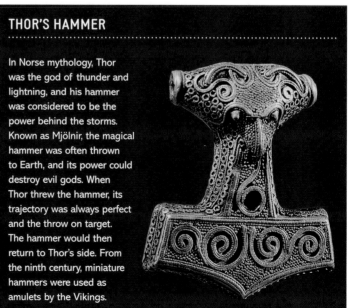

In Norse mythology, Thor was the god of thunder and lightning, and his hammer was considered to be the power behind the storms. Known as Mjölnir, the magical hammer was often thrown to Earth, and its power could destroy evil gods. When Thor threw the hammer, its trajectory was always perfect and the throw on target. The hammer would then return to Thor's side. From the ninth century, miniature hammers were used as amulets by the Vikings.

HALO

BIMARAN, AFGHANISTAN *c.* 50 CE

Worldwide symbol of divinity and holiness

The elaborate frieze bears one of the earliest depictions of the Buddha from the northwest region of Gandhara (now Afghanistan). The inscription on the steatite casket that contained the reliquary records that it had been filled with some of the actual bones of the Buddha. However, the lid of the reliquary and the bones were missing when Masson discovered it; instead it was filled with small burned pearls, beads of precious and semiprecious stones, and four coins.

A halo is also known as a nimbus or aureole, and is a ring of light surrounding a figure in art, usually indicating a sacred or holy connection but also used in images of rulers and heroes. In the sacred arts of Hinduism, Buddhism, and Islam, halos usually take the form of a circular glow or flames that leap around the head or even the whole body. Halos may be shown as almost any color, but because they represent light they are most often depicted as golden, yellow, or white.

The word "halo" originates from the Greek for "threshing floor"—a circular, slightly sloping area, around which slaves or oxen walked to

The first-century Bimaran gold casket is studded with jewels and depicts the robed Buddha surrounded by a halo.

In the 1830s, not far from Jalalabad, Afghanistan, British explorer Charles Masson discovered a small gold Buddhist reliquary. It featured a beautiful depiction of the Buddha in flowing robes with a simple halo surrounding his head, and it is this symbol—the halo—that has become an iconic sign of divinity or holiness. The casket contained coins of an Indo-Scythian king, which dated it to around 50 CE; however, the artistic decoration of the casket has led scholars to believe it may date to a hundred years later.

The fine cylindrical container is made of pure gold and is set with almandine garnets.

This painted wood Japanese Buddha from the Moromaki period (1333–1568) depicts the halo as a symbol of holiness.

thresh the grain—and it came to mean the divine bright disk. In Greek mythology, Homer described halolike lights around the heads of heroes, and a fifth-century BCE Greek vase in the Metropolitan Museum of Art, New York, depicts Perseus with halolike rays as he slays Medusa. Rays and halos appear on other mythic figures such as Lyssa, the personification of madness, Thetis the mother of Achilles, and the sun god Helios with his radiant crownlike halo.

Sumerian mythological tales mention "melam," which was described as a "brilliant, visible glamour exuded by gods, heroes, and sometimes by kings." In turn this was interpreted by Zoroastrian iconography as a "divine luster." In Chinese and Japanese Buddhist art, the halo has also been used since the earliest periods in depicting the image of the Buddha. In Tibetan art, different colored haloes have specific meanings: orange for monks, green for the Buddha. The origins of the halo may be unconfirmed but it has proved to be an archetypal symbol of divine presence.

The halo was incorporated into early Christian art around the fourth century CE with the earliest images of Christ. Initially the halo was regarded by many as a representation of Christ's divine nature. The Catholic interpretation is that

the halo represents the light of divine grace suffusing the soul, which is perfectly united and in harmony with the physical body.

In early Byzantine and Roman Christian iconography, halos were used typically to signify everything from saints and the Virgin Mary, to prophets, angels, and even Byzantine emperors. However, during the High Renaissance, when the church gradually lost cultural control, Italian painters dispensed with haloes. The disk halo was used rarely for mythological figures, apart from in stylized Mannerist and Baroque art.

By the nineteenth century, haloes had virtually disappeared from Western art, too, until Symbolist painters such as Gustave Moreau and George Frederic Watts established mythological and spiritual subjects shrouded in mysticism. Moreau's well-known painting *La Pietà* (1854) features Christ's head encircled by a glowing halo of divinity, whereas the artist's allegorical work *Jupiter and Semele* (c. 1895) depicts the god emanating radiant flames of light in all his fiery glory. In the mystical painting *The Dweller in the Innermost* (c. 1885–86), Watts revived the symbol of the body halo. Such atmospheric works rekindled the significance of the halo as the "brilliant, visible glamour" so precious to the ancients.

This detail from *La Pietà* (1854) by Gustave Moreau depicts Christ and Mary surrounded by golden halos of light.

The halo has been a symbol of divinity from early Byzantine art right through to the end of the nineteenth century.

THE EIGHT IMMORTALS

CHINA *c.* 100–900

Revered for their individual powers that granted them immortality

From the series "Myths and Legends of China" (1922) by Edward T.C. Werner, this illustration depicts the quest for immortality by Taoist sages.

the second century to the tenth century—and they were revered for their symbolic element: immortality The attainment of immortality was, and still is, sacred to Taoist belief, and each of the eight immortals is worshipped for their individual qualities that bestow them with immortality. Each immortal, or "transcendent," has a specific power and accompanying tools to wield that power. This power can give or take away life depending on the subject's innocence or guilt.

POWERS OF IMMORTALITY

Chung-li Ch'uan is regarded as the chief of the immortals and always carries a magical fan and sometimes a peach. He is said to have discovered the elixir of life and possesses the power to cure the sick and revive the dead. He is often considered to be the oldest of the group and is a symbol of longevity.

The old man with mystic powers is called Chang Kuo-lao. He carries a phoenix feather and a bamboo tube, and rides a mule (often backward) that can walk some 1,000 miles (1,600 km) a day. A symbol of wisdom, he is worshipped particularly to help childless couples conceive. Lu Tung-pin is a Taoist scholar who possesses a magic sword that is used to slay demons and evil spirits. He is also depicted with a curious whisk that cures illnesses. Lu Tung-pin bestows scholastic luck and protection on those who worship him.

The finest dressed of the eight immortals is Ts'ao Kuo-chiu, who is often portrayed with a jade tablet and sometimes a feather fan. He is said to have been connected with the Sung imperial family and therefore signifies fame and recognition. The character of Li T'ieh-kuai (also known as Iron-crutch Li) is depicted as

Chinese mythology is filled with an array of gods and spirits, but the eight immortals are among the most popular and powerful characters in ancient Chinese culture. The immortals probably originated some time during the early Taoist schools of thought—dating from a beggar with an iron crutch and sometimes a gourd that serves as a bedroom and also contains medicine. Often accompanied by a deer, he is believed to be the most powerful of the eight characters and symbolizes divine wisdom. He received his iron crutch from Han Hsiang, who is the happy immortal. The latter is often shown carrying or playing a flute and is symbolic of healing energy.

The only two female immortals are Lan Ts'ai-ho and Ho Hsien-ku. Lan T'sai-ho often wears a blue robe and carries a basket of flowers. She brings luck to young women. Ho Hsien-ku carries a magical lotus blossom. Known as the immortal maiden, she is a symbol of family and marital success.

Like many other divine beings who first appeared as symbols in ancient Taoist mysticism, the eight immortals soon became legendary folk characters when they permeated Chinese tradition. These characters are still important deities, which like many others have shaped most of Chinese culture today, and are still celebrated at the most important festivities.

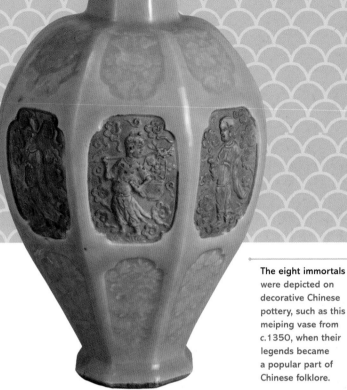

The eight immortals were depicted on decorative Chinese pottery, such as this meiping vase from c.1350, when their legends became a popular part of Chinese folklore.

IMPORTANT CHINESE GODS

JADE EMPEROR
The Jade Emperor of Taoist mythology (also known as Yuhuang) was originally the supreme being, Shang Di, the powerful one who initiated the creation and the universe, as well as the force that generated the continuation of all life. Shang Di was generous, intelligent, and wise, and was considered a heavenly equivalent to an emperor on Earth and presided over vast arrays of deities and servants.

GUAN YIN
Merciful and compassionate, Guan Yin is depicted with flowing white gowns and a beautiful benign face. In Taoist myth she was a fertility goddess and she made it possible for humans to eat rice for the first time. Every year she squeezed milk from her breasts to make edible grains of rice.

FU XI
After a terrible flood sent by demons to destroy the world, Fu Xi and his sister or consort, Nu Gua, escaped by floating in a gourd. Once the waters had receded, they returned to Earth and re-created civilization. Nu Gua made mortals from clay, and Fu Xi showed the mortals how to farm and fish, chart the seasons, hunt, and forge metal.

SHENNONG
A cultural hero and mythical emperor, Shennong was the son of a mortal princess and a sky dragon. He was also a shape-shifter, and usually took the form of a human with an ox head. However, he also had the ability to change into a scorching wind and create huge forest fires to teach mortals how to lay waste the land for agricultural purposes.

YAO
Yao ruled the world when it changed from a place of savagery to that of civilization, but he still continued to inhabit a thatched hut, to eat porridge, and to live an austere life. He had many battles with storm gods and water monsters, and was well known for employing Yi, the archer god, to destroy the demon Fei Lian and Ho Po the water god.

TEFILLIN

ISRAEL c. 200–500

Jewish ritual object that contains holy scrolls

Observant Jews still wear the tefillin, a symbolic talisman that reminds them how God brought the children of Israel out of the desert.

Worn as a talismanic symbol, tefillin serve to remind the wearer that God brought the children of Israel out of Egypt. The Talmud, the main text of Rabbinic Judaism, commanded that holy scrolls be worn by observant Jews during morning prayer. The scrolls—also known as phylacteries, meaning "amulet" or "charm" in Greek—are placed within cubic black leather boxes with leather straps worn on the head and arms. Observant Jews consider wearing tefillin to be a very great honor.

The boxes contain four hand-written texts from the Bible, in which believers are commanded to wear these sacred words either on the hand or arm, or between the eyes. The texts are known to be from Exodus 13:1–10 and 13:11–16, and Deuteronomy 6:4–9 and 11:13–21. The hand tefillin has all four texts written on a single parchment strip but the head tefillin has four separate compartments, with a single text in each. As with all ritual objects, there are very specific rules about how to make tefillin, and how to wear them.

Tefillin can be made only by trained specialists and often come with a certificate from a rabbi to prove that they have been made properly. This is to ensure that an article of such enormous religious significance is perfect in every way. Texts from the Torah have to be written according to Jewish law, on acceptable parchment and with acceptable ink. There are precise rules for writing the texts and any error automatically invalidates it. For example, the letters of the text must be written in order; if a mistake is found later, it cannot be corrected as the replacement letter would have been written out of sequence. There are 3,188 letters on the parchments, and it can take a scribe as long as fifteen hours to write a complete

The square box is carefully made only by specialists who understand its spiritual significance to the wearer.

set. The scribe is required to purify himself in the mikvah (ritual bath) before he starts work. Comprising the first five books of the Old Testament, the Torah is the book of law of the Jewish faith. In synagogues it appears as a sacred scroll, and the power of the words is used as a magical talisman, believed to heal children and pregnant women.

The tefillin must be completely black, and the boxes must be perfectly square when seen from above. All the stitches have to be perfectly square, too, and both thread and leather must be, according to Jewish law, acceptable. The arm tefillin is put on first, on the upper part of the weaker arm. A blessing is recited and the strap is wrapped around the arm seven times. The head tefillin is fastened loosely on the head about ⅜ inch (1 cm) above the wearer's original hairline (the fact that a man's hair may have receded is ignored). A blessing is recited and the strap is tightened, with the knot at the back of the head. The strap of the hand tefillin is then wound three times around the middle finger while reciting Hosea 2:21–22.

In synagogues, the Torah is the sacred scroll of law of the Jewish faith, made up of the first five books of the Old Testament.

JEWISH SYMBOLS

SHOFAR
Used to signal the start of the Jewish New Year, this symbolic musical instrument is made from a ram's horn. Based on the biblical horn that blew down the walls of Jericho, the shofar is also used to signify the start of Yom Kippur, the Day of Atonement.

NER TAMID
Also known as a sanctuary lamp, the ner tamid—meaning "eternal light"—is a sacred lamp that symbolizes the omnipresence of God. The lamp burns constantly in Jewish synagogues, and the flame itself equates the spirit of God to the power of fire and light.

MEZUZAH
The mezuzah is a small container that is attached to the doorposts of Jewish buildings. It is long and narrow in shape and contains a rolled-up piece of parchment that has two specified verses from the Torah written on it in indelible ink. Inscribed on the reverse side is the word "Shaddai," which equates the name of God with the phrase "guardian of the doors of Israel." It is traditional for Jewish people to touch or kiss the mezuzah as they walk through the doorway.

GANESHA
INDIA 300–400

Hindu elephant god of wisdom

The elephant-headed god Ganesha is shown with eight hands carrying some of his many symbols, such as an ax, a goad, and fruit.

Ganesha, and it is said that if you touch the highly polished trunk and then your forehead, your creativity will be increased tenfold.

Many legends surround Ganesha. Some stories state that Ganesha was born with an elephant head, but most relate that he was born with a human head that was later replaced by an elephant one. The most popular myth tells how Ganesha was created by the goddess Parvati as a guardian. Incensed by the refusal of her husband, Shiva, to respect her privacy while she was having her bath, Parvati decided to settle matters herself. Before going for her bath, she rubbed off the sandalwood paste on her body and out of it created a figure of a young boy. She infused life into the figure and told him that he was her son and that he should guard the entrance while she bathed. When Shiva returned home, he was so angry about a stranger blocking his access that he cut off Ganesha's head. Parvati was struck with grief, and in order to console her Shiva restored Ganesha to life, giving him an elephant head. Shiva also granted Ganesha a blessing: that he would be revered as a god of good fortune and success.

Ganesha is usually depicted with the body of a man and the head of an elephant, often with one tusk intact and the other broken. His unique features, besides the elephant head, are his large belly and a sacred thread running around him, often in the form of a snake. According to the strict rules of Hindu iconography, Ganesha figures are most commonly seen with four hands, which signify their divinity. Some figures may be seen with six, eight, ten, twelve, or even fourteen hands, each one carrying a symbol that differs from the symbols held in the other hands. There are about fifty-seven different symbols in all.

Ganesha emerged as a distinct deity in the fourth and fifth centuries, during the Gupta Period. He is a favorite god of intelligence and wisdom in the Hindu pantheon, but the elephant god also has the ability, if worshipped and venerated appropriately, not only to remove obstacles, but also to place obstacles in the way of people so that they learn how to deal with trials and tribulations. In Prambanan, Indonesia, there is a ninth-century statue of

Ganesha's head symbolizes the Atman, or the soul, which is the ultimate supreme reality of human existence, and his human body signifies Maya, or the earthly existence of human beings. The elephant head denotes wisdom, and its trunk represents "om," the symbol of the music of the cosmos. Symbols that Ganesha may hold in his hands include a goad, which helps him to propel humankind forward on the eternal path and to remove obstacles from the way, and a noose, which captures all difficulties. A broken tusk is a symbol of sacrifice, whereas a rosary suggests that the pursuit of knowledge should be continuous. The snake that runs around Ganesha's waist represents energy in all forms. Ganesha appears in Mahayana Buddhism not only in the form of the Buddhist god Vinayaka, but also as a Hindu demon form. As the Buddhist god Vinayaka, he is often shown dancing.

JAPANESE GANESHA

Kangi-ten is the Japanese version of Ganesha, and is often represented as an elephant-headed male and female pair, standing embracing each other in sexual union. The female wears a crown, a patched monk's robe, and a red surplice, while the male wears a black cloth slung over his shoulder. He has a long trunk and tusks, whereas she has short tusks. The male is reddish-brown in color, but the female is white and usually rests her feet on his, while he rests his head on her shoulder. The dual Kangi-ten may have been inspired by the Hindu Tantric portrayal of Ganesha with his consorts.

Another legend surrounding the Kangi-ten pair tells how the Indian king of Marakeira ate only beef and radishes. When these became rare, he started feasting on human corpses and then living beings. Eventually he turned into the great demon king Vinayaka, who commanded a huge army of demons known as the vinayakas. The people prayed to the god Avalokiteshvara, who took the form of a female demon, and she seduced Vinayaka, filling him with joy. Consequently, in union with her, he became the dual Ganesha, or Kangi-ten.

From Eastern Deccan, India, this painting (1780) shows the gods, Shiva and Parvati, who were responsible for Ganesha's elephant head.

Kangi-ten, the Japanese version of Ganesha, is an elephant-headed male and female pair of gods.

The Hindu om symbol represents the immanent unmanifest and manifest aspects of Brahma.

HINDU DEITIES

BRAHMA

Brahma lived on Mount Meru, the tip of the heavens, thousands of miles above the mortal world. He was all that happened, everywhere and at the same time. Because Brahma is all that is, he spends most of his time in meditation, which keeps the universe alive. Brahma was usually depicted riding a swan or peacock, or on a lotus.

SHIVA

Shiva was the destroyer, yet he was also a merciful judge. He sided with demons and outcasts and had invincible weapons such as a terrible third eye, trident, sword, and thunderbolts. At each cycle of the universe, Shiva opened his eye and danced, destroying everything in his sight, including the universe, until creation began again.

VISHNU

Vishnu is the god of preservation and personifies sacrifice. Lakshmi was his wife and they lived in heaven among the lotuses. Vishnu had hundreds of avatars (when visiting the mortal world to save it), but his most important forms were Matsya, the fish; Kurma, the tortoise; Varaha, the boar; Rama, the hero; the god Krishna; and Buddha.

LAKSHMI

The goddess of luck and good fortune, Lakshmi was popular among women and was originally the goddess of prosperity in Vedic myth. Lakshmi could become anything or put herself wherever she wanted in the mortal world, even hiding in bodies to bring luck to areas of life associated with that part of the body.

DURGA

Durga had the power of the cosmos on her side, and was the embodiment of all warlike energy. She came into being at a gathering of all the gods into a powerful army to rid the universe of demons. Not only did she destroy a demon king (also called Durga), but also went on to destroy the gigantic demon Mahisa.

KRISHNA

Krishna was the eighth incarnation or avatar of Vishnu, and came into the world solely to destroy the demon king Kansa. However, his popularity as a deity meant he also became the object of "bhakti" worship (a devotion to a supreme god). His nature was both sensuous and lustful, and he was the only god who genuinely fell in love with a mortal, the cowgirl Radha.

DEVI

Sometimes known as the great goddess, Devi was Shiva's consort. She may well have predated Brahma, Shiva, and Vishnu. Devi means "goddess," and she had many roles, such as the peaceful creator Jaganmatri (divine mother). As Shiva's consort she was both Sati (virtue) and later Sati's reincarnation Parvati (sweetness).

KALI

Kāli was the goddess of time and change, and her earliest incarnation was as a figure of annihilation of evil forces. Drunk on the blood of her victims she was about to destroy the universe when Shiva lay down in her way. In her fury, she stepped on his chest, but when she realized he lay beneath her feet, her anger was pacified.

TARA

In Hindu mythology Tara was the beautiful consort of Brihaspati, the teacher or guru of the gods. Tara was lusted after and abducted by Soma, the moon god, which led to war. Brahma persuaded Soma to return Tara to Brihaspati, who finding her pregnant refused to have her back. The child was so beautiful he claimed it as his own.

INDRA

With 1,000 eyes and 1,000 testicles that no one ever sees, Indra was a glutton, seducer, and heavy drinker of soma, which often made him irritable. In art he is often shown riding his warrior elephant or in his chariot as the chief god. His huge appetite for sex and food made him a rather bawdy deity and he became popularized in many later legends.

CHANDRA

Chandra was the original Vedic god of the moon. He drove the moon chariot across the sky with ten white horses. Young, beautiful, and fair, he carried a club and a lotus. According to Hindu myth, Chandra was born in the Ocean of Milk and nearly blinded the gods with his bright body, so the gods sent him into the cosmos as the moon.

AGNI

With thousands of aliases, Agni was the supreme god of fire, whether the flames of desire or the lightning in the sky. He appeared as a glistening prince riding a sacred ram or sometimes driving a wild chariot. With red flesh, cloaks of smoke, and his hair licking flames, he had two faces, gold teeth, and fourteen tongues.

CHALICE OF DOÑA URRACA
BASILICA OF SAN ISIDORO, LEÓN, SPAIN 1080

Alleged to be the Holy Grail, from which Jesus drank at the Last Supper

Housed in the Basilica of San Isidoro, León, Spain, since the twelfth century, this chalice is believed to be the true Holy Grail.

In 2014, Margarita Torres and José Miguel Ortega del Río published *Los Reyes del Grial* (*The Kings of the Grail*) in which they describe how a Spanish historian found two medieval Egyptian documents in Cairo. These documents, written in Arabic, suggest that the Holy Grail was taken to the city of León in the eleventh century. The writers claim that the Chalice of Doña Urraca, which historians believe has been in

León since that time, is in fact the true Holy Grail. Before this theory came to light, the mysterious grail was believed to have first appeared in the book *Perceval*, or *Le Conte du Graal*, an unfinished twelfth-century romance by Chrétien de Troyes that combined Christian lore with Celtic myth. It became an important symbol in Arthurian literature, which told how the knights of King Arthur searched for the Holy Grail, and only Sir Galahad was granted a vision of the grail because of his spiritual purity. This tale was essentially an allegory or a symbolic quest surrounding the search for immortality.

Late medieval writers also invented a false etymology for the word "grail," suggesting that it was a corruption of the word *sangréal*. *San gréal* means "holy grail" in Old French, but *sang réal* means "royal blood," and it was this latter phrase that suggested the legendary grail was something more than a goblet.

STORIES AND THEORIES

Chrétien's story attracted many interpreters and literary embellishers in the later twelfth and thirteenth centuries, including Wolfram von Eschenbach who envisaged the grail as a precious stone that fell from the sky. The connection of the Holy Grail with Joseph of Arimathea, the Last Supper, and the crucifixion of Jesus dates from the late twelfth century. In Robert de Boron's poem, Joseph receives the grail from the ghost of Jesus and sends it with his followers to Britain for safekeeping. Later writers recounted how Joseph used the chalice to catch Christ's blood at the crucifixion.

Ownership of the chalice has been attributed to various groups, including the Knights Templar, who were most influential around the time that grail stories started circulating and may have

hidden the Holy Grail in Nova Scotia. Some claim that the Holy Grail is buried beneath Rosslyn Chapel, Scotland, or that it lies deep within the springs of Glastonbury Tor in Somerset, England. Other legends claim that there is a secret line of hereditary protectors who keep the Holy Grail.

LEGENDARY QUESTS

GILGAMESH
This epic Sumerian story is one of the most ancient of quests, dating to around 3000 BCE. Two-thirds divine, Gilgamesh went on a quest to discover immortality, only to discover the futility of the desire to live forever.

ODYSSEUS
Homer's Greek poem describes the ten-year voyage of Odysseus after the Trojan war. The hero attempted to set things right on his return home and reunited with his faithful wife, Penelope, even though he had fallen in love with the lonely nymph Calypso.

AENEAS
The hero of the *Aeneid* by Virgil represents the sad fate of many lovers. After fleeing Troy, Aeneas traveled far and wide, and fell in love with Queen Dido of Carthage. However, love was not strong enough, and his destiny forced him to abandon her and sail for Italy.

More recent accounts state that Irish partisans of the Clan Dhuir transported the grail to the United States during the nineteenth century and that the grail was kept by their descendants in secrecy in a small abbey in southern Minnesota.

Conspiracy theories have led to a series of written accounts by authors who are convinced that Jesus and Mary Magdalene were ancestors of the Merovingian royal lineage, whose descendants secretly continue to guard the grail today. The "grail," in this case, is also a series of ancient documents revealing Jesus's and Mary Magdalene's lineage.

Such works have been the inspiration for a number of popular modern fiction novels. The best known is Dan Brown's novel *The Da Vinci Code* (2003), which, like the best-selling *Holy Blood, Holy Grail* (1982) by Michael Baigent, Richard Leigh, and Henry Lincoln is based on the idea that the real grail is not a cup but the womb and earthly remains of Mary Magdalene, plus a set of ancient documents that tell the true story of Jesus, his teachings, and his descendants. In Brown's novel, it is hinted that Jesus was merely a mortal man with strong ideals, and that the Holy Grail was buried originally beneath Rosslyn Chapel. In recent decades its guardians had it relocated to a secret chamber embedded in the floor beneath the glass pyramid at the entrance to the Louvre Museum in Paris.

From the series "The Quest for the Holy Grail" (1894) by Edward Burne-Jones, this painting shows Sir Galahad accompanied by Sir Bors and Sir Perceval. Thanks to his purity Sir Galahad was the only one allowed to see the Holy Grail.

TREE OF LIFE
CATHEDRAL OF OTRANTO, ITALY 1163–1165

Mosaic depiction of an allegory of life

The curious tree of life that sprawls across the cathedral floor in Otranto is one of the most eclectic of all tree-of-life imagery found in churches in Europe—and certainly the biggest. It was created by a monk named Pantaleone, who signed the mosaic at the bottom. Commissioned in 1163 by Archbishop Gionata d'Otranto, Pantaleone employed local and Norman craftsmen and other artisans from Tuscany to do the work. By 1165 the entire floor had been covered with the central tree trunk, which runs up the middle of the nave floor, and the many branches that spread out from its center.

The mosaics portray biblical characters (including Adam and Eve), warrior kings (Alexander the Great and King Arthur, for example), the Last Judgment, mythical beasts, pictorial representations of the working activities of the seasons, and the associated zodiac sign of the year. There are also vivid depictions of the building of Noah's ark and the Tower of Babel. Many of these mosaic narratives were restored and enhanced during a lengthy project that took place in the early 1990s.

Located at the southernmost point of Italy, the town of Otranto is well known for having been besieged, conquered, and sacked in 1480 by the Turks. Initially some 800 men withheld the siege, but they were finally captured and beheaded. They are known as the Otranto martyrs, and their skulls are stored in glass shrines beside an altar in the cathedral. The Turkish forces may have demolished the

The mosaic Tree of Life in Otranto Cathedral is the largest depiction of this symbol in Europe, at around 52 feet (16 m) long.

114 THE DIVINE WORLD

church's facade but they did not destroy the interior and therefore left its most precious treasure, the monumental mosaic.

Like a decorated carpet of colorful jewels, the mosaic stretches from the church entrance to the altar and is approximately 52 feet (16 m) long. Between the branches and leaves, biblical stories such as the tale of Cain and Abel are depicted, along with a mélange of scenes from pagan myths, including those of Samson, Atlas, and the huntress Diana. Other references to Greek mythology include an image of Deucalion and Pyrrha (protagonists of the Greek version of the flood story) being rescued on the back of a great fish.

Some sixteen medallions hold the whole medieval bestiary and its ambiguous symbolism together like a chain of tales and events, while domestic, ferocious, and exotic creatures run around the tree and clamber through its branches. Stranger though are the tree roots: they rest on two elephants—apparently a male and female—a bizarre cat wearing boots, and a bearded centaur with a chessboard on his head, as well as the word "PASCA" next to a winged griffin.

SCHOLARLY INTERPRETATION

The attributions of obscure meanings to the mosaic have divided scholars, but the overall message is thought to be an allegory of life: a pictorial symbol of all that is, has been, and will be. Some scholars believe the mosaic is a tribute or a historical record of ideas, events, and scenes from many different cultures at a time when Byzantine and Europe were opposed to one another. In medieval churches visual decoration served the dual purpose of educating the worshippers. The mosaic also tells about the main Christian teachings, the battle between good and evil, the virtues and vices of the human condition, and man's spiritual outcome. But is the work a moral representation of life, a record of historical events, or simply the manifestation of one man's fantasy world and love of culture?

The tree of life is a common symbol and it is recognized in many religions: it appears in the Hindu scriptures as Ashwattha, the symbol of the neverending universe, for example. The sacred tree is also a symbol of life, wisdom, and creation itself, and manifests as the Kabbalah of esoteric Judaism; the holy sycamore of ancient Egypt; the Norse ash, Ygdrassil; the Bodhi tree in Buddhism; and the Maya Yaxche, whose branches support the heavens.

The mosaic in Otranto is a universal symbol of life and its many pathways, including looking to the past and the present to record for posterity what life was all about. Many scholars have attempted to discover deeper meanings behind the imagery of the tree of life, from Kabbalistic associations to secret heresies, and even more ingeniously a complete map of how to find the Holy Grail. It may be that Pantaleone was simply documenting events, but scholars and historians are still unable to identify some of his more curious symbols.

The Tree of Life (c. 1310) by Pacino di Buonaguida depicts the crucifixion of Christ as the central symbol for an allegory of life and death.

The tree of life symbol is used in many mystical religions to represent universal oneness.

CALENDAR STONE
MEXICO c. 1427–1479

A calendar system representing the sun eras and their accompanying gods

Tonatiuh is shown holding a human heart in each of his clawed hands, and his tongue is represented by a stone sacrificial knife. Far more common than any other kind of ritual, sacrificial rites ensured that the sun continued to move across the sky.

The calendar system depicted on the stone was used not only by the Aztecs, but also by other pre–Columbian peoples of central Mexico. The calendar consisted of a 365-day cycle known as *xiuhpohualli* (year count) and a 260-day ritual cycle called *tonalpohualli* (day count). One solar year consisted of 360 named days and five nameless days. These "extra" days were thought to be unlucky and were days when people fled to their homes. The year was broken into eighteen periods of twenty days each, and this system is sometimes compared to the Julian month. Through Spanish usage, the twenty-day period of the Aztec calendar has become known as a *veintena*.

The *xiuhpohualli*, or year count, calendar was considered to be the agricultural calendar because it was based on the sun, and the day count calendar, or *tonalpohualli*, was considered to be the sacred calendar. According to experts, the calendric year began at some point in the distant past with the first appearance of the Pleiades star cluster to the east immediately before dawn. However, due to the precession of the Earth's axis, this reference point fell

The Aztec stone was based on solar cycles, sun eras, and ruling solar gods, and was used in ceremonial sacrificial rituals.

The Aztec Calendar Stone, or Piedra del Sol, is one of the best-known Aztec sculptures. Having been buried in Mexico City after the Spanish Conquest, it was rediscovered in 1790 during the restoration of the city's cathedral.

From the center of this huge stone—it is 11 ¾ feet (358 cm) in diameter and a massive 3 ¼ feet (98 cm) thick—shines the face of Tonatiuh, the Aztec solar god, surrounded by glyphs. Toward the edge of the circle are the four previous sun gods, along with symbols of the twenty-day cycle of the Aztec calendar.

out of favor and a more constant point was used, such as the solstice or equinox.

The four squares that surround the central deity Tonatiuh represent the four previous sun eras and their gods. Each era ended with the destruction of the world and humanity, and creation was restored in the next era. The top right square represents 4 Jaguar, the day on which the first era ended. It had lasted 676 years, after which time monsters devoured all of humanity. The top left square shows 4 Wind. After 364 years, hurricane winds destroyed the world and humans were turned into monkeys. The bottom left square shows 4 Rain. After 312 years this era was destroyed by a rain of fire, which transformed humanity into turkeys. The bottom right square represents 4 Water. This era lasted 676 years and ended when the world was flooded and humans were turned into fish. It is thought that the current sun era will end when the world is destroyed by earthquakes.

Although it is known as the Calendar Stone, archaeologists believe that the stone may have been used primarily as a ceremonial ritual altar for sacrifices, rather than as an astrological or astronomical reference. Other theories include a belief that the figure at the center of the stone represents Tlaltecuhtli, an earth god from creation myths. Another view is that the stone may have a geographic significance, and that the four points may relate to the four corners of the Earth or the cardinal points, and the inner circles may express space as well as time. One theory suggests that there are political associations for the stone that may have been intended to show that the city-state of Tenochtitlan was the center of the world and more powerful than any other civilization.

The Calendar Stone image has since been adopted by modern Mexican and Mexican American/Chicano culture figures and is used in folk art. It is also a symbol of cultural identity.

This volcanic stone carving depicts the solar god, Tonatiuh. Human sacrifices to Tonatiuh ensured his continued presence in the sky.

IMPORTANT AZTEC GODS

TEZCATLIPOCA
The most well-known sun god is Tezcatlipoca, who ruled the direction north and stalked the Earth at night wearing a gray cloak. He sometimes appeared as a jaguar, as depicted below. His positive aspect was that he ripened the harvest, but his negative aspect was that he created drought.

HUITZILOPOCHTLI
The god of the south was an important warrior god. The Aztecs were ferocious warriors, and Huitzilopochtli's association with fire and war meant that he was worshipped more than any other god. Such was his terrifying power that it was safer to propitiate him than ignore him.

TIALOC
The eastern god watered the earth with four vast jars of liquid, and each vessel signified various aspects of the seasons, such as growth, blight, frost, and destruction. Because Tialoc governed the mountains and all forms of water, he was the god to whom most sacrifices were made.

QUETZALCOATL
The god of the west was personified as a snake bird. He invented metalworking, and as the god of every craft and skill he was the civilizing influence on humanity. Quetzalcoatl was driven out of his domain by the other gods, and he headed east to the land of the rising sun promising one day to return.

INTIHUATANA STONE
MACHU PICCHU, PERU *c.* 1450

Believed by the Incas to hold the sun in place along its annual path in the sky

The Incas symbolically "hitched" the sun to the Intihuatana stone (shown here) at various times in the astronomical year so the world would not turn upside down.

The Inca believed that the Intihuatana stone anchored the sun in its place in order to keep it set on its annual path through the sky. They also believed that they were chosen by the sun itself to begin a new civilization at a time when all that had been before was doom and gloom, and so they called themselves the "children of the sun." The sun was the most important symbol to the Inca, both as a people chosen by the sun and as a powerful influence as a life-giver and creator of the world.

The remarkable city of Machu Picchu was once invisible from the mountainside below and was completely self-contained. Surrounded by agricultural terraces sufficient to feed its population and watered by natural springs, the hidden city seems to have been utilized by the Inca as a secret ceremonial site. Although some say that the city of Machu Picchu was a holiday resort for elite Inca, others that it was a prison, it was most probably a sacred religious site for the worship of Inti, the sun god.

HITCHING POST

In a startling solitary place high among the ruins of Machu Picchu, and astronomically aligned with the sun, is the sacred Intihuatana stone, meaning "hitching post of the sun." It is arranged so that it points directly at the sun at the winter solstice of the southern hemisphere, and the stone has been shown to be a precise indicator of the date of the two equinoxes and other significant celestial periods.

Also called the Saywa or Sukhanka stone, the Intihuatana stone is designed to hitch the sun at the two equinoxes. At midday on both March 21 and September 21, the sun stands almost directly above the pillar, thereby creating no shadow at all. At this precise moment the sun "sits with all his might upon the pillar" and is for a moment "tied" to the rock. The Inca performed rituals here to keep the sun hitched to the Earth so that the world would never turn upside down.

If the Intihuatana stone were ever destroyed or broken, the Inca believed that their gods would depart. In the sixteenth century, Atahuallpa, the last Inca emperor, greeted the Spanish conquistador Francisco Pizarro as the creator god Viracocha, believing that he had come back to honor the children of the sun. By the time Atahuallpa discovered his fatal error it was too late, and the Inca empire was already being destroyed. Machu Picchu was the only Inca city that the Spanish never found.

The ruins of Machu Picchu—some 2,000 feet (610 m) above the rumbling Urubamba River—include palaces, baths, temples, storage rooms, and more than one hundred houses, all in a remarkable state of preservation. Perilously high up in the mountains, the ruins are often shrouded in clouds, and many visitors say that it is like being among the gods themselves. There is even a legend that if you touch your forehead on the Intihuatana stone, you will be able to see into the spiritual world.

This early Nazca cotton mantle from coastal Peru features a design representing the sun deity, Inti (100–300).

IMPORTANT INCA GODS

INTI
Usually represented as a shining disk, the god of the sun was feared for his great powers: solar eclipses were an omen of his anger. The Inca believed that specks of gold found in the earth were drops of Inti's sweat, and the gold therefore became a precious spiritual force.

VIRACOCHA
The pre-Inca sun, creator, and storm god is usually depicted as a small man with a big halo. Viracocha created the universe, sun, moon, and stars. He also created time by commanding the sun to move over the sky, and then made civilization itself. He carries thunderbolts to show he is also a storm god.

MAMA QUCHA
The sea mother Mama Qucha was the sea and fish goddess as well as the protectress of sailors and fishermen. In one legend she was the mother of both the sun god Inti and his sister, the moon goddess Mama Killa, through her liaison with the powerful creator god Viracocha.

A'a

Reliquary figure of a creator god

The eighteenth-century carved wood reliquary figure of the god known as A'a reveals the symbolic importance of creation gods among indigenous peoples.

This late eighteenth-century carved wooden figure known as A'a originated in Rurutu in French Polynesia. The god is depicted in the process of creating other gods and men, and his creations cover the surface of his body in thirty small figures. The statue itself is hollow, and a removable panel on its back reveals a cavity that originally contained twenty-four small figures.

However, these were removed and destroyed in 1882. Experts are unsure as to which god A'a represents, but he was undoubtedly an important creator god, such as Rangi the father of all things.

In Polynesian mythology, Rangi and Papa were the primordial parents—sky father and earth mother—who lay locked together in a tight embrace. All the male children were forced to live in the cramped darkness between them. As they grew older and bigger, the children wanted to live in the light. A solution was proposed to kill the parents, but one of the children, Tane, disagreed and suggested pushing them apart. First Rongo, the god of food, tried to push his parents apart but nothing happened; then Tangaroa, god of the oceans, and his brother, the god of wild plants, joined him. In spite of their offspring's efforts Rangi and Papa stayed close together in their loving embrace. After many attempts, Tane, god of forests and birds, lay on his back and pushed with his strong legs. Stretching every sinew, he managed to pry Rangi and Papa apart.

RIVAL REALMS

The statue of A'a may also be likened to Tangaroa, who was the creator god of all the sea creatures. Tangaroa's son, Punga, had two children: one was the ancestor of all fish, and the other the ancestor of all reptiles. Terrified by the separation of the sky and the earth, the fish sought shelter in the sea, and the reptiles retreated to the forests. From that moment onward, Tangaroa held a grudge against Tane because he had offered refuge to Tangaroa's runaway children in the opposite domain. This dispute between Tangaroa and Tane indicates that the Maori believed the ocean and the land to be rival realms. When people went out to sea to fish or to travel, they were seen to be Tane's "creations," entering the realm of his enemy. For this reason, offerings were always made to Tangaroa and the ocean before any fishing or traveling expedition.

CREATION MYTHS

Creation myths are concerned about *how* humankind and the universe came into being. For many cultures the *why* does not enter into the myth, perhaps because myth tellers assumed that creation did not need to be questioned. Most creation stories focus on the creator god, shaping the world from himself or arising out of the waters of the primordial ocean or from chaos. In one of the oldest Greek myths, dating from around 3500 BCE, Eurynome danced the universe into being. Other stories tell of creators willing the world into existence, such as the Thinking Woman of the Keres peoples in the southwest United States. Some myths recount the cyclical nature of creation, in that creation does not happen once, but time and

time again. In the Hindu belief system, what we perceive as the world is thought to be merely an illusion.

Many myths focus on either primary or secondary creation gods. Primary creation was when gods or beings acted on their own, as in the Chinese tale of P'an Ku and the cosmic egg, or the Melanesian creator god, Qat. Secondary creation occurred when several gods got together or had offspring who they could put to work to bring humanity into being. Sometimes it was the forces of nature that created the world, but in some beliefs creation came about because of the dismembering of a creator, as in the myth of the Indian god Purusha or Ymir in Norse mythology. The giant Ymir is symbolic of the violence of creation because the giant's body represents the earth, his skull the sky, and his blood the sea—and all are torn apart.

In some Egyptian myths, the world was created when a mound of land arose from Nun, the watery abyss at the beginning of time. The mound was usually depicted as a pyramidal shape and was the perch for the mysterious benu bird, symbolizing the dawn of the world.

The Polynesian creator gods Tangaroa of the seas and Tane of the forests were always at war with one another.

This nineteenth-century Maori carving shows Rangi and Papa, the primordial parents of humankind, who were locked together in a tight embrace until pushed apart by the god of forests, Tane.

Floating in the void was the cosmic egg. P'an Ku managed to break his way out and begin to fashion the universe.

DEVIL STATUE
RENNES-LE-CHÂTEAU, FRANCE 1897

One of many secrets thought to be encoded at Rennes-le-Château

Carved on the lintel above the entrance to the mysterious church at Rennes-le-Château are the Latin words *terribilis est locus iste*. This has been translated most often as "this place is terrifying," but it can also be translated as something more cryptic: "this is a place of awe." Inside the church, however, there is a mysterious and quite alarming image: a statue of a horned devil. Legend tells that inside the Roman Catholic chapel at Rennes-le-Château there is a secret trap door in the stone floor. This door leads to the fiery abyss of hell itself, and from this entrance Satan comes and goes.

In addition to the statue, many secrets are believed to be encoded in the church, and the once quiet village on the edge of the French Pyrenees has been transformed recently into an epicenter of esoteric mysteries and riddles.

SAUNIÈRE'S SECRETS

Legend and truth are interwoven at Rennes-le-Château, but according to most records the local priest, François Bérenger Saunière, installed the diabolic statue in his church in 1897. He told close friends that he had discovered a strange coded parchment, including a document known as "Le Rouge Serpent" (The Red Dragon), which revealed many secrets, including the truth about evil. Seeking assistance in deciphering the codes, Saunière went to Paris and visited the Louvre to consult experts in ancient manuscripts. Strangely, on his return, the priest began to receive vast sums of money to refurbish the local church, and also to build other structures in the area, such as the Tour

This terrifying statue of the devil confronts all who enter the church at Rennes-le Château, France.

Magdala. Speculation was rife on the source of the parish priest's money. Was it lost treasure or was the priest blackmailing the Church with some terrible secret? Saunière's confession before his death was so shocking that the priest who heard it denied him absolution and last rites. On his death in 1917, Saunière left the secret behind his fabulous wealth with his housekeeper, Marie Dénarnaud. Marie promised to reveal the details on her deathbed, but sadly a stroke left her paralyzed and unable to speak.

Saunière's secrets can only be speculated upon, but they are believed to include the whereabouts of the treasures of the Knights Templar, the Cathars, or King Solomon. Some say that the information also reveals that Mary Magdalene was Christ's wife and the mother of his children, and that the holy couple are buried near Rennes-le-Château. A series of parchments was found by the priest's cleric in 1891, which contained an easily discovered cipher. One reads, "This treasure belongs to Dagobert II king and to Sion and he is there dead." Another cipher is the curious lettering D. O. U. O. S. V. A. V. V. M., which has never been decoded.

In his book *The Accursed Treasure of Rennes-le-Château* (1968), Gérard de Sède claims that the devil statue is that of the demon of lust, known as Asmodeus. He believes that Saunière may have been inspired by myths of Asmodeus that link the demon to showing the way to hidden ancient treasures. When Saunière ordered the demon statue in 1897, a bill for the work describes it as a *bénitier avec diable*, meaning a baptismal font with devil. According to historians, it is likely that Saunière commissioned the piece as a symbol of how one's belief in God can conquer all temptations by Satan, and how Satan, a fallen angel, must therefore pay the price. In 1996, a treasure hunter decapitated the devil statue, probably expecting to find a clue or a treasure inside. The original head was never found, and it has since been replaced by a replica.

Throughout the centuries, it is hardly surprising that the Church's mass persecution of anything pagan or heretical has filled the

collective mindset with the idea that evil exists independently, outside of man himself. With the persecution and execution of thousands of innocent people from the early Middle Ages through to the twentieth century, the devil archetype and symbol have been as powerful as people want to believe. Although mainstream Judaism has no obvious concept of a devil, Christianity and Islam have both considered the fallen angel as a rebel who tempts humans to sin and to commit evil deeds.

In many other cultures, there is a wide range of demonic spirits, such as the asuras of Hindu mythology, who are constantly in battle with the gods, and the seven demons known as the Galla of Mesopotamian myth, who roamed the night in search of victims to drag to the underworld. These demons were symbolic of death and gloom and were highly feared. However, there were few gods who were purely representative of evil until the influential Zoroastrian god of evil Ahriman came along. Zoroastrianism was the first religion to truly acknowledge and create the opposing forces and gods of good and evil, which were to become a permanent feature of Christianity.

This Zoroastrian tomb can be seen in Sulaymaniyah province in Kurdistan. Zoroastrianism changed religious belief, and the pantheons of earlier gods were replaced by two opposing gods: one good, the other evil.

In Zoroastrian belief Ahriman is the personification of evil; his name means "fiendish spirit."

The nautilus shell is one of the finest examples of a logarithmic spiral, one of the many curious systems and proportions found in nature.

SIGNS AND SYSTEMS

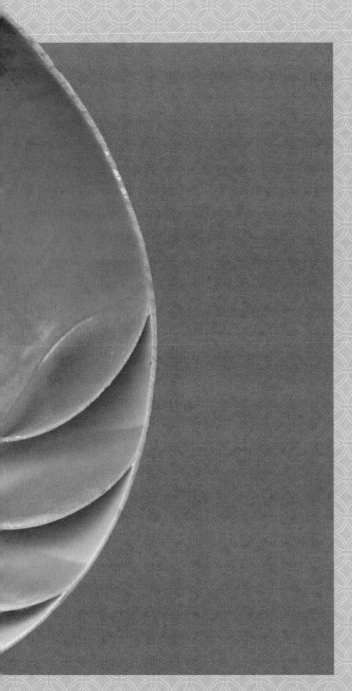

As pantheons of gods were absorbed into one god, ancient archetypal motifs appeared in a new guise. The cross became Christianity's major symbol, and ancient writing systems, such as Sumerian cuneiform script and Egyptian hieroglyphs, were integrated into religious and cultural systems. Patterns in nature were not only seen to reveal something about the divine, but also about humankind. The flower of life, for example, was a potent symbol of oneness, and the patterns on a turtle's back were seen by Taoist mystics as signs used to determine the future. Number systems took on meaning and significance after Pythagoras tried to prove that numbers resonated to the music of the planets and by association to the oneness of the universe. Sound, too, such as the Vedic om was in tune with the triad of Brahma, Vishnu, and Shiva, and wheels of life, mandalas, and other spiritual templates brought civilizations in touch with the divine. Divination, oracles, the golden ratio, and Vitruvian proportions introduced new symbolic systems to art, music, literature, and personal spiritual quests.

I CHING

CHINA twenty-ninth century BCE

An oracle that is consulted to determine one's future

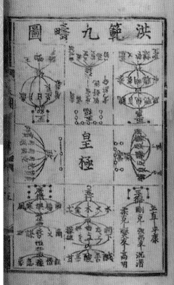 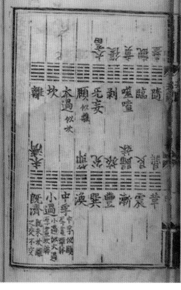

This ancient Chinese book, held at the Library of Congress, Washington, D.C., explains the use of the Bagua based on the Lo Shu magic square.

Thousands of years ago, Chinese fortune tellers consulted patterns and signs in nature to determine someone's future. They used the lines and markings on a tortoise's shell, scattered yarrow reeds or coins, and looked at the patterns of swarms of birds in the sky. These methods eventually evolved into an oracle called the "Book of Changes," or the I Ching, a mysterious concept that probably dates back to the early Taoist philosophers and the legendary first emperor of China, Fu Hsi, although some say to the later influential Duke of Zhou.

A rare book known as the "Bagua" is an explanation of a specific pattern used in the I Ching. The Bagua is based on the Lo Shu Square, a magic number square used in divination. Each number translates as one of the eight trigrams or symbols of the I Ching plus the central number, which is the single principle, the Tao or the way itself.

The concept of Tao is divided into two complementary but apparently opposing principles: yin and yang. All phenomena can be understood using yin and yang and five associated elements that affect the movements of the stars, the workings of the body, the landscape, and the nature of change. Yin is associated with all things feminine, such as the moon, darkness, intuition, feelings, and right-brain thinking. Yang is associated with all things masculine, such as the sun, noise, light, action, and left-brain thought processes. Yin and yang should be thought of as complementary forces that interact to form a dynamic system in which the whole is greater than the assembled parts. The whole is the Tao, or the way of Taoist philosophy, and that which interconnects all things.

The two opposing energies of yin and yang make up the I Ching's eight primary trigrams. Believing that nature's basic patterns were a language that revealed everything we do, these eight trigrams represent the fundamental energies of nature.

CHINESE ORIGINS

Fu Hsi reigned in ancient China during the mid-twenty-ninth century BCE. He was a cultural hero and invented writing, fishing, and trapping. He discovered the secrets of the I Ching from markings on the back of a mythical dragon horse, or some say from a turtle that emerged from the Lu River. This discovery is said to be the origin of calligraphy, too. Fu Hsi lived for 197 years and died in Chen, now known as Henan, where his monument can still be visited. Some scholars believe that the origins of the I Ching date to the Duke of Zhou, who lived in the eleventh century BCE. The Zhou dynasty ruled what is now part of Shanxi Province, known as the cradle of Chinese civilization. The duke was known as the "god of dreams," who told people via their dreams when something important was going to happen to them.

In the sixth century BCE, Chinese philosopher and sage Confucius integrated the I Ching into Chinese culture, but it remained relatively unknown until the nineteenth century when German missionary Richard Wilhelm translated the obscure texts. At the beginning of the twentieth century, psychologist Carl Jung considered the I Ching a confirmation of his own theory of synchronicity. He believed that meaningful coincidences take on greater significance when more than one occurs simultaneously, such as the throwing of the coins and the oracle's result. This is when the random throwing of the coins connects the querent to the storehouse of universal knowledge, and the revealed oracle offers insights into your future.

The Bagua reveals the positions of the eight trigrams, surrounded by the heavens, with the yin yang symbol of oneness at the center.

The legendary hero Fu Hsi discovered the secrets of the I Ching and re-created the world with his sister Nuwa.

THE EIGHT TRIGRAMS

A trigram is a group of three yin and yang lines. Yin or feminine lines are broken lines and yang or masculine lines are unbroken. These are the building blocks of a system that represents the eight energies of the universe.

CHEN
Thunder
Ancient meaning – The Arousing
Associated color – Yellow
Keywords: Initiative, spontaneity, insight, surprises

SUN
Wind
Ancient meaning – The Gentle
Associated color – Green
Keywords: Justice, flexibility, fairness, compromise

CHIEN
Heaven
Ancient meaning – The Creative
Associated color – Gold
Keywords: Achievement, focus, strength, power

K'AN
Water
Ancient meaning – The Abysmal
Associated color – Blue
Keywords: Desire, feeling, emotion
Symbolic of instincts and feelings

LI
Fire
Ancient meaning – The Clinging
Associated color – Orange
Keywords: Clarity, passion, inspiration, positive action

K'UN
Earth
Ancient meaning – The Receptive
Associated color – Black
Keywords: Receptivity, nurturing, acceptance

KEN
Mountain
Ancient meaning – Keeping still
Associated color – Purple
Keywords: Silence, solitude, withdrawal, reflection, objectivity

TUI
Lake
Ancient meaning – The Joyous
Associated color – Red
Keywords: Sexual healing, inner calm, secret power

SWASTIKA
MEZINE, UKRAINE c. 10,000 BCE

Powerful ancient symbol associated with the sun, good luck, and persecution

This striking Etruscan gold pendant (c. 700 BCE) from Bolsena, Italy, reveals an ancient swastika design as part of its decoration.

Sauwastikas were popular throughout the ancient world, and were often incorporated into ancient Greek and Roman interiors, as seen in this mosaic detail.

Throughout Europe, swastikas have been discovered on decorative items, on rocks and in caves. The earliest known swastika was found in Mezine in the Ukraine. Carved on a late paleolithic figurine of mammoth ivory, it is dated as early as 10,000 BCE. In England, neolithic stone carvings of swastikas have been found in Yorkshire, and mirror-image swastikas (clockwise and anticlockwise) have been found on ceramic pottery in the Devetashka Cave, Bulgaria, dating to 6000 BCE. Other early archaeological evidence of swastika-shaped ornaments dates back to the Old European Vinca culture of 6000 to 5000 BCE and also to the Indus Valley Civilization of around 3300 BCE. It is not clear what the symbol was used for originally, but swastikas appeared in a number of ancient civilizations

around the world, including Turkic, Indian, Chinese, European, and Celtic cultures.

The complete range of symbols and signs used by the Vincas has, to date, been controversial, and there is no certainty as to their meaning. However, in Sanskrit the word *svastika* means "well being." It has always been a sign for a lucky or auspicious object, and in particular is a mark made on persons and things to denote auspiciousness. In Hinduism, the swastika represents the principle of the origin of the universe, or creation itself. The four swirling arms represent the four directions of the manifest universe or the four faces of Brahman, God. It is a common practice for Hindus to draw swastika symbols on the doors and entrances to their houses during festivals, thereby symbolizing an invitation to the goddess Lakshmi to bring them good luck. When the arms are left facing, the symbol is called a "sauwastika."

The swastika is often linked to the development of the cross symbol in Bronze Age pagan religions, in which the cross was first thought to be a powerful early symbol of the sun. There are

various theories from archaeologists to suggest that the four arms represent the four aspects of nature: the sun, wind, water, and earth. Others believe that they represent the four seasons, the four compass directions, or the ninety-degree angles of the zodiac corresponding to the solstices and equinoxes.

According to archaeoastronomer Reza Assasi, the swastika is a geometric pattern in the sky representing the north ecliptic pole centered to the fixed star Zeta Draconis. He argues that this primitive astrological symbol was later called the four-horse chariot of Mithra in ancient Persia. In ancient Iranian mythology, the cosmos was believed to be pulled by four heavenly horses revolving around a fixed center in a clockwise direction. This was perhaps a geocentric representation of an astronomical phenomenon known as axial progression. Assasi suggests that this notion was transmitted to the West and flourished in the Roman cult of Mithraism, where the swastika symbol appears widely in the cult's iconography and astrological representations.

During the millennium that followed, the image of the swastika was used by many cultures around the world, including in China, Japan, India, and southern Europe. By the Middle Ages, the swastika was a well-known, if not commonly used, symbol but it was referred to by many different names. In China it was known as "wan," in England the "fylfot," and in Greece the "tetraskelion" or "gammadion."

Swastikas have been found worldwide, from the area of Kush in Africa to the Caucasus Mountains of Russia. After becoming a popular good luck symbol in European culture in the Middle Ages, the swastika's association with Aryan and Indian origins became popular with the newly unified Germany in 1871, because the country wanted to prove that it had its roots in an ancient empire, such as the pre–Vedic civilization known as the Aryans. By the end of the nineteenth century, the swastika could be found on German *völkisch*, or nationalist, periodicals and it was the official emblem of the German Gymnasts' League. By the beginning of

the twentieth century, the swastika had become a common symbol of German nationalism and it was adopted by the Nazi party in Germany in the 1920s as a symbol of its links with the Aryan race. A right-facing forty-five-degree-rotated swastika was incorporated into the German flag when Adolf Hitler came to power in 1933. In many Western countries the swastika has since been stigmatized and associated with Nazism, anti–Semitism, persecution, death camps, violence, and mass murder.

Although the swastika is still denounced in the West, it has become popular again as a Hindu symbol, not only for its representations of Brahman, but also for its representation of Dharma (natural order), Artha (wealth), Kama (desire), and Moksha (liberation).

At the end of the nineteenth century, Germany included the swastika among many of its emblems, and it is still associated with Nazism, Hitler, and mass murder.

As a spiritual symbol in Hinduism, the swastika has become an accepted and popular symbol again.

CUNEIFORM
SUMER, MESOPOTAMIA c. 8000 BCE

The earliest known form of writing

The Manishtusu obelisk is dedicated to the Akkadian god, Enlil, and is covered in cuneiform script.

Sumerian cuneiform is the earliest known writing system. Its origins can be traced back to about 8000 BCE, and it developed from the pictographs and other symbols used on clay tablets to represent trade goods and livestock. Originally the Sumerians made small tokens out of clay to represent the items. The tokens were kept together in sealed clay envelopes, and to show what was inside the envelopes, traders pressed the tokens into the clay on the outside to mark the amounts.

The name "cuneiform" simply means "wedge shaped," from the Latin *cuneus* and *forma*, and the term came into English usage via the Old French word *cunéiforme*. Cuneiform script is distinguished by its wedge-shaped marks. The characters were usually imprinted on a wet clay tablet with a stylus made of reed. Some tablets were dried in the sun or air, and remained fragile. Later, these unfired clay tablets could be soaked in water and recycled into new clean tablets. Other tablets, once written upon, were fired to make them hard and durable. Collections of these fired clay documents made up the first archives and libraries.

Cuneiform developed significantly in Sumer between 3000 and 2000 BCE, but it was gradually replaced by the Phoenician alphabet during the Neo-Assyrian Empire (934–609 BCE). Certain signs were used to indicate names of gods, countries, cities, vessels, birds, and trees, as well as other important words. The earliest known Sumerian king whose name appears on a cuneiform tablet is Enmebaragesi of Kish, in c. 2700 BCE.

A superb stele, or monumental stone, known as the Manishtusu obelisk, was made by Manishtusu, son of the Akkadian emperor Sargon the Great who ruled from 2270 to 2255 BCE. Manishtusu had to suppress widespread rebellions against his rule, but he also conducted long-distance trade and was credited with the foundation of the Ishtar Temple at Nineveh. According to some ancient stories, Manishtusu was hacked to death by his courtiers with cylinder seals.

The Manishtusu obelisk is made of deep black diorite, and is incised in Akkadian cuneiform in horizontal rows within a total of 1,519 boxes on all sides. It was recorded that in order to make the obelisk, black stone was taken from the mountains and transported by boat to the quay in Akkad, where the stone was crafted and dedicated to the god Enlil. When Enlil was a young god, he was banished from the land of the gods to the underworld Kur, for seducing a goddess named Ninlil. Ninlil followed him to the underworld where she bore his first child, the moon god Sin. After fathering three more underworld deities, Enlil was allowed to return to Ekur, the home of the gods. Enlil was known as the inventor of an agricultural hoe or digging tool, and was also the god of breath and wind, and height and depth.

MAJOR CHANGES

From about 2900 BCE, many of the cuneiform symbols began to lose their original meaning, and a given sign could have a wide variety of meanings depending on the context in which the symbol was placed. The sign inventory was reduced from some 1,500 symbols to about 600. By 2500 BCE, the writing direction had changed to left to right in horizontal rows. In the process, the pictographs were rotated ninety degrees counter-clockwise, and a new wedge-tipped stylus was used, pushed into the clay to produce the series of signs. These two major changes made writing quicker and easier. By adjusting the relative position of the tablet to the stylus, the writer could use a single tool to make a variety of impressions.

Although the cuneiform writing system was in common use for more than three millennia, up until the second century CE, it was replaced completely by alphabetic writing during the course of the Roman era. By the third century CE, cuneiform script had become extinct, and all knowledge of how to read it was lost until it began to be deciphered by scholars in around 1857. Since then, between half a million and two million cuneiform tablets are estimated to have been excavated in modern times. However, of these, only approximately 100,000 have been published.

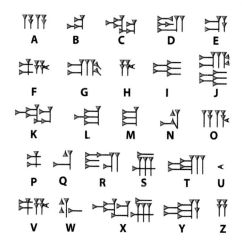

The earliest form of cuneiform writing dates back to 8000 BCE, when the Sumerians recorded information on wet clay tablets with a wedge-shaped stylus or reed.

Cuneiform developed over the centuries, and it was eventually identified with other alphabets.

OM

INDIA c. sixth century BCE

Ancient Sanskrit sign of the vibration of divine energy at creation

Brahma, Vishnu, and Shiva are the triad of gods from the beginning of creation, and resonate to the mystical sound "om."

Om, sometimes written as aum, is a mystical mantra that was recorded in the ancient Vedic sacred texts known commonly as the *Rigveda*. This Sanskrit sound originated in India, and it is sacred to a number of religions such as Hinduism, Buddhism, and Jainism. The syllable is also referred to as *aumkara*, which translates as "aum syllable," and in Sanskrit it is sometimes referred to as *pranava*, meaning "that which is sounded out loudly."

The om is placed at the beginning of most Hindu texts as a sacred mantra to be intoned at the beginning and end of a reading of the Vedas or prior to and after any prayer. It was first described as an all-encompassing mystical entity in the *Upanishads*, a collection of Vedic texts, and om can be seen everywhere in Hindu art as a generic sign for the philosophy and religion of the Hindus.

When creation began, the divine, all-encompassing consciousness took the form of the first and original vibration manifesting as the sound "om." Before creation, there was the void. The void was known as Shunyakasha, meaning "no sky," and this was more than nothingness because everything existed in a latent state of potentiality.

In one form of Hinduism known as Puranic Hinduism, om is the mystic name for the union of the three gods. The letter "a" stands for Brahma, the "u" for Vishnu, and the "m" for Mahadeva, better known as Shiva. The three sounds also symbolize the three Vedic texts *Rigveda*, *Samaveda*, and *Yajurveda*. According to Hindu philosophy the letter "a" represents creation, when all existence issued forth from Brahma's golden nucleus; the letter "u" tells how Vishnu preserved this world by balancing Brahma on a lotus above himself, and the letter "m" symbolizes the final part of the cycle of existence, when Brahma falls asleep. This is when Shiva has to take an in-breath so that all existing things have to disintegrate and are reduced to their essence. Om is also said to be the original sound that contains all other sounds, all words, all languages, and all mantras.

In some Hindu schools, when one gains true knowledge, there is no split between the knower and the known: one becomes knowledge itself. In essence, om is the signifier of the ultimate truth that all is one.

Many of the hymns recorded in the sacred texts known as the *Rigveda* involve the use of chanting the om mystic sound.

OM MANTRAS

The om symbol is today used by many Western spiritual groups as a chant or mantra to aid meditation or to help with spiritual development, and the symbol is usually drawn using the Vedic script. For example, the om sound is a familiar element in the practice of many forms of yoga. It is a supreme mantra and the most sacred of holy words. It is used as a meditation on the nature of the universe, and involves using every part of the lung when chanted during breathing techniques. In the yoga sutras of Patanjali, which form the basis of Ashtanga yoga, the om is seen as god's voice.

In the Advaita Vedanta school of Vedic philosophy, the om is used to represent the triad as one, and it also implies that our existence is "false." Chanting om reminds us that in order to see beyond the veil of so-called reality, we must learn to understand that the true nature of infinity lies beyond this illusion. With liberation from the cycles of birth, death, and rebirth, known as "moksha" or "samadhi," we are able to see existence for what it is, and we can also become at one with the whole. When one gains true knowledge, there is no split between the knower and the known: one becomes knowledge itself. Om is therefore the sound or symbol of the ultimate truth that all is one.

One of the most profound mantras in Tibetan Buddhism, and often engraved on mani stones, is *Om mani padme hum*, or "om to the jewel in the lotus, hum." These words are also written on scrolls of paper and placed in prayer wheels. The living om symbol also exists in varying forms in Taoist and Sikhist beliefs. Sometimes it has been translated as "so be it," similar to the concluding Hebrew praise "amen" and the Druid "awen." The Ek Onkar symbol, meaning "god is one," used by Sikhs is a different version of the om symbol and encompasses another sign for healing and protection.

The Hindu symbol for om is now popular in jewelry design in the West.

PENTAGRAM
URUK, MESOPOTAMIA *c.* 4000 BCE

A sacred symbol of renewal, regeneration, and transformation

In Uruk in ancient Mesopotamia, this symbol of a pentagram dating to about 4000 BCE signifies the universe.

Some of the earliest known pentagrams were found in archaeological excavations in Uruk, Mesopotamia, and date from 4000 BCE. In the Sumerian language the pentagram, and its cuneiform derivative, meant "the regions of the universe." Moreover, in early Sumerian script from around 2500 BCE a pentagram glyph can be found for a word meaning corner, angle, small room, cavity, or hole. Studies of cuneiform tablets discovered in Susa, Iran, in the 1930s, and dating to the second millennium BCE, leave little doubt that the Babylonians knew at least an approximate mathematical formula for the area of a pentagon.

In Greek, the word "pentagram" comes from the words for "five" and "line," and it is sometimes used synonymously with the words "pentacle" and "pentangle." One interpretation of the pentagram is that each of the five points represented the initial Greek letters of the five elements. The five-pointed star is the most common form of geometric star. It is a symbol of renewal, regeneration, and transformation, whether it represents the biblical star of Bethlehem or Venus, as the morning star and the bringer of dawn. However, the symbol also seems to have been used as a magical or mystical sign by the ancient Greek philosopher Pythagoras and his followers, who would cross themselves using the pentagram, just as Christians do using the Latin cross. Whenever Pythagoras met someone in the street, he would make the sign of the pentagram accompanied by a greeting of "good health."

During the medieval period the pentagram was used as a Christian symbol for the five wounds of Christ. In the fourteenth-century English tale of Sir Gawain and the Green Knight, the pentagram decorates the shield of the hero, Gawain. The anonymous author of the romance credits the symbol's origin to King Solomon, saying that the pentagram is the key to understanding the work. In explanation, Gawain is keen in his five senses, dextrous in his five fingers, faithful to the salvation provided through the five wounds of Christ, takes courage from the five joys that Mary had of Jesus, and exemplifies the five virtues of knighthood.

In Renaissance grimoires dealing with magical invocations and spell casting, the pentacle is described as being hung about the neck, providing protection and authority to the magician. Magus Johannes Trithemius suggested that a pentacle should be hung around one's neck before casting a magic circle. He advised that the pentacle was to be drawn on virgin parchment, or engraved on a square plate of silver, and suspended from the neck to the breast. Renaissance magus Agrippa and other Hermetic magicians perpetuated the popularity of the pentagram as a magic symbol, attributing the five Neoplatonic and Pythagorean elements to the five points. Freemasonry also draws on Pythagorean symbolism in the pentagram, although it is also regarded as a reminder that Christ was spirit descended into matter.

By the mid nineteenth century a distinction had developed among occultists regarding the pentagram's orientation. With a single point upward, it depicted spirit presiding over the four elements of matter, and was essentially "good." Influential French occult author Eliphas Levi referred to the pentagram as evil whenever the symbol appeared the other way up. His symbol for Baphomet, connected with Satanism, made use of this upside-down pentagram, and it has been considered an iconic symbol of black magic ever since.

The pentagram is also used commonly as a protective symbol, such as the five-point form of the Seal of Solomon in medieval Islamic tradition, and many varieties of pentacle can be found in grimoires of Solomonic magic, or used in modern Wicca and other witchcraft traditions. Although the pentagram and the pentacle are considered synonymous in most scholarly circles, they are differentiated in Wicca and other modern pagan systems. For example, a pentacle refers to a pentagram circumscribed by a circle. This form of pentacle is drawn on a disk, which may be used either upon an altar or as a sacred space of its own.

In Middle French the word "pentacle" was used to refer to any magical talisman, whereas in many tarot decks one of the four suits is known as coins, or sometimes pentacles. These tarot decks depict the suit as disks marked with a pentagram. In this context they represent the element of earth or divinity manifesting in matter.

With its fifth point oriented upward, the pentagram symbolizes "spirit" presiding over the four elements of the material world in occult circles.

The pentagram is among the symbols used by the Carboneria, an Italian secret society and offshoot of the Freemasons.

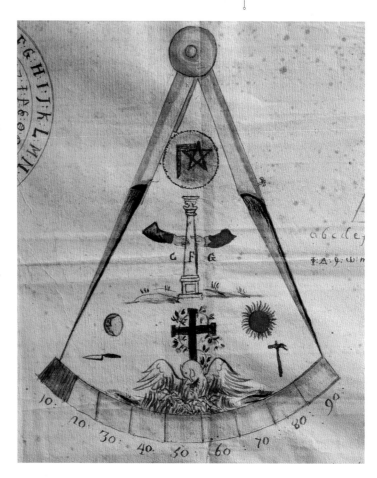

YIN AND YANG

CHINA fourth–third century BCE

Ancient Taoist symbol of duality

This detail of a seventeenth-century Chinese porcelain dish shows sages with the yin and yang symbol used for divination.

The symbol shows the white yang or masculine energy and the black yin or feminine energy as one in harmony.

Everyone is familiar with the yin and yang sign, but what does it actually symbolize? The yin is the black side with the white dot, and the yang the white side with the black dot. In ancient Taoist philosophy, these two apparently opposing yet interwoven energies were thought to be the dark, northern side of a mountain (yin) and the bright, sunny southern side of the mountain (yang), united by the mountain itself.

Yin and yang symbolize the duality that we see, such as light and dark, high and low, hot and cold, fire and water, life and death, male and female, sun and moon. However, these pairs are simply physical manifestations of the duality of yin and yang. We see both sides of the mountain, but in fact the mountain is one. Yin and yang are complementary forces (rather than opposing ones) interacting to form a dynamic system of oneness. Everything has both yin and yang aspects, and balancing these forces creates harmony and health, as well as, in the ancient Taoist pathway, the experience and understanding of the Tao: the driving force behind everything that exists.

Yin symbolizes feminine principles and as such is slow, soft, yielding, diffuse, cold, wet, and passive. It is also identified with water, earth, the moon, and nighttime. Yang, by contrast, is masculine, potent, fast, hard, solid, focused, hot, dry, and aggressive. It is associated with fire, sky, the sun, and daytime.

Chinese astrology is closely associated with Taoist philosophy and uses the principles of yin and yang to determine a person's horoscope, along with the five elements—fire, earth, metal, water, and wood—and the twelve zodiac animal signs that are based on the lunar calendar. The sixty-year cycle consists of two separate cycles interacting with each other. The first is the cycle of the five elements in either a yin or a yang form, and the second is the cycle of the twelve animal signs. These are as follows: rat, ox, tiger, rabbit, dragon, snake, horse, goat, monkey, rooster, dog, and pig; the last is replaced by the cat in Vietnam. This combination creates the sixty-year cycle starting from yang wood rat and continuing until its return, sixty years later.

Since the zodiac animal cycle of twelve is divisible by two, every zodiac sign can only occur as either yin or yang. For example, the dragon is always yang, and the snake is always yin, and so on. Years that end in an even number are yang; those that end with an odd number are yin.

As the zodiac follows the lunar calendar, the actual date of the new yin or yang year falls on a different date each year, sometime between the middle of January and the middle of February. So, for example, someone born on February 2, 1981 (according to the Western calendar) may well think that they were born in the year of the rooster and are therefore yin metal. In fact the year of yin metal rooster did not start until February 5 in 1981, so they are actually yang metal, and born in the year of the monkey.

CHARACTERISTICS

Yin or yang softens or enhances the characteristics of the personality. It can, according to the energy of the elemental year, invoke courage and stamina when aligned with fire or metal, for example, as these are both strong-willed and self-centered energies. Yin would internalize the energy; it would still be potent, but more reflective or inward looking. A yin metal or yin fire person is often someone who is a highly creative artist or thinker, whereas a yang metal or yang fire person would be a warrior for themselves or for a cause.

Yin and yang principles are also applied to the human body in traditional Chinese medicine. Good health is directly related to the balance between yin and yang energies within oneself.

This mother-of-pearl inlay on a piece of Chinese furniture at the Haiphong Museum, Vietnam, shows the yin and yang symbol guarded by two dragons.

YEARS AND YIN OR YANG ELEMENTS

If the year ends in 0 it is yang metal.
If the year ends in 1 it is yin metal.
If the year ends in 2 it is yang water.
If the year ends in 3 it is yin water.
If the year ends in 4 it is yang wood.
If the year ends in 5 it is yin wood.
If the year ends in 6 it is yang fire.
If the year ends in 7 it is yin fire.
If the year ends in 8 it is yang earth.
If the year ends in 9 it is yin earth.

The twelve animal signs and the five elements form the Chinese sixty-year astrological cycle.

TRISKELION

NEWGRANGE, IRELAND *c.* 3200 BCE

Ancient emblem comprising spiral symbols

Outside the 5,000-year-old temple of Newgrange, Ireland, a lone entrance stone bears the curious motifs of the triskelion.

The spirals of the triskelion represent the power of the divine one, plus the merger of the masculine and feminine principles.

A triskelion is a motif consisting of three interlocked spirals, and the term originates from an ancient Greek word meaning "three legged" or "three times." It appears throughout Celtic and European Iron Age art and decoration. The triskelion symbol also features in many other early cultures, including on the decoration of Mycenean jugs and drinking ware, on the coinage of Lycia, and as a heraldic emblem on the shields of warriors on Greek pottery. With the arrival of Christianity, the symbol took on a new meaning, as that of the Trinity: Father, Son, and Holy Spirit. Its popularity continues today as a decorative symbol of faith for Christians of Celtic descent around the world. It is also the symbol of Sicily, where it is called the *trinacria*.

The triskelion appears as a motif in ancient rock art. Around 5,000 years ago, as the sun reached the winter solstice, a large group of priests, initiates, and lords squeezed into the passageway and inner chamber of a mystical temple at Newgrange, Ireland. It was a place of astrological, spiritual, religious, and ceremonial magic, and the moment that the sun began to climb in the sky again in the depths of winter was a time for special celebration: a time to give thanks to the sun and for the new fertility of the year ahead. It is here that the triple spiral motif, known as the triskelion, is found carved on the passageway and on the lozenge-shaped entrance stone as well as on several of the surrounding curb stones.

The number three is also a sacred symbol worldwide and considered magical. In ancient Greek mythology there were three Fates, three Graces, three Gorgons, and three Furies. Even Apollo's Pythia sat on a three-legged chair, and Cerberus was a three-headed dog. In Celtic mythology and early Indian philosophy, threeness or the triad is a magical number, considered to be the merger of the power of two—the masculine and feminine—plus oneness, or the divine itself. A threefold nature materializes in a mysterious fashion but still obeys universal laws, which is why it is also associated with various forms of magic and spell casting.

The triskelion in Celtic mythology is said to symbolize the past, present, and future embraced in the now. This probably derives from the manifestation of three goddesses—maiden, matron, and crone—who became the triple goddess Brigid, and from earlier triads of gods in Indian mythology. The triskelion is also one of the primary symbols of the contemporary movement known as Celtic Reconstructionist Paganism, which uses the symbol to represent a variety of triplicities in its cosmology.

The Three Graces (c. 1505) by Italian artist Raphael is one of many depictions of a triad of deities important in ancient spiritual beliefs.

OTHER SYMBOLS ASSOCIATED WITH "THREE"

DRINKING HORNS
A 10-foot (3 m) high Danish runestone dating from the ninth century CE called Snoldelev Stone is decorated with a design of three interlocking drinking horns, similar to the symbol known as Diane de Poitiers's three crescent emblem. Diane de Poitiers was an influential French courtier who advised Henry II in the sixteenth century. She only ever wore black and white clothing as a symbol of the dark and light of the moon, and her emblem was three interlocking crescent moons.

THREE HARES
In sacred sites as far apart as the Middle East and the United Kingdom is found a symbol of three hares in a circular surround. Primarily used as an architectural or religious motif, it is viewed as a puzzle or visual challenge. The symbol features three hares, or sometimes rabbits, chasing each other in a circle. Each of the ears is shared by two hares, so that only three ears are shown. It has a range of symbolic and mystical associations with fertility and the lunar cycle.

TRIQUETRA
The word "triquetra" originally meant triangle, and it was used to refer to various three-cornered shapes. Nowadays, it has come to refer exclusively to a particular, more complicated shape formed of three vesica piscis, sometimes with an added circle in or around it. Also known as a "trinity knot," the design is used as a religious symbol by both Christians and polytheists.
Christians refer to the triquetra as a symbol that unites the Father (God), the Son (Jesus), and the Holy Spirit.

CADUCEUS
GREECE *c.* 3000 BCE

Magical wand that was carried by the messenger of the gods

A caduceus is a short staff or wand that has magical properties. As a symbolic object it represents the qualities of both Hermes and Mercury, and by extension symbolizes trades, occupations, or undertakings associated with them. In late antiquity, the caduceus was the basis for the symbol for the planet Mercury, both in astrology and alchemy, and it was later used to denote the element Mercury, too. The caduceus has also been used as a symbol to represent printing, and incorrectly as a symbol of health care and medical practice. This is due to its confusion with the traditional medical symbol, the rod of Asclepius, which has only one snake and is never depicted with wings.

Entwined by two serpents, the caduceus is sometimes surmounted by wings. In Roman iconography it was often depicted being carried in the left hand of the god Mercury, the Roman equivalent of Hermes. Mercury was not only the messenger of the gods, but also the divine guide and protector of merchants, shepherds, gamblers, liars, and thieves. It is said that the wand would wake the sleeping and send the awake to sleep. If applied to the dying, their death was gentle; if applied to the dead they returned to life.

The Greek messenger god Hermes was a psychopomp, a god who guided souls to the underworld, but he was also god of magic, merchants, boundaries, and journeys. In most depictions Hermes is shown carrying a caduceus. The same staff was also carried by the goddess of the rainbow, Iris, who descended frequently to Earth with messages from the goddess Hera. It is believed by many mythologists and historians that Hermes developed from an ancient Babylonian deity, most likely an underworld snake god. From this perspective, the caduceus was a symbol

The caduceus has two serpents coiled around the rod and symbolizes harmonious agreement and peace.

Mercury (1550) by Giambologna is a bronze statue of the god with a caduceus, a magic wand that could bring the dead to life.

of the god himself, in his early form as the Mesopotamian deity Ningishzida. On a libation vase dating to around 2000 BCE, Ningishzida is depicted as two entwining snakes around a staff. However, many early Greek philosophers believed that Hermes developed from the Egyptian god Thoth, who was also a god of magic, communication, astrology, philosophy, knowledge, astronomy, and science. Later, in esoteric and mystical traditions, Hermes and Thoth were amalgamated into the legendary mystic Hermes Trismegistus.

One ancient Greek myth tells how Hermes came to have the magical wand due to the frustrations of the blind prophet Tiresias. When Tiresias came across two snakes copulating on Mount Cyllene, he killed the female with his staff. Tiresias was immediately turned into a woman by the goddess Hera, and remained female until he was able to repeat the act and kill the male snake seven years later. His staff later came into the possession of Hermes, along with its transformative powers. Another myth suggests that Hermes (or Mercury) saw two serpents entwined in mortal combat. Separating them with his wand he brought about peace, and as a result the wand with two serpents was associated with harmonious agreement.

ROD OF ASCLEPIUS

Whatever the origins of Hermes, it is in Homer's work that we learn of the story of how Hermes offered his lyre to his half-brother Apollo, and in return Apollo gave him the caduceus. The association with the serpent thus connects Hermes to Apollo, as later the serpent was associated with Apollo's son, Asclepius, the Greek god of healing. The association of Apollo, Hermes, and Asclepius with the serpent is a variant of the ancient pre-classical tale of the earth dragon, Python, who with the rise of classical mythology is slain by Apollo.

The rod of Asclepius, also known as the asklepian, is a serpent-entwined rod wielded by Asclepius and associated with healing and medicine. The symbol has continued to be used

This eighteenth-century engraving by Martin Engelbrecht shows a doctor carrying the rod of Asclepius.

in modern times, where it is associated with medicine and health care. When Asclepius was rescued from his dead mortal mother's womb, Apollo carried the baby to the centaur Chiron, who raised Asclepius and instructed him in the art of medicine. It is said that in return for kindness rendered by Asclepius, a snake licked Asclepius's ears clean and taught him secret knowledge. Snakes were sacred beings of wisdom, healing, and resurrection to the ancient Greeks. From then on, Asclepius bore a rod wreathed with a single snake.

ANKH

EGYPT *c.* 3000–2500 BCE

Ancient Egyptian symbol representing the key to another world

Part of the collection of Tutankhamun's Tomb in the Cairo Museum, Egypt, this superb gilded mirror box is shaped like an ankh.

The ankh symbol takes the shape of a tau cross with a loop on top.

The ankh, also known as the "key of life," the "key of the Nile," or in Latin *crux ansata*, meaning "cross with a handle," not only symbolized life, but in tomb art it also represented eternal life. A gilded mirror box in the shape of the ankh was found in Tutankhamun's tomb when it was discovered in the Valley of the Kings by archaeologist and Egyptologist Howard Carter in 1922. It once contained a mirror but this was stolen by tomb raiders long before the site was excavated.

An inscription with Tutankhamun's names, epithets, and relationships to specific gods is written around the loop of the upper sections of both parts of the box and in a column in the vertical part. The corresponding area on the lid has the king's throne name written alongside a winged beetle. This is flanked by two serpents whose heads are surmounted by solar disks and whose tails terminate in the hieroglyphic sign for infinity known as "shen." Below the name is a lotus, and the entire composition—inlaid in glass and semiprecious stones—was thought to be a reference to a myth involving the birth of the sun god. Interestingly, the Egyptian hieroglyph "ankh" not only means "life," but also "mirror."

ORIGINS

Theories on the ankh's origins range from its ancient use as a sex and fertility symbol to it as a representation of the common sandal strap, thus invoking the power of movement and therefore life. Prior to the Egyptian dynastic usage, the ankh may have been a knot with a specific religious or mythical significance. Indeed, some scholars agree that it was a symbol of the life-giving elements of air and water, the latter so precious in the Nile delta. It was often shown being offered to the pharaoh as a symbol of the "breath of life."

Well-known English Egyptologist E. A. Wallis Budge believed that the ankh originated from a symbolic image of the goddess Isis's belt buckle. This developed into a separately known symbol: the tiet, or knot of Isis. The tiet was often paired with the djed pillar—a symbol of Osiris—and together the djed and the tiet represented the dual nature of life. The tiet was also called the "blood of Isis," and amulets of

Anubis-like gods hold protective ankhs, often thought to be keys to the afterlife, which were painted on the interior of tombs.

A similar symbol to the ankh has been found on Minoan figurines from Knossos, Crete.

the sign were made from red stones such as carnelian and jasper. Ankhs were often carried as an amulet either alone or with two other hieroglyphs that mean "strength" and "health." Mirrors of beaten metal were also made in the shape of an ankh, either for decorative reasons or to symbolize the eternal world that lay beyond the beholder.

Various decorative images on temples show a personified ankh holding an ostrich feather fan behind the pharaoh. Similarly, chains of personified ankhs were shown pouring out of water vessels and descending over the king as a symbol of the regenerating power of water. Early libation vessels used in religious ceremonies were sometimes produced in the shape of the ankh. Other objects such as spoons and musical instruments were also made in this shape.

Egyptian gods were often portrayed carrying the ankh symbol by its loop, or bearing an ankh in each hand, arms crossed over their chest.

Many ancient gods were depicted with ankhs, such as Ptah, Satet, Tefnut, Osiris, Ra, Isis, and Anubis. The ankh sign was depicted being offered to Queen Nefertiti by the sun disk, Aten, as a symbol of life in the netherworld. The dead were often referred to as "ankhu," and a term for a sarcophagus was "neb-ankh," meaning possessor of life.

A symbol similar to the ankh has been found in Minoan and Mycenaean archaeological sites. It is a combination of the sacral knot, a symbol of holiness, and the double-edged ax, a symbol of matriarchy that was highly sacred to the Minoan culture and essentially based on goddess worship. This symbol can also be recognized on the two well-known figurines of the underworld snake goddess discovered in the palace of Knossos, Crete. Both snake goddesses have a knot with a projecting loop cord between their breasts. The ankh also appeared frequently on coins from ancient Cyprus, where the ankh symbolized the planet Venus.

CELTIC CROSS

The Celtic cross is a symbol that combines a simple cross with a ring surrounding the intersection. When Christianity replaced ancient pagan beliefs in Europe, the old Celtic cross was combined with the Christian cross, and the design was often used for freestanding crosses made of stone, particularly in Ireland.

CROSS

The simple cross, also known as the Latin cross, is the principle Christian symbol used worldwide. It is believed to predate Christianity by thousands of years, and was once the symbol of sacred fire or the daily rotation of the sun according to the four cardinal points. It has also been interpreted as the emblem of the primitive Aryan civilization.

CRUCIFIX

The crucifix (from the Latin *cruci fixus* meaning "one fixed to a cross") is an image of Jesus on the cross itself. Western crucifixes usually have a sculpted body upon the cross, but in Eastern Orthodoxy Jesus's body is normally painted, or sculpted in low relief. In order for the cross to be a crucifix, it must be three-dimensional.

MARINER'S CROSS

Also known as an Anchored cross, the Mariner's cross is a symbol that is shaped like a plus sign with anchorlike protrusions at the end of each arm. The symbol is used to signify a fresh start or hope. The Mariner's cross is also referred to as St. Clement's cross, referring to the way in which the saint

BASQUE CROSS

This cross is often known as a "lauburu." Its origins are obscure, but it may once have marked the tombs of healers of animals and souls. At the end of the sixteenth century, the lauburu was popular as a Basque decorative element on wooden chests or tombs. Each arm of the cross can be drawn with

COPTIC CROSS

The Coptic cross was adopted by early Christian Gnostics and may have been influenced by the Egyptian ankh. Old Coptic crosses often incorporate a circle of various proportions in relation to the cross. For the Coptic Church, the circle represents the eternal and everlasting love of God, as shown through Christ's crucifixion, halo

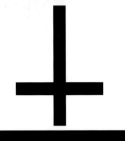

ST. PETER'S CROSS

St. Peter is believed to have been crucified upside down at his own request, as he did not feel worthy to die the same way as Jesus. Therefore many Christian sects use an inverted Latin cross as a symbol of humility. Sometimes this cross is called Satan's Cross. It is used by pagans as the Nordic hammer of Thor.

CHI-RO CROSS

A sign appeared to the Roman Emperor Constantine as a light in the sky, and within it he saw the symbol of the Savior's name and two letters indicating the name of Christ at the center. He made it the emblem for his army. Various versions of this cross exist, including the Christogram used by Christians as a reminder of the fight against evil.

MALTESE CROSS

In Italy, this symbol is associated with the Knights Hospitaller of Malta. The cross is eight-pointed and has the form of four V-shaped elements. Its design is based on crosses used since the First Crusade. It has also become the modern symbol of Amalfi, a small Italian republic that arose during the eleventh century.

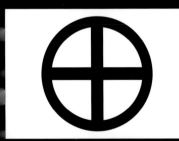

SUN CROSS

A sun cross, solar cross, or wheel cross is a cross inside a circle. It is frequently found in the symbolism of prehistoric cultures, particularly during the Neolithic and Bronze Ages. It is currently used in neopagan religions to represent the sun and the four quadrants, or the wheel of the year. The same symbol

BRIGID'S CROSS

Associated with St. Brigid of Kildare, Ireland, this small cross is usually made from rushes or straw. It comprises a woven square in the center and four radials tied at the ends. Many rituals are associated with the making of the crosses. It was traditionally believed that a Brigid's cross protected the house

ARMENIAN CROSS

An Armenian cross is a symbol that combines a cross with floral embellishments or elements. In Armenian Christianity, this design was used for freestanding crosses made of stone, often richly decorated with additional motifs such as rosettes and interlaces, as well as botanical motifs such as

LO SHU SQUARE
CHINA *c.* 2200–2100 BCE

Number square used in feng shui to divine auspicious energy

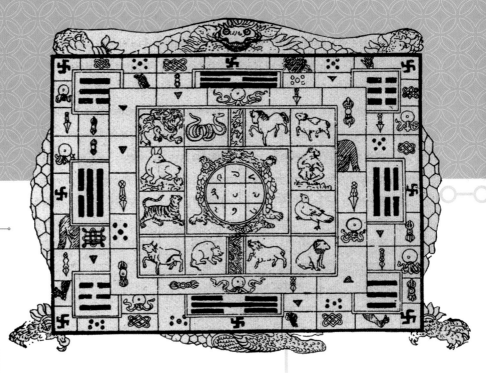

The Lo Shu Square is an important symbol of the harmony and balance of the elements in the art of feng shui.

4	9	2
3	5	7
8	1	6

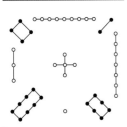

Magic number squares were used extensively in occult or magical texts, and became popularized as mathematical puzzles.

The Lo Shu Square is an important emblem in feng shui, the art of object placement and the flow of chi, or universal energy, in the home and landscape. Feng means "wind," and shui "water," and it is the simple balance of these two energies that brings auspicious energy to the world.

Chinese legend tells how about 4,000 years ago there was a huge flood in China, and people began to offer sacrifices to the god of the river, Lo, to calm his anger. Each time they made an offering, a turtle would appear from the river. It had a curious figure or pattern on its shell; there were circular dots of numbers that were arranged in a three by three grid, such that the sum of the numbers in each row, column, and diagonal was the same: fifteen. This number is considered to be magical and

powerful in the East, and one reason for this is that fifteen is the number of days between the new moon and the full moon, and also between the full moon and new moon, which mark the twenty-four phases of the solar year. This cycle was highly respected and was used in ancient traditional divination methods to work out auspicious times to sow seeds, dig gardens, and build houses.

The "Bagua" is an ancient grid system based on the Lo Shu Square and it is still used today in feng shui. Bagua represents the invisible patterns of energy in anything from a city block, landscape, house, or room to a bed. Each of the Bagua areas corresponds to part of the home or landscape and also to one of the five Chinese elements: earth, water, fire, metal, and wood. By reinforcing an area with its corresponding element enhancers, feng shui practitioners can help create positive and harmonious energy in the office or home. These five elements represent the kind of chi manifest throughout the environment, and they work in tandem with the yin and yang qualities and the Bagua energies.

CREATION AND DESTRUCTION

This elemental system is based on the Chinese cycle of creation and destruction. In the creative cycle, wood creates fire, which creates earth, which creates metal, which creates water, which creates wood. So fire and earth, because they are creatively moving forward, are compatible. In the destructive cycle, wood destroys earth, which destroys water, which destroys fire, which destroys metal, which destroys wood. So metal and wood for example are not compatible.

Fire is dynamic motion and action. It gives us light and awareness and is associated with the color red. Wood energy is quite magical, which is why trees and plants have been symbols for growth and fertility in many different cultures. Earth energy is concerned with nourishment, the here and now, nature and peace, whereas metal is concerned with communication and prosperity and relates to the west and northwest. The ancient Chinese mystics were very fond of this energy and put it to its most positive use: to make money. Water is always fluid and symbolic of energy that is reflective and instinctive. This element is concerned with feelings, emotions, and the dark side of life.

The Bagua usually has key words that correspond to the nine energies or pathways

according to their compass point direction and the number associated with the Lo Shu Square. So to the south is fire, and this is associated with success and fame. To the southwest is earth, associated with marriage, love, and romance; to the west is lake, associated with children and creativity. Heaven is to the northwest, representing communication, mentors, and friends, and to the north is water, representing careers and professions. To the northeast is mountain, symbolizing education and knowledge, to the east is thunder, which deals with family and well-being, and to the southeast is wind, representing wealth and prosperity. The center of the Bagua is generally known as the core, concerned with universal life-giving energy.

A feng shui compass is an intricate map of constellations, elements, heavens, Bagua numbers, and other information used to calculate the potential of a landscape or home.

This ancient Chinese scroll from the Southern Song dynasty depicts people making offerings and sacrifices to the nymph or god of the River Lo.

HIEROGLYPHS
THEBES, EGYPT *c.* 1275 BCE

An ancient writing system of powerful symbols

The Papyrus of Ani in the British Museum, London, reveals the intricacies and decorative work of hieroglyphs.

Egyptian hieroglyphs are part of one of the oldest writing systems in the world. Unlike Sumerian cuneiform, the hieroglyph's origin is more obscure. Hieroglyphic script was held to have been invented by the god Thoth, and all words were therefore magical, powerful symbols. The Egyptian word for "hieroglyph" meant "words or speech of the gods."

On the death of important Egyptians in society, such as kings, officials, and scribes, a text—commonly known as the Book of the Dead—was compiled to help the dead make their way through the underworld to the afterlife. Hieroglyphs and illustrations described magic spells, incantations, and hymns, and the book was part of a tradition of funerary texts, painted on objects and later papyrus. The Egyptians also believed that knowing the name of something

gave power over it. So the Book of the Dead equipped its owner with the mystical names of many of the entities he would encounter in the afterlife, giving him power over the gods.

The beautiful Papyrus of Ani is a manuscript with hieroglyphs and illustrations, compiled for the Theban scribe Ani. He most likely commissioned this book for himself, knowing that the magical power of words was crucial for the afterlife. It includes hymns, praises to Osiris, hails to Thoth, homages, and funeral chamber texts and spells.

In hieroglyphics, the inventory of signs is divided into three major categories. These are logograms—signs that reveal morphemes (morphemes are units of language that cannot be divided, such as the "ing" of "drinking"; phonograms—signs that represent one or more sounds; and determinatives—glyphs that carry no phonetic value but instead are added at the end of a word to clarify the meaning of the word. This is because the hieroglyph writing system does not record vowels, so different words with the same set of consonants (but different vowels) can be written by the same sequence of glyphs.

TYPES OF HIEROGLYPH

Traditionally Egyptologists divided hieroglyphs into three types based on appearance: hieroglyphic, hieratic, and demotic. Hieroglyphic was always inscribed on large-scale monuments. Hieratic was used extensively on manuscripts and paintings, and is a less formal form of hieroglyphics. Demotic is a highly cursive script that replaced hieratic as the script for everyday use from 600 BCE. Pure hieroglyphic writing was not, however, eclipsed, but existed alongside the other forms, especially in formal writing.

Hieroglyphs continued to be used under Persian rule in the fifth century BCE, as well as after Alexander the Great's conquest of Egypt and in the following Macedonian and Roman periods. Greek and Roman writers believed that hieroglyphs distinguished real Egyptians from their foreign conquerors. But Greco-Roman authors also believed that because hieroglyphs were sacred writing, this complex but rational system was an allegorical even magical one, transmitting secret mystical knowledge.

In the fifth century CE the Egyptian priest Horapollo wrote *Hieroglyphica*, an explanation of almost 200 glyphs. Later attempts at understanding the glyphs were fruitless until the decipherment by European scholars such as Johannes Becanus in the sixteenth century, Athanasius Kircher in the seventeenth century, and Danish archaeologist Jørgen Zoëga in the eighteenth century. The discovery of the granodiorite Rosetta Stone in the Nile Delta

in 1799 provided critical missing information, gradually revealed by a succession of scholars, which eventually allowed French Egyptologist Jean-François Champollion to determine the nature of this mysterious script.

LETTER	HIEROGLYPH	DEPICTED	MEANING OF HIEROGLYPH
A		Egyptian vulture	strong personality
B		feet	loves to travel
C K X		basket	lucky
D		hand	friendly
E		reed leaf	knightly
F V		viper	purposeful
G		jug stand	stabile
H	or	courtyard, flax wick	artful
I		two strokes	single-eyed
J		cobra	intelligent
L		lion	sedate

MEANING OF HIEROGLYPH	DEPICTED	HIEROGLYPH	LETTER
wise	owl		M
pure soul	Red Crown, water surface	or	N
optimist	lasso		O
able to create	wicker seat		P
—	hillside		Q
talkative	mouth		R
independent	folded cloth, bolt	or	S
loves to eat	bread		T
obstinate	quail chick	or	U W
equitable	two reed leaf		Y
capricious	belt		Z

European scholars did not begin to decipher Egyptian hieroglyphs until the sixteenth century.

With the discovery of the Rosetta Stone in 1799, the mysterious code was finally cracked.

VESICA PISCIS
GREECE *c.* sixth century BCE

The intersection of the two worlds, the spiritual and the manifest

In the Codex Bruchsal (thirteenth century), Jesus is depicted surrounded by a mandorla-shaped aureola, symbolizing him as being in, and coming from, the womb of Mary.

One of the many popular forms in the sacred geometry of gothic, medieval, and Renaissance architecture, the vesica piscis is the shape made by the intersection of two circles. It is also a strange mathematically organized container of other geometric shapes, such as the triangle, tetrad, square, pentacle, and polygon. The term "vesica piscis" translates as "the vessel of the fish."

To the ancient Egyptians vesica piscis was first known as the hieroglyph Ru. Ru symbolized the female vagina as a doorway through which the spirit of life entered the tangible world. Pythagoras, who lived at the end of the sixth century BCE, was believed to have spent much time in Egypt in contact with Alexandrian mystics, and he later developed the idea that the mystical symbol represented the intersection of two worlds: the spiritual world and the manifest world, which came into being after the initial creation. To the Pythagoreans, the vesica piscis was the symbol of the "dyad," or twoness: the manifestation of the entire universe from the one, the Monad.

In mythology, the symbol has long been associated with the great goddess, the Hindu yoni—meaning vagina or womb—and feminine fertility. The yoni is the symbol of the Hindu goddess Shakti, the divine mother, and the consort of Shiva who is symbolized by the linga or the phallus. The great goddess was associated with fish, seashells, the sea, and fishermen. In ancient mythology, she often appeared as a mermaid or siren.

A twentieth-century example of the vesica piscis can be found on the inside of the cover of the Chalice Well at Glastonbury, Somerset, England, a popular destination for neopagan pilgrims who believe in the divine feminine. The design is finely sculpted in wrought iron and the vesica piscis is bisected by a sword or spear. Wells were considered to be gateways to the spirit world in Celtic mythology, and the interchange of these two worlds is represented by the vesica piscis. Designed by architect and archaeologist Frederick Bligh Bond, the well cover was presented as a gift to Glastonbury Abbey in 1919.

In Gothic architecture, the arches within many cathedrals, such as Reims Cathedral, France, are based on the vesica piscis, and the shape was used by architects to reveal their association with the Pythagorean theory that numbers were sacred aspects of the divine. The shape can also be seen in the seals used in Freemasonry in the Middle Ages, and in emblems such as the Flag of the Church of Scotland.

The vesica piscis also dominates Christian art, and early depictions of Christ show him within the vesica. In this context the shape is usually referred to as a *mandorla*, an Italian word meaning "almond," and it represented the womb of Mary. It was also thought to represent the merger of heaven and Earth in the body of Jesus. Again, in Christianity, the vesica piscis became a symbol of the doorway between worlds, or the intersection between heaven and Earth. It was popular in Byzantine, Romanesque, and early medieval Church decoration and was used extensively by artists and architects during these periods. In the Eastern Orthodox Church, the mandorla is used to depict sacred moments that transcend time and space, such as the resurrection, the transfiguration, and the "falling

The symbol was used as a secret sign between Christians when trying to avoid Roman persecution.

The vesica piscis design on the cover of the Chalice Well at Glastonbury, England, represents the Celtic gateway to the spirit world.

asleep" or death of Mary. It was often painted in several concentric patterns of color rather than a single surrounding aura.

The well-known version of the vesica piscis—known as the ichthys, which is Greek for "fish"—consists of two intersecting arcs, the ends of which extend beyond the meeting point so as to resemble the profile of a fish. This was used by early Christians as a secret symbol and it is known as the sign of the fish or the Jesus fish. When Christian traders were first persecuted by the Romans, they would draw one half of the symbol in the dust in order to see if the person with whom they traded recognized the symbol. If they were Christian, the other party would complete the symbol of the fish and trade could begin. However, before long, the more shrewd Romans discovered this secret sign and found themselves a huge untapped market for executing Christian martyrs. After the Romans had converted to Christianity, the sign continued to be used as an emblem or motif and it is still in common usage today. The center of the ichthys is often filled with five Greek letters that stand for "Jesus Christ, Son of God, Savior."

MEANINGS AND USAGE

Essentially the intersection of two overlapping spheres, the vesica piscis (including the interior portion of it, and/or the more common two-dimensional version) represents, among other things:

1. The joining of god and goddess to create an offspring.
2. A symbol for Jesus Christ.
3. A pointed oval used as an aureole in medieval sculpture and painting.
4. The vagina of the female goddess.
5. The basic motif in the flower of life.
6. An overlay of the tree of life.
7. The formative power of polygons.
8. A geometrical description of square roots and harmonic proportions.
9. A source of immense power and energy.

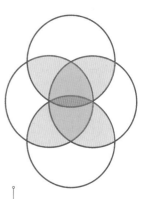

Four interlocking circles with a shared radius create five vesica piscis, which form the basis of another geometrical symbol, the flower of life.

GOLDEN RATIO
GREECE c. 500 BCE

Mathematical ratio used in art and architecture

Italian artist Jacopo de' Barbari's painting *Portrait of Fra Luca Pacioli* (*c.* 1500) reveals the monk's interest in geometry.

Φ

Fra Luca Pacioli discovered the strange number known as "phi," which was concerned with divine proportion.

The mathematical magic of the so-called golden ratio was used in classical antiquity in the building of temples, churches, and cathedrals, and it became a standard means of construction employed by medieval architects in such awe-inspiring places as Chartres Cathedral in France. Although architects took a great interest in geometry, artists during the Middle Ages had little interest in the golden section and in mathematics as a whole. However, in the late fifteenth century, a Franciscan mathematician and friend of the great Renaissance painters, Luca Pacioli, rediscovered the golden secret. His publication devoted to the number phi, and titled *Divina Proportione* (*c.* 1509), was illustrated by no less an artist than Leonardo da Vinci. One of his other artist friends was Jacopo de' Barbari, whose *Portrait of Fra Luca Pacioli* (*c.* 1500) confirms the monk's passion for geometry.

The painting shows Fra Pacioli, an expert on perspective, demonstrating geometry at a table on which lies one of his works and a book by Euclid. He is accompanied by an unidentified student. The table is covered with geometrical instruments and tools: slate, chalk, compass, and a small dodecahedron model, for example. Suspended from the ceiling is a rhombicuboctahedron half-filled with water, which Pacioli is using to demonstrate a theorem by Euclid.

Greek mathematician Euclid was the first to write a definition of the golden ratio: "A straight line is said to have been cut in extreme and mean ratio when, as the whole line is to the greater segment, so is the greater to the lesser." However, it was Greek mathematician and mystic Pythagoras who first proved that the golden ratio was the basis for the proportions of the human figure. He showed that the human body is built with each part in a definite golden proportion to all the other parts. His discoveries of the proportions of the human figure influenced Greek architects, and every element of their major buildings, down to the smallest detail of decoration, was constructed around this proportion.

The golden ratio is also referred to as the golden section (Latin: *sectio aurea*) or golden mean. Other names include divine proportion, divine section (Latin: *sectio divina*), golden proportion, golden cut, and golden number. With the Renaissance and the rediscovery of the ratio's magical power, golden ratios or rectangles were employed by a number of important artists.

The ratio appears not only in da Vinci's *Mona Lisa* (*c.* 1503–1506), but Michelangelo and Raphael also constructed a number of their compositions around golden proportions. For

The Sacrament of the Last Supper (1955) by Salvador Dalí reveals the use of the golden ratio and how the figure of Jesus dominates the composition.

example, the proportions of Michelangelo's *David* (1501–1504) conform to the golden ratio, from the location of the navel with respect to the height to the placement of the joints in the fingers. Whereas Michelangelo's painting *Doni Tondo*, or *The Holy Family* (c. 1507), is notable for its positioning of the principal figures in alignment with a pentagram or golden star, in Raphael's *The Mond Crucifixion* (c. 1502–1503), the principal figures outline a golden triangle that can be used to locate one of its underlying pentagrams.

GOLDEN RECTANGLE

During the twentieth century, artists and architects such as Le Corbusier and Salvador Dalí proportioned their works as aesthetically in line with the golden ratio by using the golden rectangle, in which the ratio of the longer side to the shorter is the golden ratio. Dalí explicitly used the golden ratio in his masterpiece *The Sacrament of the Last Supper* (1955). The dimensions of the canvas are proportioned as a golden rectangle, while a huge dodecahedron, in perspective so that the edges appear in golden ratio to one another, is suspended above and behind Jesus and thus dominates the composition.

Architects also frequently used the golden section in their work. In the United Nations Building in New York (1952), the ratio of the width of the building compared with the height of every ten floors is golden. The CN Tower in Toronto (1976), the tallest tower and freestanding structure in the world, features the golden section in its design. The ratio of its total height of 1,815.4 feet (553.33 m) to the height of the observation deck at 1,122 feet (342 m) is 1.618.

Although many people believe that the nautilus shell is constructed as an exact golden spiral, there is a subtle difference between a golden spiral and the nautilus's spiral structure. The shell can be modeled in a spiral form, which expands the golden ratio at every 180-degree turn of the spiral. However, the normal golden spiral is constructed from a series of golden rectangles that increase in dimension by the golden ratio at every 90-degree turn of the spiral. The 180-degree expansion of the ratio certainly appears in the first few rotations of the nautilus shell spiral. However, this is the reason why it is wrongly considered to be an example of a golden spiral when, in fact, it is a logarithmic spiral, like many other spirals found in nature.

Michelangelo's statue *David* (1501–1504) conforms exactly to the proportions of the golden secret.

SATOR SQUARE
POMPEII, ITALY 79 CE

Said to provide protection against the devil

The Sator Square found in the ruins of Pompeii had magical powers long before Christians used it as protection against evil.

The Sator Square is a magic word square that has baffled scholars, linguists, and historians since its discovery in the 1930s. The mysterious inscription carved in stone was found in the ruins of Pompeii and had lain hidden beneath the ash since the eruption of Mount Vesuvius in 79 CE. Its meaning has caused much speculation, but it is now generally thought that the Sator Square has mystical pagan roots.

A mysterious collection of letters, the square is arranged in five lines of Latin words of five letters each, which can be read both forward and backward, and up and down. This powerful palindrome (a sentence or word that reads the same forward and backward) has long been believed to ward off evil, and it is imbued

with magical properties. Throughout medieval Christian Europe, it was inscribed on amulets, walls, and homes as a protective talisman, but there is a more esoteric and mysterious layer of meanings hidden in the strange words.

Many translations have been suggested for the Latin phrase. One of the words, "arepo," confuses most scholars, who can only suggest that it is someone's name. The simplest translation of the square reads, "The farmer, Arepo, holds and works the wheels," and this is often translated as the maxim "you reap what you sow." The letters contained within the square can also be seen to form part of a cross, and two words, "pater" and "noster"—the start of a Christian prayer—form the cross. This leaves two As and two Os, which are considered to be the Greek letters alpha and omega. Known as the "first and the last," these symbols relate to a passage in the Book of Revelation.

Many scholars now link the Sator Square to the mystery religion, known as the Mithraic Mysteries, practiced in the Roman Empire from the first century to the fourth century. The high priest of the Mithraic cult was known as "pater," and it is thought that the "pater noster" and the hidden cross within the square are symbols of these earlier Mithraic secret rites. There is also another theory that the first word, "sator," is a corruption of Saturn, and one translation reads, "Saturn laboriously draws the wheels of the wagon of the sun." This indicates an even earlier cult surrounding the earth god Saturn, who was identified with sowing the land and his rule over the Golden Age.

Magic squares can be found throughout Europe, such as in the Duomo of Siena, Italy, and in a wall in the old district of Oppède, in France's Luberon. Also in Italy, the Benedictine Abbey of St. Peter ad Oratorium near

Capestrano has a fine marble square, while in Valvisciolo Abbey, the letters curiously form five concentric rings, each one divided into five sectors. Valvisciolo Abbey was occupied by the Knights Templar in the thirteenth century, and this strange version emphasizes the power of cosmic oneness, symbolized by the five circles and the word "rotas."

Throughout medieval Christian Europe, the Sator Square was often placed above doorways and inscribed on various objects for protection from evil. With the magical positioning of the letters in the grid, the Sator Square was considered a powerful palindrome. Palindromes were considered to be immune to the devil because it was thought that, in an attempt to unravel the magic spell, he would become confused by the repetition of the letters.

In France the earliest example of the magical use of the Sator Square occurs in a Carolingian Bible of 822, originally the property of the monastery of Saint-Germain-des-Prés. According to a thirteenth-century parchment from Aurillac, the square apparently helped women in labor. By the fifteenth century, it had put out fires in the Château de Chinon. However, one of the most extraordinary examples of the properties of the square is an account of a citizen of Lyons who recovered from insanity after eating three crusts of bread, each inscribed with the magic square.

There are numerous possible codes hidden in the Sator Square. Attempts have been made to decipher hidden messages and to rework geometric formulae and mystical numerology, all in an attempt to reveal the secret of cosmic truth. For example, the letters and lines and their corresponding numerological value add up to 666—to some the number of the devil, to others a number of divine connection.

According to one account, the wall in Pompeii where the inscription was found was part of a tradesman's shop selling bags to weary Roman travelers. Starting from the fourth letter, the symbolic number of hidden secrets, the message would read, "Orare pote neto pera rotas sat." Although no longer palindromic, this is an encrypted message that means "You may pray (or ask) for the right number of wheels on your bag." On a street level, customers were perhaps being sold wheels to attach to their bags, but on an esoteric level this is an encrypted message for those who wanted to journey toward the cosmic truth. The message reveals that with the right number of "wheels," or secrets, you, the "bag carrier," will be led on the pathway to enlightenment.

Associated with the Mithraic Mysteries, a scene from which is depicted here in a second to third-century relief, the square may be part of the ritual of the high priest or a dedication to the god Saturn.

ZERO
INDIA 458

A symbol to denote the absence of all magnitude or quantity

Brahmagupta was a seventh-century Indian mathematician who first introduced zero and algebraic concepts to negative numbers.

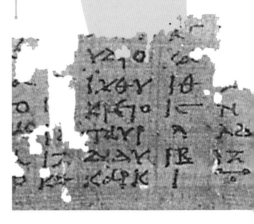

Zero was conceived as a blank space in ancient Indian philosophy.

Before zero was represented by a symbol, it had been represented as a blank space in India during the fourth century BCE. However, the concept of zero being used as an actual number is also attributed to India. The oldest known text to use a decimal place system including a zero is the Jain text from India titled the *Lokavibhaga*, of around 458 CE, in which "shunya" or void was used for this purpose. The rules governing the use of zero appeared for the first time in Indian mathematician Brahmagupta's book on the universe written in 628 CE. Brahmagupta considered not only zero, but also negative numbers, as well as the algebraic rules for arithmetic with such numbers. Finally, around 825 CE, Persian scholar Muhammad al-Khawarizmi amalgamated the Indian and Greek concept of zero as we know it today. His book on arithmetic was eventually translated into Latin in the twelfth

century, and his new numerical system, known as Arabic, was introduced to the Western world.

As the last number to be invented, or perhaps discovered, zero has always fascinated scholars in that it encompasses everything, and nothing. In Buddhism and early Hinduism, it represented the void. To the ancient Greek philosophers, who were usually mathematicians and often dabbled in a variety of cosmological subjects, it seems that the question of zero being a number was something that caused them great confusion and concern. They asked themselves, "How can nothing be something?" This paradoxical argument led to further theological and religious debates throughout Western Europe right up to the medieval period. Even the radical paradoxes of Greek philosopher Zeno of Elea depended mostly on the uncertain interpretation of what zero was. Greek mathematician and philosopher Pythagoras believed that zero represented not a number but perfect form, whereas in Islamic belief zero represented the essence of divinity.

This second-century Greek papyrus reveals an early use of a sign for zero (lower right).

BABYLONIAN ZERO

Several thousand years before the Greeks had postulated theories about nonexistent numbers, the Babylonians had used a space to mark the nonexistence of a digit. However, they understood that the idea of nothingness was merely the lack of a number. In a tablet unearthed at Kish dating to 700 BCE, the scribe Bêl-bân-aplu wrote his zeros with three hooks, but by 300 BCE, the later Babylonians were using a symbol of two slanted wedges to reveal a "nothing" space. By 130 CE, Greek astronomer and mathematician Ptolemy, influenced by the Babylonians, was using a symbol for zero that resembled a small circle with an over bar. Because it was used alone, not just as a placeholder, this zero was perhaps the first documented use of the number zero in the European world.

Much earlier, around 1740 BCE, the Egyptians used a hieroglyph for zero in accounting texts. They introduced the "nfr" symbol, which also referred to beauty, and it was used in plans and drawings to indicate the base level for the measurement of tombs and pyramids. The Maya were also using a form of zero at least a thousand years before the number was used in Western Europe. In Maya calendars of around 36 BCE, zero is represented by the spiral symbol of a snail shell. Even the Romans has a word for nothing, "nulla," and by around 720 CE, this had been abbreviated to "N."

It seems that zero has always mystified both the layman and the philosopher alike. Akin to a magic circle, it appears to encompass everything and yet signifies nothing. However, the form as we know it today is absolutely right for the very confusion surrounding the number, or rather lack of number. It represents, like a seed, the potential and possibility of what can happen after zero and also what has happened before it. Like the Chinese, Pythagoras believed that numbers hold the key to understanding the harmony of microcosm and macrocosm, but without the crucial number zero, the mathematical world of science would never have developed as it has today.

The ancient Egyptian "nfr" symbol was used to indicate zero as well as things of beauty.

NUMBERS

1 Not only has this number been equated to the Christian God, the creator in many mythologies and religions, but also to the undifferentiated oneness of primordial chaos.

2 Cosmic dualities, mother and father gods, spirit and matter, light and dark, and yin and yang are associated with the number two.

3 Three is the number of perfect completeness. It is associated with various trinities, such as the Christian Father, Son, and Holy Ghost; the Hindu Brahma, Vishnu, and Shiva, and Buddhism's three jewels: Buddha, Dharma (teachings), and Sangha (disciples.)

4 Four symbolizes the four directions, four seasons, and four elements in Western traditions. It is associated with Earth, equality, common sense, and trust. In Buddhism there are four noble truths.

5 Associated with the pentagram, five represents action, passion, creativity, and movement. In Chinese astrology there are five elements, and there are five pillars of Islam.

6 Linked with divine creative power, six is the double trinity, and the six days of active creation in the Bible. In China it represents heaven, and it is also the number of points in the magical Star of David.

7 Traditionally associated with magic and religious days, seven is the number of days that elapse between Passover and Shavuot in Jewish traditions. In ancient Greece, seven was sacred to Apollo.

8 Eight symbolizes infinity and perfection. The Buddhist wheel of life has eight spokes, and it is an auspicious number in the Far East.

9 The nine-layered Chinese pagoda represents the ascent to heaven, and for Hindus nine is the number of Lord Brahma. In Judaism, nine symbolizes truth and wisdom.

SOLOMON'S KNOT
JORDAN sixth–seventh century

Decorative motif that has a range of symbolic meanings

A superb example of a Solomon's knot, thought to represent eternity in mystical circles, can be seen in the mosaic floor of the Aquileia Basilica in Italy.

Two versions of the symbol can be seen in the recently excavated Yattir Mosaic in Jordan, and the British Museum in London has a fourteenth-century Egyptian Koran with a Solomon's knot as its frontispiece. The University of California at Los Angeles Fowler Museum of Cultural History has a large African collection that includes nineteenth- and twentieth-century Yoruba tradition glass beadwork crowns and masks decorated with Solomon's knots.

Considered one of the finest examples of metalwork and decorative art of its period, the Cross of Cong is an early twelfth-century Irish jeweled processional cross that was made for the King of Connacht, the High King of Ireland. Designed to be placed on top of a staff, it is also a reliquary, a special kind of casket that holds a sliver of the apparent true cross upon which Jesus was crucified. The reliquary aspect gave it additional importance as an object of

A Solomon's knot consists of two closed loops, which are linked in an interlaced manner. The symbol looks like two links of a chain, set at right angles to one another. In other words, if laid flat the Solomon's knot is seen to have four crossings where the two loops interweave under and over each other. In most artistic representations, the parts of the loops that alternately cross over and under each other become the sides of a central square, while four loops extend outward in four directions.

Scholars have mixed opinions about why the symbol is called Solomon's knot, but it may have been associated in the Middle East with the biblical monarch Solomon and his reputation for wisdom and occult powers.

Across the Middle East, historical Islamic sites have revealed examples of Solomon's knot as decorative work in Muslim tradition.

The twelfth-century processional cross, known as the Cross of Cong, is adorned with two Solomon's knots.

reverence, undoubtedly the reason behind the elaborate craftsmanship and elegant beauty. The cross is adorned with two very small Solomon's knot symbols at the junction of the cross, one on either side of the quartz crystal–covered hollow that once held the piece of the true cross. The cross was moved from Connacht to Cong Abbey in County Mayo, from where it gets its name.

SYMBOLIC MEANINGS

Among the Yoruba people, Solomon's knot often denotes royal status and it is featured on crowns, tunics, and other ceremonial objects. Also in Africa, the knot is found on kasai velvet, the raffia woven cloth of the Kuba people who attribute mystical meaning to the symbol. The Akan people of West Africa use a version of the symbol stamped on their sacred adinkra cloth. Adinkra is a symbol system representing specific words and phrases. The Akan's symbol of Solomon's knot means "one being bad makes all appear to be bad." Other adinkra examples include a symbol of a yellow flower, known locally as the fofoo (botanical name, *bidens pilosa*), which drops its petals and turns into a black spiky seed. This symbol is used to describe a jealous person. A fern-shaped symbol means "I am not afraid of you."

In Italy, a group of medieval stonemasons called the Comacines adopted the knot as a protective symbol. Deriving from Roman times, the symbol was already imbued with mysticism and protective powers. The Freemasons also used this knot in their symbolism, claiming descent from the guilds of the Comacines. The knot has no visible beginning or ending, and for this reason it represents immortality and eternity—as does the more complicated Buddhist endless knot—across a wide range of cultures and beliefs.

The endless knot appears frequently as a decorative motif throughout Buddhist, Chinese, and even Celtic artwork and decoration. In Buddhism, it is symbolic of the spiritual path

taken by the adherent, as well as the flowing of all that is eternal. It is also equated with the flow of the mind and Samsara: the endless cycle of suffering of birth, death, and rebirth. Because the knot has no beginning or end, it also symbolizes wisdom and enlightenment as gained by the Buddha as he sat under the Bodhi tree.

In Celtic decorative knotwork, often found on crosses and in illuminated manuscripts, the broken and reconnected braid work originated in northern Italy and southern Gaul, and then spread to Ireland around the seventh century. Scholars have identified eight elementary knots that form the basis of nearly all the interlaced patterns in Celtic decorative knot art, including the endless knot.

The knot appears in various forms on the cloth, tunics, and regal paraphernalia of indigenous peoples, such as the Yoruba of Africa.

A double Solomon's knot is a complex weaving of two knots and seems to be created with one single line.

PLAYING CARDS
CHINA c. 618–906

Decks of cards used for trading, entertainment, and divination

This fifteenth-century Flemish set of playing cards confirms the early use of cards for entertainment.

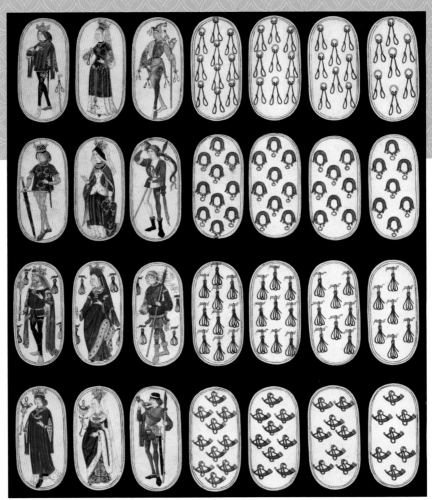

The Chinese were using a primitive form of motif for gaming as far back as the seventh century; this card from *c.* 1400 shows how cards have developed.

Playing cards are believed to have been "invented" in China during the Tang dynasty (*c.* 618–906). A certain Princess Tongchang is said to have played the "leaf game," which was probably a paper form of dominoes rather than true cards, but Emperor Muzong, who reigned from 821 to 824, is recorded as shuffling and dealing actual cards. During the Song dynasty of 960 to 1279, scholar Ouyang Xiu noted that the invention of playing cards coincided with the development of separate paper sheets, used instead of long scrolls.

Ancient Chinese "money cards" had four suits: coins (or cash), strings of coins (which may have been misinterpreted as sticks from crude drawings), myriads (of coins or of strings), and tens of myriads (a myriad is 10,000). These were represented by ideograms plus various numerals. Scholars have suggested that these cards may have been actual paper currency and used for betting and trading. The designs on modern mahjong tiles probably evolved from these earliest playing cards.

By the early fourteenth century, playing cards were seen in Europe, originating probably from Egypt or the Middle East. These cards had four suits, and were similar to tarot cards. The suits were swords, staves, cups, and coins (also known as disks or pentacles), and these suits are still used in traditional Italian, Spanish, and French decks. The early Egyptian-style packs contained fifty-two cards comprising four suits: sticks, coins, swords, and cups. Each suit contained ten "pip" cards (cards identified by the number of suit symbols they show) and three "court" cards.

By the late fourteenth century, the use of playing cards had spread rapidly throughout Europe, but the decks were used only by the wealthy. The earliest cards were made by hand. Initially this was very expensive, but gradually, over the next fifty years or so, the technique of printing woodcuts to decorate fabric was also used to print on paper. Playing cards even competed with devotional images as the most common usage for woodcuts in this period. From about 1418, professional card makers in Nuremberg and Augsburg made the first printed decks. However, no examples of printed cards from before 1423 survive.

An anonymous engraver, known as the "master of the playing cards" was the first major celebrity in the history of printmaking, and his beautiful engravings for card decks gave him iconic status. He was active in southwestern Germany from the 1430s to the 1450s, and it is probable that he was also a painter. Various attempts to identify him have been unsuccessful, but his set of playing cards in five suits survives in unique impressions in the National Library of France in Paris and in the Museum of Prints and Drawings in Dresden.

In the middle of the fifteenth century, suits began to vary, and typically a pack of cards had four suits. In Germany, hearts, bells, leaves, and acorns became the standard suits, and these are still used in eastern and southeastern German

packs today. Italian, French, and Spanish cards used swords, batons, cups, and coins. The four suits in most common usage across the world—spades, hearts, diamonds, and clubs—originated in France in about 1480. Playing cards rapidly became an extremely popular activity, and in 1534, French writer Rabelais could name thirty-five different card games, including the Spanish bezique; the Italian primero, which evolved into whist; the British cribbage; and the Amish euchre.

The popularity of card games is reflected in the work of Georges de La Tour, a seventeenth-century French Baroque painter dedicated to creating powerful chiaroscuro scenes lit by dramatic candlelight. La Tour painted images of cheats, charlatans, fortune tellers, and tricksters in popular settings, at a time when card games were being played among the wealthy and poor alike. By the time he produced one of his masterpieces, *The Cheat with the Ace of Clubs* (c. 1630–1634), the playing card and its symbols were well known throughout the West.

Across in the New World, pilgrim fathers were manufacturing their own card decks within decades of their arrival, and it was U.S. devotees who created rounded edges, the joker card (originally a special card in the game called euchre), the process of lamination, and dozens of games including poker, pinochle, and bridge.

The Cheat with the Ace of Clubs (c. 1630–1634) by Georges de La Tour reveals how seventeenth-century Europe was a place for tricksters and gamblers to make their fortune.

The symbols of the playing cards—spade, diamond, heart, and club—have remained unchanged for centuries.

WHEEL OF LIFE
TIBET 1000

Symbolizes the cyclical existence of life and death

Also known as the "wheel of becoming," the Tibetan wheel of life decorates the walls of temples and monasteries such as the Monastery of Rongwo in Tongren, China.

The wheel of life, also known as the bhavacakra, is a symbolic representation of samsara, the cyclic existence of life and death to which most mortals are condemned. It is usually found on the outside walls of Tibetan Buddhist temples and monasteries to teach the Buddhist philosophy of life to the less philosophically minded people of the countryside. The bhavacakra can also be translated as the "wheel of cyclic existence" or "wheel of becoming."

Legend tells of how the Buddha created the first depiction of the bhavacakra. King Rudrayana, also known as King Udayana, offered a gift of a jeweled robe to King Bimbisara of Magadha. King Bimbisara was concerned that he did not have anything of equivalent value to offer in return. Bimbisara went to the Buddha for advice, and the Buddha gave instructions to have the first drawing of the bhavacakra made. He told Bimbisara to send the drawing to Rudrayana, and it is said that Rudrayana attained enlightenment through studying this drawing.

ANIMAL REPRESENTATIONS

The images of three animals in the hub of the wheel represent the three unwholesome roots, or the three poisons. These are ignorance, attachment, and aversion. Usually the animals are the pig, snake, and bird. The pig stands for ignorance; this comparison is based on the Indian concept of a pig being the most foolish of animals because it sleeps in the dirtiest places and eats whatever comes to its mouth. The snake represents aversion or anger; this is because it can be aroused easily and will strike at the slightest touch. The bird represents attachment (also translated as desire or clinging). In many drawings of the wheel, the

BUDDHIST SYMBOLS

USHNISHA
The hairstyle that tops most Buddha statues is known as the Ushnisha, or the wisdom bump, denoting the Buddha's superior knowledge.

TILAKA
The spot in the center of the forehead of the Buddha marks the third eye, or ajna chakra, the center of spiritual insight and clairvoyance.

EIGHT AUSPICIOUS EMBLEMS
These include the royal parasol representing the Buddha's princely lineage and pursuit of enlightenment; two fish that symbolize good fortune; the vase that denotes abundance; and the conch shell representing the call of dharma.

snake and the bird are shown as coming out of the mouth of the pig, indicating that aversion and attachment arise from ignorance. The snake and the bird are also shown grasping the tail of the pig, indicating that they in turn promote greater ignorance

The second layer of the wheel represents karma in two half-circles. One half-circle (usually light) shows contented people moving upward to higher states, possibly to the higher realms. The other half-circle (usually dark) shows people in a miserable state being led downward to lower states, possibly to the lower realms. The third layer represents the six realms of samsara, the cyclic existence of life and death. These realms include the god domain, the jealous god domain, the human domain, the animal realm, the hungry ghost realm, and the domain of hell. The fourth layer represents the twelve nidanas. These are the links between suffering, the physical body, feelings, cravings, consciousness, and so on.

Symbolically, the three inner circles, moving from the center outward, show that the three poisons of ignorance, attachment, and aversion

lead to positive and negative actions; these actions and their results are called karma. Karma in turn leads to the six realms, which represent the different types of suffering within samsara. The fourth and outer layer of the wheel symbolizes the twelve links of dependent origination; these links indicate how the sources of suffering—the three poisons and karma—produce lives within cyclic existence.

The fierce-looking figure holding the wheel represents impermanence, whereas the moon above the wheel represents liberation from samsara. The Buddha points to the moon to indicate that liberation is possible. The figure most commonly depicted holding the wheel is Yama, the god of death, revealing that the entire process of cyclic existence (samsara) is transient: everything within this wheel of life is constantly changing. Yama wears a crown of five skulls that symbolize five poisons. Often adorned with a tiger skin, representing fearfulness, his third eye symbolizes the understanding of impermanence, whereas his four limbs represent the universal sufferings of birth, old age, sickness, and death.

Buddhist symbols refer to the cycles of life and death, liberation from that cycle, and the pursuit of enlightenment.

The Buddhist Wheel of Dharma has eight spokes, eight being the number of renewal and regeneration.

FLOWER OF LIFE
ABYDOS, EGYPT *c.* second century

Geometric pattern of overlapping circles that reflects ancient spiritual beliefs

This acrylic painting by James Wyper titled *All That Is* (2012) depicts the flower of life, the basic pattern of everything in existence.

The flower of life is believed to be one of the most sacred patterns in the universe, and it consists of seven or more overlapping circles, in which the center of each circle rests upon the circumference of up to six surrounding circles of the same diameter. However, the surrounding circles need not be clearly or completely drawn. Some ancient symbols contain only a single circle or hexagon. When adapted to make thirteen circles, the pattern is known as the fruit of life, each circle representing an aspect of reality. These systems are supposedly able to give us access to everything ranging from the human body to the galaxies. Said to be the blueprint of the universe, the fruit of life contains the basis for the design of every atom,

every molecular structure, and every life form—in fact everything in existence.

The flower of life and its offspring, the seed of life symbol, have been linked to the angel Metatron and the biblical prophet Enoch, to the vesica piscis religious symbol, and to the Borromean rings: three interconnected circles commonly used as a symbol of the Trinity. However, its precise origins are unclear.

At the rear of the main Seti I temple at Abydos, Egypt—built during Seti's reign from *c.* 1290 to 1279 BCE—is a very strange structure called the "Osirion," which predates the temple by at least 1,000 years. Inscribed on some of the Osirion's blocks are a number of patterns of interlocking circles. This honeycomb design involves a circle cluster that is known as the "flower of life," which is found throughout the history of geometric design.

Some barely noticeable text that adjoins the Osirion patterns may indicate the possible origin of the designs, and the text includes the Greek letters "θ" theta, "ϵ" epsilon, and "λ" lamda. There are also two Greek words—*Theos Nilos*—meaning "god of the Nile." Another letter appears to be the archaic Greek letter digamma, which was used occasionally as a symbol in later Greek mathematical texts.

Due to the height of the columns at Abydos, it appears that the graffiti could have been inscribed only after the temple had fallen into disuse, when the Osirion had begun to fill up with sand. Recent research shows that these symbols can be no earlier than 535 BCE, and most probably date to the second and or even fourth century CE.

The flower of life is often linked to the tree of life, a well-known image throughout world mythologies and philosophies. Along with the seed of life, in contemporary Kabbalistic

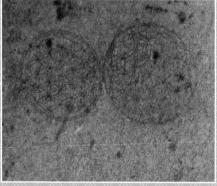

traditions the tree of life is believed to be part of the geometry that parallels the cycle of the fruit tree.

According to some new-age groups, the seed of life is a symbol of the six days of creation, and it is formed from seven circles being placed with sixfold symmetry. This forms a pattern of circles that acts as a basic component of the flower of life's design. The first day is believed to be the creation of the vesica piscis, meaning "fish bladder." The second day corresponds to the creation of the tripod of life, followed by one sphere added for each subsequent day until all seven spheres make up the seed of life. New-age groups have also interpreted the vesica piscis pattern of two interlocking circles as a yonic symbol, common in Indian religions and representative of femininity.

METATRON'S CUBE

Metatron's cube (in Judaism Metatron was Epoch, a descendant of Noah who was transformed into an archangel; he is mentioned in apocryphal texts including the Second Book of Enoch) depicts the five so-called Platonic solids that may be derived from the flower of life. The five solids are geometrical forms that are said to act as a template from which all life springs. The structures are crucial because they are the building blocks of organic life. These five structures are found in minerals, animated and organic life forms, sound, music, and language. Metatron's cube is also considered to be a holy glyph, used to ward off evil spirits.

The flower of life holds many mathematical and geometrical laws that represent the interconnection of the universe. Giving the flower of life to someone, as an engraving on a piece of jewelry or as a motif in a painting, is like giving them the entire universe in one jewel. In the pagan sense, the flower of life is believed to contain a type of Akashic record of basic information of all living things, and it is the visual expression of the connections of life that run through all beings.

The egg of life is a simpler symbol, taken from the design of the flower of life but usually composed of seven interconnecting circles. The shape of the egg of life is said to be the same as a multicellular embryo in its first hours of creation.

Metatron's cube is a geometric arrangement of the five Platonic solids thought to be the building blocks of all organic structures in life.

CHAKRAS
INDIA *c.* sixth century

System used for healing and spiritual development

This eighteenth-century silk painting, titled *Shiva Purana*, from Badgaon depicts the ancient Sanskrit system of the seven chakras.

In Sanskrit chakra means "wheel," and most Eastern spiritual traditions use the chakras as the basis for self-healing, healing others, and spiritual development. Chakras are part of the subtle body, not the physical body, and as such are the meeting points of the nonphysical or subtle energy channels called nadis. Nadis are channels in the subtle body through which the life force or prana moves.

Whether or not we are aware of them, the chakra centers are said to be always active, and different states of mind arise as energy travels through the chakras from the base chakra to the crown of the head and the place of supreme enlightenment. For most people, the five lower chakras dominate the subtle body energy, and the aim of Tantric yoga is to cultivate the subtle body so that energy rises to activate the two highest chakras.

Various scriptural texts and teachings present a different number of chakras. According to tantric texts, there are numerous chakras in the subtle human body, but there are seven chakras in most traditions and these are considered to be the most important ones.

SEVEN CHAKRAS

The base chakra is located at the bottom of the spine, centered between the last disk of the spine and the pubic bone to the front. It vibrates to the color red and is concerned with the sense of being grounded. It provides a firm base and sense of security, and it also controls the basic functioning needs of the body. Next, located approximately a hand's breadth below the navel, the sacral chakra is concerned with one's sex drive, creativity, and emotional state. It vibrates to the color orange. Situated between the navel and the breastbone, the solar plexus chakra relates to the color yellow, and is the seat of personal power.

The heart chakra is situated behind the breastbone and in front of the spine; it vibrates to the colors green and pink and is the center of warm, loving feelings. This chakra is about true compassion, love, and spirituality. The heart chakra also directs one's ability for self-love, and one's ability to give and to receive love. This is also the chakra that connects the body and mind with the spirit. The throat chakra is located in the lower end of the throat and is the center for thought, communication, music, speech, and writing; it vibrates to the color blue.

Located in the center of the brow, the third eye or brow chakra vibrates to the color indigo and is concerned with inspiration, imagination, and psychic ability. The final chakra is the crown chakra, situated on the top of the head. This is the center for true spirituality and enlightenment, vibrating to the color violet. It allows for the inward flow of wisdom, and brings the gift of cosmic consciousness.

Austrian philosopher Rudolf Steiner considered the chakra system to be dynamic and evolving. He described a sequence of development that begins with the upper chakras and moves down, rather than up. He gave suggestions on how to develop the chakras through disciplining the thoughts, feelings, and will. There are those who believe that chakras have a physical manifestation, too. One of the influential members of the Theosophical Society

Each chakra is associated with the astrological planets, gods, herbs, and specific crystals to aid in all kinds of healing.

in the late nineteenth century, C. W. Leadbeater, associated the crown chakra with the pineal gland itself. More recently, author Gary Osborn has described the chakras as metaphysical manifestations of the endocrine glands, and in psychophysiology—the study of physical causes behind states such as fear or joy—chakras are considered to be part of the process of this form of reaction.

CHAKRA CORRESPONDENCES

CROWN CHAKRA
Element: None (transcends the material level). **Petals**: 1,000. **Planet**: Ketu. **Deity**: the Inner Spirit. Relates to enlightenment and transcendence of self.

BROW CHAKRA
Element: All. **Petals**: Two. **Planet**: Saturn. **Deity**: Shiva-Shakti. Relates to cosmic insight.

THROAT CHAKRA
Element: Ether. **Petals**: Sixteen. **Planet**: Jupiter. **Deity**: Panchavaktra Shiva, lord of oneness. Relates to truth.

HEART CHAKRA
Element: Air. **Petals**: Twelve. **Planet**: Venus. **Deity**: Rudra Shiva, lord of peace. Relates to emotional maturity.

SOLAR PLEXUS CHAKRA
Element: Fire. **Petals**: Ten. **Planet**: Sun. **Deity**: Old Shiva, lord of destruction. Relates to personal power.

SACRAL CHAKRA
Element: Water. **Petals**: Six. **Planet**: Mercury. **Deity**: Vishnu, lord of preservation. Relates to procreation.

BASE CHAKRA
Element: Earth. **Petals**: Four. **Planet**: Mars. **Deity**: Child Brahma, lord of creation. Relates to pure survival.

MANDALA
JAVA, INDONESIA ninth century

Hindu and Buddhist symbol of the universe, and used to access the spirit world

The ninth-century Borobudur Temple in Java, Indonesia, is a unique template for a giant mandala when seen from above.

The mandala derives from a Sanskrit word meaning "circle," and it is a symbol of the universe used in rituals and spiritual work in Hinduism and Buddhism. The basic construction of most mandalas is made up of a square with four gates contained within a circle or containing a circle. Each gate is in the general shape of a letter "T." In various spiritual traditions, mandalas may be employed for focusing attention or used as a spiritual teaching tool. They are also used for establishing a sacred space and to aid

meditation and altered states of consciousness. In common use, "mandala" has become a generic term for any plan, chart, or geometric pattern that symbolically represents the cosmos.

The Borobudur Buddhist Temple in Java is a curious but remarkable feat of ninth-century construction, and it is unlike any other Buddhist temple. When viewed from above, it takes the form of a giant mandala, simultaneously representing the Buddhist cosmology and the nature of the mind. Until it was discovered in the nineteenth century, Borobudur lay hidden for hundreds of years under layers of volcanic ash and jungle growth. The facts behind its abandonment remain a mystery.

The temple has nine platforms, of which the lower six are square and the upper three are circular. The upper platform features seventy-two small stupas surrounding one large central stupa. Each stupa is bell-shaped and pierced by numerous decorative openings that house 504 Buddha statues. A main dome, located at the center of the top platform, is surrounded by seventy-two Buddha statues seated inside a perforated stupa. It is the world's largest Buddhist temple and one of the greatest Buddhist monuments in the world. Walking around the temple in a certain direction is, for pilgrims, a meditative and enlightening journey in itself. Pilgrims are guided by the system of staircases and corridors ascending to the top platform. Each platform represents one stage of enlightenment.

As a symbol of the universe, the mandala is traditionally depicted with Mount Meru at the center, surrounded by the continents. The outer circle of fire represents wisdom, and the ring of eight charnel grounds represents the Buddhist expression to be always mindful of death. Charnel grounds were specific locations for decomposing human bodies and they were utilized in order to confront and to realize the transient nature of life. Inside this ring are the walls of the mandala palace itself, specifically thought to be a place populated by deities and Buddhas.

The mandala is not always circular in shape, and other shapes such as triangles and squares can be contained within it, as well as animals, flowers, and plants. However, a mandala is usually aesthetically pleasing, and it can be as simple or as complex as the designer wants it to be. The unfolding petals of the lotus flower in which the Hindu gods are often depicted are also considered to be mandalas.

In Christianity, there are several symbolic "wheels" similar to the mandala: for example, the halo, the crown of thorns, and the labyrinth

This fourteenth-century Chinese silk tapestry of a mandala in the form of the Tibetan cosmos has Mount Meru at the center.

in Chartres Cathedral. The latter represents a journey from the outer world to the inner sacred center where the divine is found. The mandala is considered by many new-age adherents to be a mystical and magical map of the universe, and it is constructed in such a way that the focus of attention is drawn to the center and then back to the outer edge.

Swiss psychoanalyst Carl Jung explored the unconscious through his own art and was fascinated by the psycho-spiritual dimension of the mandala. He believed the drawings reflected both his and his clients' inner state at the moment of their creation. Familiarity with the philosophical writings of India prompted Jung to adopt the word "mandala" to describe these circle drawings. In his autobiography *Memories, Dreams, Reflections* (1963), he wrote: "I sketched every morning in a notebook a small circular drawing. which seemed to correspond to my inner situation at the time. . . . Only gradually did I discover what the mandala really is . . . the self, the wholeness of the personality, which if all goes well is harmonious."

Mandalas are often drawn by individuals seeking spiritual or psychological enlightenment.

FIBONACCI SERIES
ITALY 1202

A number sequence that appears throughout the natural world

Within flowers, fruit, branches, and the reproduction of bees lies the secret of the Fibonacci sequence of numbers.

This engraved portrait depicts Fibonacci, a thirteenth-century mathematician who wrote a book on arithmetic.

The Fibonacci sequence first appeared in *Liber Abaci* (also spelled *Liber Abbaci*), a medieval book on arithmetic by Italian mathematician Leonardo of Pisa, who was later known by his nickname Fibonacci. *Liber Abaci* was among the first Western books to describe the merger of Hindu and Arabic numbers, traditionally described as "Arabic numerals." In its attempt to prove to commercial tradesmen and mathematicians the value of this system, the text eventually convinced the public of the superiority of the new numerals.

Fibonacci explains this by considering the growth of an idealized (biologically unrealistic) rabbit population. He assumes that there is a newly born pair of rabbits—one male, one female—and they are put in a field. Rabbits are able to mate at the age of one month, so at the end of its second month a female can produce another pair of rabbits. Rabbits never die (in this idealized world) and a mating pair always produces one new pair—one male, one female—every month from the second month onward. The puzzle that Fibonacci posed was: how many pairs will there be in one year?

FIBONACCI FORMULAE

At the end of the first month, the first pair of rabbits mates, but there is still only one pair. At the end of the second month the female produces a new pair of rabbits, so now there are two pairs of rabbits in the field. At the end of the third month, the original female produces a second pair, making three pairs in total in the field. At the end of the fourth month, the original female has produced yet another new pair, and the female born two months ago produces her first pair, too, which makes five pairs of rabbits. At the end of the nth month, the number of pairs of rabbits is equal to the number of new pairs (which is the number of pairs in month n − 2) plus the number of pairs alive last month (n − 1). This is the nth Fibonacci number.

The Fibonacci sequence often appears in botanical or biological settings, such as the branching pattern in trees, the arrangement of leaves on a stem, the fruitlets of a pineapple, the flowering of an artichoke, the arrangement of a pine cone, and the family tree of honeybees. The Fibonacci numbers are a simple sequence, starting with 0, then 1, and continuing 2, 3, 5, 8, 13, and so on, each new number being the sum of the previous two. For example, if each number is the sum of the two previous numbers the sequence goes like this:

$$0 + 1 = 1$$
$$1 + 1 = 2$$
$$2 + 1 = 3$$
$$3 + 2 = 5$$
$$5 + 3 = 8$$
$$8 + 5 = 13$$

The Fibonacci numbers are also a theme in popular culture. In Dan Brown's novel *The Da Vinci Code* (2003), the numbers are used to unlock a safe and they are also placed out of order in a message to indicate that the message is an anagram.

The sequence of numbers is found in the spirals of shells and sunflower seeds, and corresponds to many biological patterns in the natural world.

NUMERICAL LANGUAGE

Letters, number codes, and planets associated with the numbers.

1	2	3	4	5	6	7	8	9
A	B	C	D	E	F	G	H	I
J	K	L	M	N	O	P	Q	R
S	T	U	V	W	X	Y	Z	

One	The Sun	Innovation
Two	The Moon	Negotiation
Three	Jupiter	Creative thinking
Four	Uranus	Organization
Five	Mercury	Versatility
Six	Venus	Compassion
Seven	Neptune	Mysticism
Eight	Saturn	Power
Nine	Mars	Vision

Throughout history numbers have been linked to letters, and the occult use of numbers in this way is known as numerology. The father of Western numerology was Greek philosopher and mathematician Pythagoras, born around 590 BCE. According to Pythagoras, numbers have a language of their own and have been considered powerful symbols of universal energy ever since the ancient Babylonians, Chinese, Greeks, Egyptians, and Hebrews developed their own unique systems of using numbers to divine the future.

The numerical language was encoded into the alphabet system and this is the most popular way of using numerology today. Each letter of the alphabet is designated a number from one to nine. Any words, names, or whole sentences can be decoded and analyzed by using this code, by reducing the numbers down to a single digit.

The Fibonacci series has associations with the golden ratio of sacred geometry.

GEOMANCY
SYRIA 1241–1242

Geomantic instrument used to divine oracles

This geomantic instrument from Syria or Egypt, dating to the thirteenth century, was used as an oracular device.

In Syria, in the thirteenth century, Muhammad ibn Khutlukh al-Mawsili constructed a strange device that was one of many curious instruments invented in the medieval period to aid magicians in the divination of oracles. When turning the dials, random designs of dots would appear, which were then interpreted and predictions made. This popular form of geomancy was considered to be as important as astrology and other divination techniques at the time.

In medieval Europe, a well-known magician and astrologer named Cornelius Agrippa developed sixteen mystical symbols from ancient shamanic patterns. Similar to the Taoist oracle the I Ching, Agrippa's geomancy symbols corresponded to the astrological elements, planets, and their associated crystals. These symbols were used in rituals to harness the Earth's positive energy through the vibrational alignment of crystals. Geomancy also uses earth acupuncture. Earth acupuncture has the same principles as Chinese acupuncture, in which the Earth's meridians are realigned to create balance in the environment.

During the Middle Ages and the Renaissance geomancy was one of the most popular forms of divination throughout Africa and Europe. Books and treatises on the subject were published up until the seventeenth century, when most occult traditions fell out of popularity or went underground. This was due not only to the Church's deliberate attempts to wipe out all forms of magic, but also to the debut of the Age of Reason and the growing favor of intellect and science over pagan beliefs and the esoteric arts. In the Renaissance, geomancy was classified as one of the seven "forbidden arts," including necromancy, chiromancy (palmistry), and hydromancy.

The practice of geomancy originated with ancient Middle Eastern shamans who drew mystical patterns in the sand to invoke earth energies. Translated from ancient Greek, geomancy literally means "divination by earth," and it is a way to align harmoniously the environment with existing sacred earth energies.

Geomancy is thought to have established its roots in the Middle East when traders brought the esoteric knowledge from Eastern Asia. The original names of the sixteen figures were traditionally given in Arabic, but the reference in Hermetic texts to the mythical king Ṭumṭum al-Hindi potentially points to an Indian origin.

According to one Arabic text, the ancient prophet Idris witnessed the angel Jibril in a dream. Idris asked for enlightenment, so Jibril drew a geomantic figure in the earth. When Idris asked what he was doing, the angel began to teach Idris the geomantic arts. Keeping this secret, he sought out Ṭumṭum al-Hindi, who then wrote a book on geomancy. This book was passed down through clandestine circles until it reached Khalaf al-Barbari, who traveled to Medina and converted to Islam. Confessing to knowing a divinatory art, he explained that pre–Islamic prophets knew geomancy, and that by learning geomancy, one may know all that the prophets knew.

METHODS OF GEOMANCY

Traditionally, geomancy is drawn in the surface of sand using the hands or a stick, but it can be done equally well with a wax tablet and stylus or a pen and paper. Ritualized objects may or may not be desired for use in divination. Modern methods of geomancy include computerized random number generators, counting bricks on a wall, throwing unknown amounts of stones on a flat surface, counting the eyes on potatoes, drawing a number of beans from a sack, and a wide range of creative numbering devices. Some practitioners use specialized cards, with each card representing a single geomantic figure; in this case, only four cards are drawn after shuffling. Specialized machines have also been used to generate full geomantic charts, such as the geomantic instrument that originated from Egypt or Syria.

The Arabic tradition of geomancy consists of sketching sixteen random lines of dots in sand, whereas in Africa another traditional form of geomancy involves throwing handfuls of dirt in the air and observing the way in which the dirt falls. Originating in West Africa, Ifa, one of the oldest forms of geomancy, uses the same sixteen geomantic figures as in Arabic and Western geomancy but they have different meanings and names.

Although it stems from a distinct tradition, the term "geomancy" now commonly includes the Chinese art of feng shui. Furthermore, the introduction of vastu shastra, a similar Indian system of positioning items, and even the construction of houses, to harmonize the local energies, has come under the name "geomancy." Due to the definition of the term having changed over the years, geomancy nowadays can refer to any spiritual, metaphysical, or pseudoscientific practice that is related to the Earth.

SYMBOLS OF CORNELIUS AGRIPPA

| Via | Cauda Draconis | Puer | Fortuna Minor |
| change | completion | passion | resolution |

| Puella | Amissio | Carcer | Laetitia |
| fertility | losing | protection | joy |

| Caput Draconis | Conjunctio | Acquisito | Rubeus |
| profit | relationship | financial luck | power |

| Fortuna Major | Albus | Tristitia | Populus |
| success | negotiation | strength | people |

Late fifteenth-century magician and astrologer Cornelius Agrippa devised magical symbols as a way to harness the powers of the planets.

ROSE CROSS
GERMANY *c. fourteenth century*

Symbol associated with the Rosicrucian Order

This seventeenth-century engraving *Temple of the Rosy Cross*, **by Daniel Mögling, is filled with obscure symbolic imagery.**

derives from the Latin *rosae* and *crux*, and some groups, such as the Ancient and Mystical Order Rosae Crucis, suggest that the symbol predates Christianity. It has also been suggested by some orders that the rose represents silent magic whereas the cross signifies the love of God and the beauty of brotherhood. Other mystical sects, who claimed Rosicrucian descent, considered the rose cross as a symbol of spiritual sexuality, whereas others believed it to be the philosopher's stone, the ultimate goal of the alchemist.

In 1618, alchemist and Rosicrucian Daniel Mögling wrote a work titled *The Mirror of the Wisdom of the Rosy Cross*. An engraving from this publication has become one of the more curious yet essential images in understanding the secret symbolism of Rosicrucianism. It features a bizarre winged temple and other weird imagery, and like many other alchemical engravings it is filled with obscure and mysterious symbols, such as a ship atop a mountain, a swan, and shooting stars. The temple is on wheels to signify that it can go anywhere, and it is suspended from heaven by a rope because it is moved by the will of God. The rose is delicately drawn above the left-hand window and the cross is shown above the other.

This engraving was one of the few ostensible signs of the esoteric movements, such as Rosicrucianism and alchemy, that were bubbling beneath the apparent solid ground of the Church. Many modern Rosicrucians believe that the order began as a Hermetic group and that it had been active since the beginning of the Renaissance. In fact, the Rosicrucians were merely continuing a long-held mystical tradition of genuises, sages, and magi in the literary, political, art, religious, and scientific fields.

The rose cross is associated with the semi-mythical Christian Rosenkreuz, the Kabbalistic alchemist who is said to have been the founder of the Rosicrucian Order. Believed to have been formed in the fourteenth century by a group of mystic sages (chosen by Rosenkreuz), the secret society was intended "to prepare a new phase of the Christian religion to be used during the coming age."

Commonly the rose cross is represented as a cross with a white rose at its center. It

HERMETIC MOVEMENT

Hermeticism was based on the writings of a legendary prophet known as Hermes Trismegistus, who was greatly influential in Neoplatonic and Renaissance thought. The Hermetic movement began to flourish between 1300 and 1600, when its major tenets were the interconnectedness of all things, and how the world of nature could be manipulated or controlled by the magus by invoking supernatural powers. No longer was man at the mercy of God; man could make things happen. This strain of thought was a major influence on the new "scientists," who looked to magic and its associated arts (alchemy and astrology) with a hunger for its secrets. The rose cross was to symbolize its very followers: a mélange of Christian mystics and Hermetic magicians.

Nineteenth-century U.S. freemason Albert Pike believed that the rose cross taught three things. These were the immutability of God, the immortality of the soul, and the ultimate extinction of evil by a redeemer yet to come. He believed the symbol of the cross was originally associated with the ankh, the symbol of life to the ancient Egyptians. The rose was also sacred to the Roman goddess of dawn, Aurora. Thus it was a symbol of the return of light and the renewal of life, and therefore of the dawn of the first day, or the resurrection. The cross and rose together are read as the dawning of eternal life, and the advent of the redeemer.

This nineteenth-century leather apron of a Master of the Order of the Rose-Croix is at Musée Crozatier, Le Puy en Velay, France.

THE GOLDEN DAWN

The Hermetic Order of the Golden Dawn, commonly known as The Golden Dawn, was a late-nineteenth-century British movement devoted to the study and practice of magic and the occult. The order made use of the rose cross in rituals designed for spiritual protection and as a preparation for meditation. Based on the symbolism of the red rose and the cross of gold, the rose cross is a key symbol of the Golden Dawn's Second Order of initiates. The design of the Golden Dawn's rose cross contained signs of the elements, planets, zodiac, Hebrew alphabet, alchemical principles, important geometric symbols such as the hexagram and pentagram, the tree of life, and the Latin acronym INRI, which when translated means "Jesus, King of the Jews."

The symbolic layout of the Golden Dawn's rose cross works according to the elements. Air is a yellow ground with a purple pentagram and other symbols; fire is a scarlet ground with an emerald pentagram and other symbols; water is a blue ground with an orange pentagram; and Earth is citrine, olive, and black, beneath a white pentagram.

This rose cross is from a ritual notebook by the poet W. B. Yeats, who was a member of the Hermetic Order of the Golden Dawn.

VOYNICH MANUSCRIPT
ITALY 1404–1438

An example of symbols that are yet to be deciphered

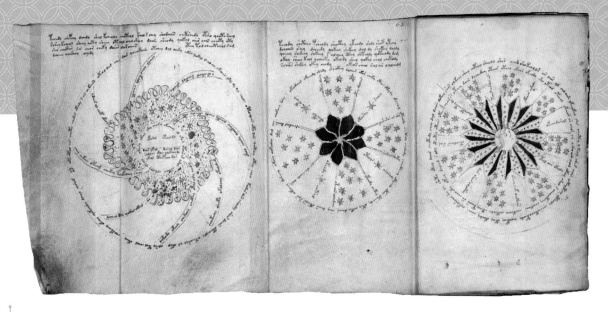

Strange symbols, still unidentified, fill the Voynich manuscript, said to have been written in the fifteenth century by an anonymous mystic.

The pages of this illustrated codex, known as the Voynich manuscript, were hand written in an unknown writing system. The document has been carbon-dated to the early fifteenth century and it is believed to have been composed in Italy during the Renaissance. Although some of the pages seem to be missing, the bulk of the work includes bizarre and sometimes comical illustrations, such as naked women frolicking in bathtubs, and fantasy herbs and plants.

It was purchased by a Polish book dealer, Wilfrid Voynich, in 1912, and the manuscript has been studied by professional and amateur cryptographers, including U.S. and British code breakers from both World Wars. Although mystics claim to understand it, and interpreters and linguists have attempted to reveal its language, no one has yet succeeded in deciphering the text, which has become an infamous case in the history of cryptography. Mystery and obscurity surround the manuscript, and the lack of answers as to its meaning

has given rise to much speculation. None of the many hypotheses proposed over the past hundred years have been verified, and many people have speculated that the book might simply be nonsense written by a madman.

The top right-hand corner of each right-hand page has been numbered from 1 to 116, probably by one of the manuscript's later owners. Although there are various numbering gaps, it seems likely that in the past the manuscript had at least 272 pages. The text consists of more than 170,000 glyphs, separated from each other by narrow gaps. Most of the glyphs are written with one or two simple pen strokes, and it appears that an alphabet of about twenty or thirty glyphs would account for most of the text, except a few rare characters that appear only once or twice. Various transcription alphabets have been created in an attempt to equate the Voynich glyphs with Latin characters to help with analysis. However, all have failed, and linguists have realized that the language is unlike any other European language. The distribution of letters within words is also rather peculiar: some characters occur only at the beginning of a word, some only at the end, and some always in the middle section.

The bizarre features of the Voynich manuscript text, such as the doubled and tripled words, the fantasy illustrations, and its lack of historical references, support the idea that the manuscript is a hoax. If no one can unravel the mystery of the book, then perhaps it had no meaning in the first place. Or it could be a double bluff, meant to deceive by its very deceptive element. However, several theories still hold that there is some meaning to the book.

CIPHER THEORIES

According to the letter-based cipher theory, the Voynich manuscript contains a meaningful text in a European language that was intentionally rendered obscure. This has been the working hypothesis for most twentieth-century deciphering attempts, including an informal team of National Security Agency cryptographers in the early 1950s. By contrast, the codebook cipher theory suggests that the Voynich manuscript "words" could be codes to be looked up in a dictionary-like book. The main evidence for this theory is that the internal structure and length distribution of many words are similar to those of Roman numerals, a natural choice for the codes to have been cross-referenced at the time. However, book-based ciphers are viable only for short messages because they are very cumbersome.

Steganography, the art of concealing a message within another message, was described by German monk and occultist Johannes Trithemius in 1499. This theory holds that the text of the Voynich manuscript is mostly meaningless, but contains meaningful information hidden in inconspicuous details: either within the words themselves or in the illustrative material. However, no one has yet been able to find this hidden message. More

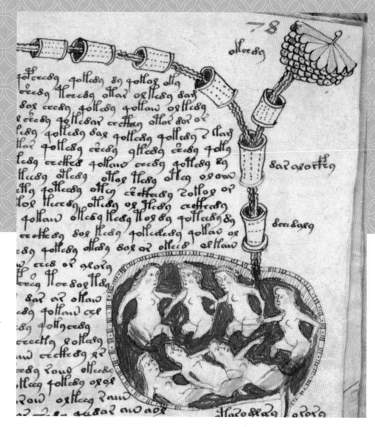

recent theories suggest that the manuscript is a map for buried treasure, a coded recipe for eternal youth, or a handbook on magic. Others believe it is a forgery by Voynich himself.

Voynich is suspected of having acquired a large supply of ancient vellum and to have used his knowledge of chemistry gained at the University of Moscow to replicate medieval inks and pigments. He is even on record at the British Museum in London for studying a book titled *Some Observations On Ancient Inks*. However, Voynich claimed to have stumbled on the manuscript at a Jesuit seminary outside Rome. Appended to the manuscript was what purported to be a letter written in 1665 by Johannes Marcus Marci, a former physician of the Holy Roman Emperor. It stated that the manuscript had previously belonged to Rudolf II, who ruled from 1576 to 1612, and that it was probably the work of Elizabethan alchemist Roger Bacon. Voynich referred to the document as "The Roger Bacon Cipher Manuscript."

Held in the Rare Book and Manuscript Library of Yale University, USA, this undeciphered script appears to refer to a bathtub scene.

Voynich believed the manuscript was the work of Roger Bacon (above).

VITRUVIAN MAN
ITALY 1490

A symbol of the symmetry of the human body, and of the universe as a whole

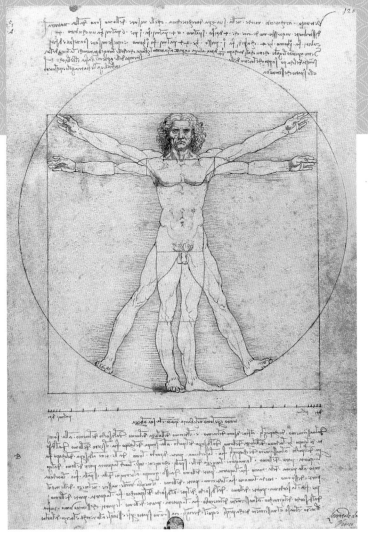

Leonardo da Vinci's *Vitruvian Man* (1490) is the perfect example of the classical proportions of man as reflected in the universe.

Leonardo da Vinci's striking image *Vitruvian Man* (1490) was accompanied by textual notes and it was based on the work of Roman architect Vitruvius. Vitruvius described the human figure as being the principal source of proportion among the classical orders of architecture. He worked out mathematically that the ideal body should be eight heads high, and recorded his findings in Book III of his treatise *De Architectura* (c. 15 BCE).

Da Vinci's pen and ink drawing famously depicts a man in two superimposed positions with his arms and legs apart drawn within a circle and square. The drawing and text are sometimes called the "Canon of Proportions" or the "Proportions of Man." The combination of arm and leg positions creates sixteen different poses. The pose with the arms straight out and the feet together is seen to be inscribed in the superimposed square. On the other hand, the spread-eagle pose is seen to be inscribed in the superimposed circle.

The artist was the ultimate Renaissance man, who relied like many of his peers on the merger of art, mysticism, magic, and science in his work. *Vitruvian Man* has not only become a cultural icon of the Renaissance, but is also a perfect example of da Vinci's deep understanding of proportion. It reiterates the Hermetic tenet "as above, so below": man as a mirror of the cosmos itself. The painter also believed the workings of the human body to be an analogy for the workings of the universe.

Da Vinci's accompanying text was written in mirror writing. Although it may have served as some form of code, the artist was left-handed, so it is more likely that he used mirror writing because it was easier: moving his hand across the wet ink from left to right would have smeared the words; mirror writing would avoid messy ink stains. The first paragraph of da Vinci's text reiterates Vitruvius's original words describing how man's proportions could be measured. According to Vitruvius, a palm is four fingers, a foot is four palms, a cubit is six palms, and four cubits makes a man. A pace is four cubits, and a man is twenty-four palms. The second paragraph reads: "If you open your legs enough that your head is lowered by one-fourteenth of your height and raise your hands enough that your extended fingers touch the line of the top of your head, know that the center of the extended limbs will be the navel, and the space between the legs will be an equilateral triangle."

In the second section of text da Vinci notes the variety of Vitruvius's proportions, such as the length of the hand is one-tenth of the height of a man; the root of the penis is at half the height of a man; the foot is one-seventh of the height of a man, and—a lesson for portrait painters ever since—"the distances from below the chin to the nose and the eyebrows and the hairline are equal to the ears and to one-third of the face."

ANATOMY

Da Vinci's drawing combined a careful reading of the ancient text with his own observation of actual human bodies. In drawing the circle and square, he correctly observed that the square cannot have the same center as the circle—the navel—but is somewhat lower in the anatomy. This adjustment is the innovative part of Vitruvian Man, and distinguishes it from earlier illustrations along the same theme. Da Vinci also departs from Vitruvius by drawing the arms raised to a position in which the fingertips are level with the top of the head, rather than Vitruvius's lower angle, in which the arms form lines passing through the navel.

Even before Vitruvius, geometric ratios had been employed in the architecture of many ancient buildings throughout the world, including in Egypt and Greece. Later medieval European cathedrals also incorporated symbolic

A 1684 depiction of Vitruvius (right) presenting *De Architectura* to Augustus.

geometry, while Indian and Himalayan spiritual communities constructed temples using the designs of mandalas and sacred numbers.

In sacred geometry, symbolic and sacred meanings are ascribed to various geometric shapes and proportions to create a worldwide pattern of recognition, a complex system of religious symbols and structures involving space, time, and form. Vitruvius recognized this proportion in man. Yet the Vitruvian Man, or rather its creator, took the sacred geometry proportions one step further, in that man himself became a microcosm of the universe. The drawing is an iconic symbol of the symmetry of the human body, and by extension the symmetry of the universe itself.

Whatever the proportions of the sacred geometry and its influence on architecture and art, there is still the question of who the man depicted actually was. Is it a self-portrait of the artist or, as some suggest, Jesus as he would have appeared on the cross? Other scholars and art historians believe that the Vitruvian Man is in fact an allusion to John the Baptist. Da Vinci was highly secretive about his alternative religious views and it is believed that he was certain that John the Baptist was superior to Jesus. To promote that idea would have been unthinkable at the time, so it may be that hidden within the painting is the artist's secret heresy.

Self-portrait by da Vinci, who saw that the microcosm and the macrocosm, or man and the universe, were one and the same.

INFINITY
ITALY 1584

Represents the quality of having no limits and no end

This ouroboros drawing is from a late medieval Byzantine Greek alchemical manuscript.

The infinity symbol first appeared in 1584 in the talismanic drawings of Italian philosopher, astrologer, and mystic Giordano Bruno, who proposed a theory of an unbounded universe: "Innumerable suns exist; innumerable earths revolve around these suns in a manner similar to the way the seven planets revolve around our sun. Living beings inhabit these worlds." In those days Bruno was considered a heretic for even thinking that the Earth and the planets revolved around the sun, let alone that there were other suns or that the universe was infinite.

The curious symbol features in a number of Bruno's drawings. A sideways eight, also known as a lemniscate, it resembles a serpent coiled across itself. This figure eight symbol has also appeared across a wide range of cultures and throughout Persian, Minoan, and Greek decorative artwork and has its roots in Egyptian serpent worship. Infinity is sometimes drawn in figure eight form to show how eternally interweaving cycles of opposites are in fact one and the same. Like the Taoist symbol of yin and yang, each is found in the other, representing the eternal unity of all things.

John Wallis is credited with giving the infinity symbol a mathematical meaning in 1655. He did not explain his choice of symbol, but in mathematical circles it is thought to be a variant form of the Roman numeral for 1,000, which was sometimes used to mean "many," or was a derivative of the Greek letter omega—ω—the last letter in the Greek alphabet. In mathematics, the infinity symbol is used to represent a potential infinity, rather than to represent an infinite quantity. The infinity symbol is also used in book binding to indicate that a book is printed on acid-free paper and will therefore be long lasting.

OUROBOROS

In mysticism the infinity symbol is identified with a variation of the ouroboros, the ancient image of a snake eating its own tail, considered to be symbolic of the eternal cycle of the cosmos, the transcendence of duality, and the union of opposites. After emerging in ancient Egypt, the ouroboros became an important symbol in religious and mythological symbolism, and it was used frequently in alchemical works in which it represented the circular nature of the alchemist's opus. The first known appearance of the ouroboros motif is in

The caption for the Strength tarot card reads:

VIII

STRENGTH.

THE MAGICIAN.

The sideways figure eight infinity symbol was used in the Rider-Waite tarot deck, created by two members of the Hermetic Order of the Golden Dawn.

The figure eight resembles a snake coiled upon itself, reminding us of its ability to be reborn.

the *Enigmatic Book of the Netherworld*, an ancient Egyptian funerary text discovered in the tomb of Tutankhamun and dating from the fourteenth century BCE. The text concerns the actions of the god Ra and his union with Osiris in the underworld. In an illustration from this text, two serpents, holding their tails in their mouths, coil around the head and feet of an enormous god, who may represent the unified Ra-Osiris. The figure is named "He who hides the hours." The ouroboros is shown to be Mehen, the protective snake god known as the Enveloper. This depiction, along with the text, refers to the beginning and the end of time and its cyclic nature. A rope upheld by seven adoring gods in the center evidently serves to pull the disk from the body of the central figure.

The ouroboros appears elsewhere in Egyptian sources, where, like many other Egyptian serpent deities, it represents either a destructive element, as the serpent god Apep, or its protective element, as Wadjet. The symbol of the ouroboros persisted through the Egyptian dynasties, and later it appeared frequently on magical talismans in Greco-Roman times. A well-known ouroboros drawing from an early papyrus manuscript known as *The Chrysopoeia of Cleopatra* dates to the second century CE. Cleopatra the Alchemist was one of a minority of female alchemists working at the time, and famously depicted the words "hen to pan," meaning "one is the all," surrounded by the ouroboros. She was reputed to be one of the few alchemists who produced the philosopher's stone, the elixir of life.

The infinity symbol also appears on several cards of the Rider-Waite tarot deck, including the magician and strength.

HARMONICES MUNDI

GERMANY *c.* 1599

A theory of the universe based on musical or geometrical harmony

The symbolic vibrations and mystical music of the spheres were taken one step further by Johannes Kepler in *Harmonices Mundi* (1619).

This portrait depicts German astronomer and astrologer Johannes Kepler.

Around 1599, German astronomer and astrologer Johannes Kepler was keen to publish a work exploring his new theories about elliptical orbits using the Copernican system: in other words, the dubious and heretical (at the time) model that the Earth and other planets revolved around the sun. Kepler was aware that including his new theories of celestial–harmonic relationships might result in suspicion and outcry from those scholars aligned with the Catholic Church. Although very different to the mystical harmonies of Pythagoras, his geometrically supported musical ratios allowed Kepler to relate musical consonance to the angular velocities of the planets. His model also wisely gave reasoned evidence for God acting as a grand geometric designer.

Pythagoras had proposed that the sun, the moon, and the planets all emit their own unique vibration based on their orbital revolution, and God was not responsible for this creation. He also argued that the quality of life on Earth reflects the celestial sounds physically imperceptible to the human ear, rather than that the quality of life was determined by God's will. This was heretical in the extreme, so it is hardly surprising that Kepler developed his theory quietly in his laboratory. Luckily, he moved to Prague, where he became advisor to Emperor Rudolf II, an infamous patron of the occult arts.

Harmonices Mundi, published in 1619, completed Kepler's work from which the three most important astronomical laws, known as the "Three Laws of Planetary Motion," developed.

These were to change the whole course of astronomy and science.

The concept of musical harmonies of the planets already existed in medieval philosophy. The *musica universalis* was a traditional philosophical metaphor that was taught in universities, and was referred to as the "music of the spheres." *Musica universalis* saw proportions in the movements of the sun, the moon, and the planets as a form of music. This music was not thought to be audible, but was some kind of symbolic vibration, or a mathematical or religious concept.

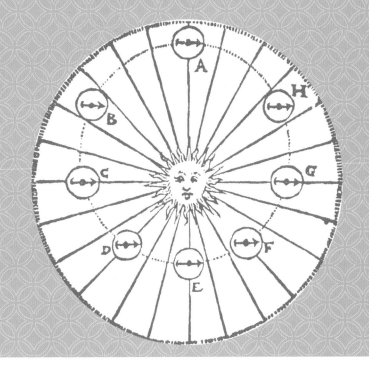

HARMONIC WORKINGS

Pythagoras first identified that the pitch of a musical note is in proportion to the length of the string that produces it, and that intervals between harmonious sound frequencies form simple numerical ratios.

Kepler was intrigued by this idea, and sought a rational explanation. It should be noted that when he used the term "harmony" he was not referring to the musical definition, but rather a broader one encompassing the workings of both the celestial and terrestrial bodies. The astronomer divided *Harmonices Mundi* into five long chapters: the first on regular polygons; the second on the congruence of figures; the third on the origin of harmonic proportions in music; the fourth on harmonic configurations in astrology; and the fifth on the harmony of the motions of the planets.

Kepler discovered physical harmonies in planetary motion. He found that the difference between the maximum and minimum angular speeds of a planet in its orbit approximates a harmonic proportion. For instance, the maximum angular speed of the Earth as measured from the sun varies by a semitone (a ratio of 16:15), from "mi" to "fa," between the greatest distance of a planet's elliptical orbit and the closest distance. He explained the reason for the Earth's small harmonic range: "The Earth sings mi, fa, mi: you may infer even from the syllables that in this our home misery and famine hold sway."

Kepler's celestial choir was made up of a tenor, the planet Mars; two bass, Saturn and Jupiter; a soprano, Mercury; and two altos, Venus and Earth. Mercury, with its large elliptical orbit, was determined to be able to produce the greatest number of notes, whereas Venus was capable of only a single note because its orbit is nearly a circle rather than an ellipse. According to Kepler, at very rare intervals, all of the planets would sing together in perfect concord. He proposed that this may have occurred only once in history, perhaps at the time of creation. Yet Kepler's theory of the universe based on musical or geometrical harmony laid the seeds of the laws of planetary motion that would later provide one of the foundations for Isaac Newton's theory of universal gravitation.

Kepler discovered the harmonic proportions of the angular speeds between the planets, from which he developed his hugely important laws of planetary motion.

UNICURSAL HEXAGRAM
UNITED KINGDOM twentieth century

Mystical symbol associated
with the key of life

The **Rosicrucian symbol** of the Hermetic Order of the Golden Dawn (nineteenth century) inspired Aleister Crowley to develop his own symbols.

Aleister Crowley believed himself to be a prophet, after a deeply spiritual experience in Egypt in 1904.

The unicursal hexagram is a hexagram or six-pointed star that can be traced or drawn in one continuous line. The standard hexagram cannot be drawn in one continuous line, but rather has to be constructed in two separate halves, by using two overlaid triangles. The unicursal version of the hexagram was probably devised by the Hermetic Order of the Golden Dawn, although occultist Aleister Crowley claimed it as his own invention and used it as a symbol for his spiritual philosophy, Thelema.

The Hermetic Order of the Golden Dawn's unicursal hexagram allocated the sun to the upper point, the moon to the bottom point, and the four elements to the remaining points. Similar to normal hexagrams, it represents the uniting of the macrocosm with the microcosm. However, as one continuous line, it creates both the divine and the manifest, further accentuating the ultimate unity of the two. Unicursal hexagrams were convenient for Golden Dawn ritual work, in which symbols were traced in the air with magical tools.

In Thelema, the unicursal hexagram is usually depicted with a five-petal flower in the center, which symbolizes a pentacle. In the early twentieth century, Crowley believed himself to be the prophet of a new age, based upon a spiritual experience that he and his wife, Rose Edith, had in Egypt in 1904. The word "Thelema" is Greek for "will," particularly the desirous nature of man. Crowley's law of

Thelema was "Do what thou wilt shall be the whole of the law. Love is the law, love under will." As Crowley developed the religion, he wrote widely on the topic, producing what are collectively termed the "Holy Books of Thelema." He also included ideas from yoga, Eastern and Western mysticism, and the Kabbalah. The unicursal hexagram is still used as a symbol of his Thelemic system and it is included in some versions of the Thoth tarot deck.

The normal hexagram is also a potent symbol of the macrocosm (God, the universe, and higher energies) and of the relationship between the macrocosm and the microcosm (humankind, the Earth, and manifest energies). In its regular form it is drawn as two intersecting equilateral triangles, and it is most commonly seen as the Judaic Star of David.

KABBALISTIC HEXAGRAM

In Kabbalah, the upward-pointing triangle (the symbol of the element fire) represents the yearning of the manifest to reach or return to the divine, and the downward-pointing triangle (the symbol of the element water) signifies the descent of the divine into matter. Where these two meet in the center of the hexagram, a point of balance and beauty is reached, corresponding to Tiferet on the Kabbalistic tree of life. The astro–Kabbalistic form of the hexagram is particularly powerful because each point shows not only a Kabbalistic sefira and its relationship to the other sefirot, but also the astrological planet that has the same sphere of influence. For example, the red point of the hexagram corresponds to the aggressive, judgmental sefira Geburah, and also to the violent, willful planet Mars.

In a number of traditions the upward-pointing equilateral triangle symbolizes the male phallus. To the Maya, it represented the sun and fertility, whereas to the Hittites it was a symbol of health. It was also a sacred mountain in Pueblo art. In numerous traditions the downward-pointing equilateral triangle symbolizes the feminine, or female sexuality. In ancient India, Greece, and Rome it represented the female pubic area, and also represented the element of water.

In alchemy, the hexagram is the sign of completion, combining all the elements needed to create the philosopher's stone. The upward-pointing triangle symbolizes fire, the downward-pointing triangle water. An upward-pointing triangle through a horizontal line represents air and a downward-pointing triangle through a line symbolizes Earth.

The hexagram in Hinduism represents the merger of male and female, and in Judaism it is familiar as the Star of David. The base of the Freemason's triangle symbolizes duration, and the two sides represent light and darkness. The whole triangle is a symbol of qualities, such as faith, hope, and charity, as well as of spiritual development. In some traditions equilateral triangles placed point to point represent the meeting of the Earth and the sky, or the union of male and female. In India they represent Shiva's hourglass drum, the *damaru*, the sound of which brought about the beginning of creation.

The normal hexagram, drawn with two triangles, reflects the merger of the spirit and the material worlds.

In Thelema, the unicursal hexagram is usually depicted with a flower at its center to symbolize a pentagram.

Ancient Chinese oracle bones inscribed with messages were an early system of divination used by emperors to determine the outcome of events.

THE MYSTIC WORLD

The mystic world encompasses humankind's creative attempts to understand better the divine world. In ancient times, magical symbols were developed to invoke the gods or spirits, primarily to ensure fertility and a good harvest. Yet as civilizations developed, these symbols were used to manipulate the supernatural and natural worlds in an attempt to be united with the divine. The common theme is that this rich symbolism was usually shrouded in great secrecy. As the stars and planets appeared to have power over humankind, so ancient cultures attempted to harness that power. Augurs or seers observed patterns in the sky and in nature and saw these as portents of coming events. Astrology, tarot, magic, divination, and other occult arts developed their own symbolic language; great Renaissance individuals such as John Dee and Giordano Bruno developed their own secret symbols, too. Persecuted by the Church, this occult force had little choice but to go underground until a renewed fascination for mysticism emerged at the beginning of the twentieth century.

NAMARRGON, THE LIGHTNING MAN

KAKADU NATIONAL PARK, AUSTRALIA *c.* 20,000 BCE

One of the creation spirits worshipped by early Aboriginal peoples

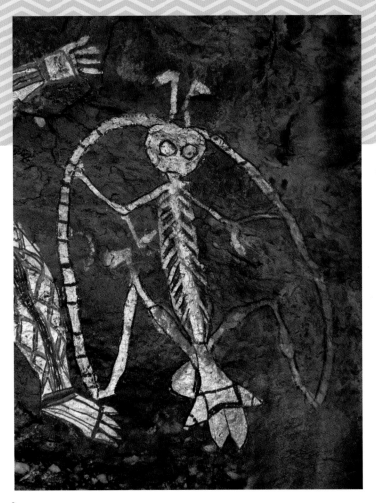

In the main painting, Namarrgon the lightning man is encircled by his white lightning bolt.

The creation spirit Namarrgon features in the ancient rock paintings found at the Anbangbang shelter at Nourlangie Rock in Kakadu National Park, Australia. He was not only a portent of the dangerous stormy season, but also respected as one of the creator ancestors. Aboriginal occupation of this remote sandstone escarpment in the Northern Territory dates back to before 20,000 BCE, and the shelter is home to some of the finest images of Aboriginal mythology. They reveal how the earliest societies worshipped the spirits and gods of nature, lightning, and storms.

Namondjok is the central figure of the main painting. This creation ancestor indulged in incest with his sister and was banished to the sky. He can be seen only at night, when he appears as a dark spot in the Milky Way. To his right sits Namarrgon, the lightning man, who also played an important role in the creation legends. The white band that surrounds him, linking his ankles, head, and hands, is his lightning bolt. According to an ancient Dreaming story, Namarrgon and his family came from the sea and traveled across Australia for hundreds of years. During his travels Namarrgon left his power in many places. On his last journey, when he approached the escarpment near Nourlangie Rock from the east, he looked over the cliff, then took out an eye and placed it on the edge where it waits for the storm season. It is said to be the large round boulder that can be seen from the Gunwarddehwardde lookout.

The lightning man is shaped like a praying mantis, and he crackles his electrical rods through the stormy skies of the tropical monsoon. He causes thunder by hitting the clouds with an ax, and when he comes to Earth he uses his ax to split trees and slice off the roofs of houses. Each year, Namarrgon arrives in late October, and his lightning bolts hit the Earth through the wet season, until he finally leaves in March. When the Aboriginal people hear the last thunder roar, it is Namarrgon saying, "Time to go, but I'll be back for more next year."

Namarrgon and his wife, Barrginj, created a ghastly race of children who were grasshoppers known as the Alyurr. Every November, these grasshoppers leap across the land as the lightning man arrives. The Alyurr are highly respected by the Aboriginal people because it is believed they gave them their language, beliefs, and cultural structure during the Dreaming.

There are three main sites at Nourlangie Rock, and according to legend the area was formed when two creation ancestors, in the form of short-eared rock wallabies, traveled through from east to west. They moved past Nourlangie Rock, across Anbangbang Billabong, and up into the rocks where they cut two crevices as they passed. Spirits such as the Mimi were said to inhabit the thin crevices between the rocks and remained there to avoid being destroyed by the high winds. Detailed, delicate rock paintings at the Anbangbang shelter depict the Mimi spirits with their thin, fragile, and elongated bodies. The Mimi are said to have taught the indigenous people of Australia how to hunt, prepare kangaroo meat, and make fire. Today, rock wallabies are often visible at Nourlangie Rock during early morning and at dusk.

DREAMING

The Dreaming was considered to be both the beginning of creation and a time when spirits gave form to the land. Hunter-gatherers have, according to archaeologists, inhabited Australia since the Ice Age of 50,000 years ago. These peoples lived in small groups, and when Western settlers arrived in the late eighteenth century it was thought there were more than 300 or so of these communities, each with its own language.

In Dreamtime, a place beyond time and space, spirits stocked the world with animals and plants, including everything that was to be born in the future, and infused a mystical dimension into everyday life. Dreamtime was intimately connected to the land, and everything in it was animated with its own spirit. For example, even a rock or hollow was invested with spirit, as was the apparent empty desert whose features were assigned spirits known as "djang." The most well-known and sacred djang location is Ayers Rock in the Northern Territory.

The boulder that sits aloft Nourlangie Rock is said to be the lightning man's eye, which he left there to remind the people of his yearly return.

Mimi spirits were fairy spirits that were so thin they could hide between crevices in the rocks to avoid the storm winds.

SHAMAN

LASCAUX CAVES, FRANCE *c.* 15,300 BCE

Figure associated with divination, healing, and the spirit world

The birdman scene in the Lascaux Caves is thought to depict a shaman who, in a trancelike state, has just encountered animal spirits in the otherworld.

Throughout many indigenous cultures, shamans are respected magicians and wise healers, able to transcend the tangible world and enter the spirit world. Shamanism is a belief that so-called "reality" is filled with invisible forces such as spirits and demons that influence the living in both positive and negative ways. These spirits play a key role in the society or culture in question. Shamans can leave their mortal body to engage in the spiritual world, and can cure illnesses and communicate with spirit guides, often animals. Once an initiate has become a shaman, he is given specific magical talismans associated with cultural needs. To travel to the spirit world, the shaman must first enter a trancelike state, induced by self-hypnosis, drugs such as ayahuasca, rapid drumming, sweat lodges, vision quests, and other rituals.

At the bottom of a 20-foot (6-m) shaft in a remote corner of one of the main caves at the Lascaux complex in France, with room enough only for a single person to view it at a time, is a depiction of an extraordinary scene of what appears to be the outcome of a bloody hunt. Among the glittering calcite crystals on the wall, a great black bison, fatally wounded, seems to be poised for attack, its tail lashing in fury. A barbed spear lies across its body, and its entrails spill to the ground. In front of the bison is a stickman wearing a bird mask, who appears to have fallen to the ground. Some scholars have interpreted the image as a portrayal of a simple hunting accident, but many others now believe that it shows a shaman in a state of ecstatic trance. His altered state of consciousness is represented by an erect penis.

In this interpretation, the bird-headed staff is perhaps a ritual instrument, and the bison spilling its entrails an animal spirit encountered and perhaps killed in the otherworld. Among the approximately one hundred painted caves of Europe, only a handful have similar enigmatic paintings of human-animal composites, possibly shape-shifters or shamans.

French researchers believe that the gallery of figurative images in Lascaux's Great Hall of the Bulls cave represents an extensive star map. Key points on major figures in the group correspond to stars as they would have appeared in the Paleolithic period. According to one theory, the eyes of the bull, the bird, and the bird man represent the three stars Vega, Altair, and Deneb, known to modern-day astronomers as the Summer Triangle. It has been suggested by archaeoastronomers that the star configuration marked the summer solstice. But is there another more mysterious story being told here?

The bird man lies prostrate on the ground with an erect phallus, one claw hand pointing to the bison, the other to a bird-headed staff or bird sitting on the end of a stick. Is the shaman bird contacting the soul of the bison to learn the mysteries of death, or is this a shamanic ritual scene and a tribal statement of a kill? Some anthropologists have theorized that the paintings could represent a mystical ritual performed to improve future hunting endeavors. This theory is thought to be supported by the overlapping images of another group of animals in the same cave location, suggesting that one area of the cave was more successful for predicting a plentiful hunting excursion.

SORCERER PAINTING

Another well-known depiction of a shaman figure is the appropriately named *Sorcerer* cave painting, found in the cavern known as the Sanctuary in Trois Frères, Ariège, France. This artwork dates to around 13,000 BCE. The figure's significance is unknown, but it is usually interpreted as either a shape-shifting shaman

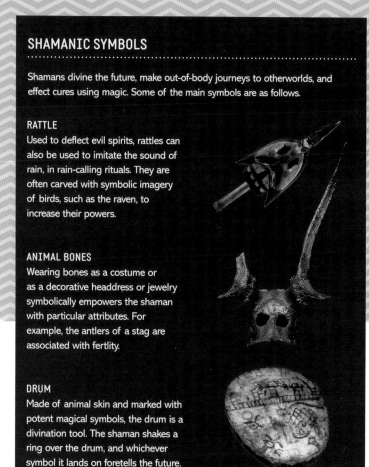

SHAMANIC SYMBOLS

Shamans divine the future, make out-of-body journeys to otherworlds, and effect cures using magic. Some of the main symbols are as follows.

RATTLE
Used to deflect evil spirits, rattles can also be used to imitate the sound of rain, in rain-calling rituals. They are often carved with symbolic imagery of birds, such as the raven, to increase their powers.

ANIMAL BONES
Wearing bones as a costume or as a decorative headdress or jewelry symbolically empowers the shaman with particular attributes. For example, the antlers of a stag are associated with fertlity.

DRUM
Made of animal skin and marked with potent magical symbols, the drum is a divination tool. The shaman shakes a ring over the drum, and whichever symbol it lands on foretells the future.

or a master spirit. Because of the other images that decorate the walls of the Sanctuary, it is likely that magical ceremonies were practiced in the chamber. French archaeologist and accomplished draftsman Henri Breuil made numerous sketches of the cave paintings. His depiction of the *Sorcerer* in the 1920s, with its horned humanoid torso and erect penis, influenced many subsequent theories about the figure. Breuil asserted that the cave painting represented a shaman or magician, whereas British archaeologist Margaret Murray referred to the image as "the first depiction of a deity on Earth," an idea that Breuil and others later adopted. Perhaps the most common interpretation of Breuil's image is that it represents a shaman performing a ritual to ensure good hunting.

Henri Breuil's *Sorcerer* is thought to be a shaman in ritual dress propitiating the spirits for a good hunt.

LABYRINTH

KNOSSOS, CRETE *c.* 1860–1814 BCE

Mazelike patterns of pathways designed to imprison or confuse

The fourth-century Roman floor mosaic from Villa Desenzano, Brescia, Italy, reveals the popular usage of the labyrinth.

The labyrinth first appeared at the heart of the Minoan civilization at the palace of Knossos, Crete, a political and ceremonial center renowned for its maze of rooms, living spaces, exquisite murals—both inside and out—and highly decorative pottery. Built during the reign of Pharaoh Amenemhat III (1860–1814 BCE), the palace was abandoned some time at the end of the Late Bronze Age between 1380 and 1100 BCE.

In Greek mythology, King Minos, the ruler of Crete, dwelt in the palace at Knossos, where he ordered the skilled craftsman Daedalus to construct a labyrinth in which to imprison his monster son, the Minotaur. In the myth of the Minotaur recounted by Homer, Theseus—a prince from Athens—sailed to Crete where he was forced to fight the Minotaur, half man, half bull. The king's daughter, Ariadne, fell in love with Theseus, and before the prince entered the labyrinth, Ariadne gave him a ball of thread that she attached to a rock at the entrance. Theseus unwound the thread on his way into the maze so that he could find his way back out again after killing the Minotaur. Later writers, such as Ovid, suggest that Daedalus constructed the labyrinth so cunningly that he himself was almost unable to find his way out.

Labyrinths are either unicursal, made with a line without a break, or multicursal, made with several or more puzzling pathways and a number of lines, much like the Knossos labyrinth. Labyrinth-like symbols have been found carved on rocks and painted or scratched on pottery dating to the Neolithic and Bronze Age periods. The depiction of a labyrinth on an Etruscan wine jar from Tragliatella, Italy, dating from the late seventh century BCE, shows armed soldiers on horseback running from a labyrinth with the word "TRVIA" (Troy) inscribed in the outermost circuit. More recently, in the late medieval period, Welsh and Cornish shepherds made unicursal labyrinths in the turf, which eventually led to a point in the center. They called them "Caer Droia," which means Troy Town, or Town of Turnings. The labyrinths may have been used for symbolic journeys of penance, related to pagan myths and the disastrous siege of Troy.

Popular throughout the Roman Empire, labyrinths were used as protective symbols often laid out in mosaics on the floors of civic buildings and villas. They were also constructed outdoors as a playground for children and as a test of skill for soldiers on horseback. However, it was during the medieval period that

This detail from a Mycenean drinking cup, or kylix, at the British Museum, London, shows Theseus destroying the Minotaur in the heart of the labyrinth.

It was laid in colored marble and tiles on the floors of cathedrals and churches, most famously at Chartres Cathedral in France. This unicursal labyrinth constructed in the early thirteenth century survives to this day. It has become an object of pilgrimage, where "walking the labyrinth" is likened to walking along a spiritual path to the center, symbolizing Jerusalem. In this way, the devotee makes a symbolic pilgrimage to the Holy City, or has an individual experience of the divine.

In Britain and Germany, from the late medieval period onward, labyrinths were created by cutting designs into the turf of village greens, rural hilltops, and town commons, such as in Saffron Walden, Essex. Mentioned by Shakespeare in *A Midsummer Night's Dream*, and employed as a dancing ground for rustic festivities, they were once widespread. However,

An ancient Cretan coin found at Knossos depicts the labyrinth.

the labyrinth symbol became equated with a mystical experience.

Medieval labyrinths in churches and cathedrals were often used by the clergy for dances, as they tiptoed, two-stepped, and twirled along their pathways. In a more intricate form, the labyrinth reflected the complexities of spiritual faith, life, and philosophy in the medieval mind.

only eight historic examples survive in England and three in Germany. Elsewhere in Europe walkable labyrinths formed of rocks on remote islands in Scandinavia are associated with the superstitious practices of fishing communities. Examples have also been found alongside prehistoric burial grounds in southern Sweden and Arctic Russia.

The thirteenth-century paving stone labyrinth at Chartres Cathedral, France, is one of the best-known examples in the world.

PHAISTOS DISK
CRETE *c.* 1700 BCE

The meaning of the elaborate symbols and signs remains a mystery

Both sides of the Phaistos disk display glyphs and symbols. Although some of them have been identified, to date no one is certain of their meaning.

The Phaistos Disk is a curious circular clay disk covered on both sides with a rough spiral of inscribed symbols that are unlike any other signs in any known writing system. It was discovered in the ancient city of Phaistos in southern Crete in 1908, and is thought to date to around 1700 BCE. Because no other similar artifacts have ever been found anywhere in Crete, it is thought that the disk may have come from distant shores.

The Minoans were great sea traders and their civilization arose on the island of Crete, flourishing from 2700 to 1500 BCE. However, their cultural contacts reached far beyond the island, from the Old Kingdom of Egypt to Cyprus, Canaan and the Levantine coast, and Anatolia. In 2009, Minoan-style frescoes and numerous other artifacts were discovered during excavations of the Canaanite palace at Tel Kabri, Israel.

Some of the symbols inscribed on the Phaistos Disk may provide important clues to the meaning of the glyphs and their origin. One depicts a helmet decorated with a crest, which was later used by the Philistines; another depicts a structure that is similar to a sarcophagus used by the Lycians of Asia Minor. The relatively detailed inscriptions were made by pressing pre-formed hieroglyphic seals into the soft clay in a clockwise sequence spiraling toward the center. The disk was then baked at a high temperature.

There are a total of 241 figures, and many of the forty-five different glyphs represent easily identifiable everyday items, such as a boat, a shield, and a staff, as well as human figures, birds, insects, fish, and plants. In addition, there is a small diagonal line that occurs eighteen times underneath the final sign in a group. In several places, the Phaistos Disk also shows traces of corrections made by the scribe, as if he had to re-stamp or include new symbols in between other glyphs.

The inscriptions are broken into sixty-one groups, and attempts to interpret them has, to date, not led to any obvious decipherment. Speculation suggests that the pictograms may be phonetic or are similar to Egyptian hieroglyphs. Another theory is that the disk is an artifact that had a ceremonial or magical religious function, and therefore does not represent a developed writing system. The use of stamps implies a mass-production capability, so it is possible that other examples may yet be discovered.

Some archaeologists claim that the disk was used as a receipt for religious favors; others that it was used for permanent records or that it was a trading disk, taken by a sea captain as he made his way around Crete. At each port he would have logged the trade or supplies requested on the disk.

Suggestions as to the meaning of the glyphs include a secret message, prayers, a narrative or adventure story, a call to arms, and a geometric theorem. In the popular imagination, there are beliefs that the Phaistos Disk is a mantra used in healing rituals, a spell for magical ceremonies, a farmer's almanac, or some form of calendar. There are also those who believe that the signs could be markings for a board game that illustrated the journeys of the sun god and the moon goddess, both in astronomical and mythological terms.

MINOAN SYMBOLS

Dating back to 3500 BCE, the Minoan civilization was not only a powerful trading force but also a goddess-worshipping culture. Minoan symbols such as serpents, bulls, and the poppy are identified with the mother goddess, also known as the mistress of the animals. Images depicting bull leaping appear frequently in Minoan art and the activity was probably part of a ritual. Other popular symbols include the Minoan genius and the labrys. The former was a fantastic mythological creature, portrayed sometimes with the head of a lion or hippopotamus, that played a role in various religious ceremonies. It is often depicted with water vessels and appeared as a libation bearer. The labrys is a double-headed ax that was used to slay the sacrificial bull, a powerful symbol that appears as decoration on walls and on pottery found at Knossos.

The labrys, or double-headed ax, was a symbol of the Minoan goddess who presided over Knossos and its labyrinth.

MINOAN BULL

A potent symbol of strength, the bull was a totemic royal beast in ancient Crete. Bull leaping, and bulls in general, is believed to have been an important part of Minoan culture. Excavations at Knossos have revealed several frescos depicting the sport of bull leaping, and the exaggerated size of the bull compared to the human leaper, reveals the Minoans' reverence for the power of the animal. Bull leaping consists of an acrobatic jump over a bull. When the bull's horns were grasped, he would violently jerk his neck upward, giving the leaper the momentum necessary to perform somersaults and other acrobatic tricks.

ORACLE BONES

CHINA c. 1500–1000 BCE

Inscribed bones used for divination

The oracle bone texts are the oldest extant documents written in the Chinese language. They are a record of the questions asked by various members of the royal house of Shang in the hope that the diviner or seer could advise them for the future. By analyzing oracle bone inscriptions and other artifacts, scholars have been able to piece together many details of the earliest Chinese civilizations. Through the oracle bones, they have confirmed the names of their kings and rulers and the styles of government, as well as military history, religious beliefs and rituals, and social behaviors.

Ancestor worship and ancestor spirits are at the core of most ancient beliefs in China, so it is hardly surprising that the first successful dynastic family, the Shang, believed that its power came through spiritual contact with its ancestors via the oracle bones. Success in wars against rivals, hunting expeditions, and harvesting all depended on the benevolence

One of the earliest methods of divination was the use of Chinese oracle bones; this one is held in the Hopkins Collection, Cambridge University Library, England.

When the site of Anyang in China was excavated at the end of the nineteenth century, more than 10,000 oracle bones, primarily ox shoulder blades and turtle shells, were found carved with archaic forms of Chinese characters. They had been used for divination between 1500 and 1000 BCE, but for centuries their secret had lain hidden beneath the city streets. According to local legend, a doctor discovered them in 1899 while searching for "dragon bones," which he intended to grind up and use in a special magic potion to cure a dangerously ill patient.

of these royal ancestors. Illness, accidental death, murder, and natural disasters were punishments inflicted by spirits who could not move on to the afterlife. Venerating one's ancestors was a surefire way of receiving their benefits rather than their vengeance.

The writing on the oracle bones reveals that professional diviners hired by the king answered a broad spectrum of questions such as "Will the king have a son?" "Will it rain tomorrow?" "If we send a thousand men into battle, will we succeed?" and even "Is the long drought caused by ancestor X?" The scribe or diviner would carve the question onto the bone. On the other side of the bone, he would carve a number of small pits. He then inserted a hot metal rod into these pits until the bone cracked, and then interpreted the patterns made by the cracked lines. Afterward, on the other side of the bone, the diviner carved the answer to the question and the eventual outcome.

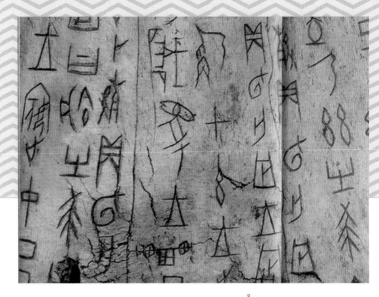

This ancient Chinese script from the Shang dynasty reveals the emperor's future in response to his many questions.

Archaeologists have discovered that some holes were drilled into the bone deliberately before firing in order to make sure that the bone would crack in a specific way so the diviner could fix the desired future. In this way, any seer who wanted to improve his lot with the ruler or family could be sure of providing a suitable forecast for both himself and the querent.

OTHER ORACLES

In ancient India, an oracle was a person known as an Akashvani or Asariri (Tamil), meaning "voice from the sky," who related messages from the gods. Oracles played key roles in many of the major incidents of the epic stories, such as the *Ramayana*, in which Kamsa, the evil uncle of Krishna, was informed by an oracle that the eighth son of his sister Devaki would kill him. There are still several Akashvanis available to the public in India.

The Yucatec Maya employed oracle priests or *chilanes*, literally meaning "mouthpieces" of the deity. One written repository of traditional knowledge is known as the "Books of Chilam Balam," which were authored by an oracle priest who correctly predicted the coming of the Spaniards and its associated disasters.

Apparent messages from the gods were interpreted by reading the patterns and cracks in the bone.

DIVINATION

RUNE CASTING

The casting of runic stones dates back to medieval times. The stones are cast onto a table or floor, and the ones that turn up— symbol side up—are read and interpreted according to the layout and the question or future outcome sought.

READING PATTERNS

There are numerous methods of oracular fortune telling that involve watching patterns in nature. These include a flock of birds flying past, ripples on water, smoke, and dripping candle wax, as well as the patterns of stars in the sky, and the observation of animal entrails, and of reflections in a mirror or water.

ORACULAR DIVINING

The future can be divined using a dowsing pendulum. This relies on the direction the pendulum moves, in response to specific questions. The four different possible swings usually correspond to each of the following responses: yes, no, don't know, try again.

ASTRONOMICAL CALENDAR
BABYLON, MESOPOTAMIA 1500 BCE

Demonstrates the Babylonian understanding of stellar movements

On these tablets, for each month, three stars were identified as rising and being visible immediately before dawn, following a period known as the "heliacal rising" when they could not be seen. Circular diagrams, or disks, were divided into twelve equal arcs by radial spokes (not unlike a modern horoscope), which represented the twelve months of the year. The disks were also divided horizontally into three zones, representing northern, central, and southern bands of the sky. The northern hemisphere pertained to the god Enlil, the equator belonged to the god Anu, and the southern hemisphere to Enki. The perimeters were at 17 degrees north and south, so that the sun spent precisely three consecutive months in each third.

The basic function of the Three Stars Each tablets was to tie each month to a specific astronomic event, such as the heliacal rising of chosen stars. Before 1000 BCE, these star maps did not show the yearly passage of the sun through the constellations of the zodiac, which had yet to be identified and named. However, some groups of stars had begun to be designated, such as the Pleiades, Orion, and the Great Bear. Although some Babylonian artifacts are inscribed with lions and scorpions and therefore may appear to refer to the constellations, awareness of the zodiac and its astronomical and astrological function lay in the future.

The Venus tablets and the Three Stars Each tablets reveal that the Babylonians had identified several dozen individual stars and charted their progress through the sky before 1000 BCE. They began the process of zoning the sky and recognized the complexity of the planetary paths. Despite being devoid of geometric paths, curves, and circles, the Babylonian system

An Assyrian star tablet (c. 650 BCE) in the Kuyunjik Collection, British Museum, London, is thought to be astro-magical in nature and may reveal an early form of divination.

Around 1500 BCE in Babylon, an early form of astronomical calendar began to emerge recorded on clay or stone tablets. These first tablets gave the movements and periods of visibility of the planet Venus, which were based on painstaking observations that had taken place over decades, usually from temple towers, or ziggurats, such as the Temple of Marduk in Babylon. Slightly later than the Venus tablets, probably dating from 1300 BCE, another group of texts giving star positions was produced. Confusingly, these texts are sometimes called astrolabes, but they are better known as Three Stars Each tablets.

charted and predicted many celestial positions centuries before Greek astronomy was born.

To the Babylonians, the planets were known as "gods of the night," and from this concept arose the correlation between the movement of the planets and humankind's actions. The stars did not issue irreversible decrees of fate, but omens, which if correctly interpreted would enable evil to be averted. In this way, the Babylonians believed that the gods were speaking to humankind, and the study of this language of the planets was the basis of ancient astrology. In the Tablet of Shamash (c. ninth century BCE), the sun god is seated on his throne holding the ring and rod of divine justice. The king is accompanied by two *ummanu* (omen advisers), and beneath the throne two *apkallu* (spirits) reveal divine wisdom to mankind.

Somewhere around the fifth century BCE, Babylonian astronomical texts began to describe the positions of the sun, moon, and planets in terms of twelve zodiacal constellations. This now provided the necessary mapping reference point, so that a star or planet could be described as being at 5 degrees Aries or 20 degrees Leo, and so on. The names of the constellations were used to describe a fixed, imaginary 30-degree section of the sky, but where did the names originate? Many theories

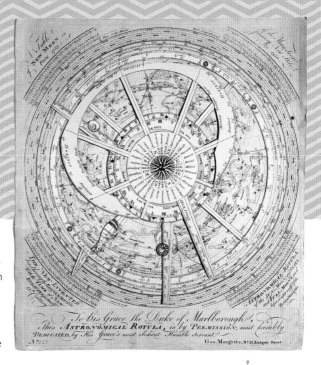

have been put forward, but it is most likely that the names of the constellations were drawn from significant cults or rituals embodied in the ancient gods, or from symbols in Mesopotamian myth in which gods were personified as half man, half animal. The lion, the goat, the fish, and so on may represent the ancient archetypes of these mythical creatures.

This astronomical calendar (1799), designed by George Margetts, could be used to predict events up to 6,000 years in the past or future.

This tablet records an auspicious moment for a Babylonian king. He is accompanied by two omen seers as they honor the sun god Shamash at the moment when Venus and the moon were in a favorable position in the sky.

ZODIAC SIGNS

ARIES

Represented by the ram and the first of the four fire signs, Aries is associated with impulsive energy, potency, and courage. Ruled by the planet Mars, people born under this sign are thought to be self-centered, independent, and strong willed. Aries is traditionally seen as a headstrong sign—act first and think about it later.

TAURUS

Taurus is a sign that represents the qualities of resilience and strength. It is one of the four earth signs, and people born under the sign are thought to be possessive and violent when roused, but also lazy, slow moving, and sensual. Taureans can be very concerned with material security, acquiring wealth wherever they can.

GEMINI

The twins of the zodiac symbolize the duality of life: light and dark, up and down, black and white, and so on. Gemini's character is thought to be versatile and communicative, but prone to rapid changes of mood and fluctuating energy levels. Those close to Geminis often feel as though they are living with at least two different people.

LIBRA

Libra is an air sign and it is the only zodiac sign that is represented by an inanimate object: the scales of balance and harmony. Libra is concerned with both justice and compromise. However, Libra's airy reputation for indecisiveness stems from a desire to evaluate everything so that a perfectly balanced judgment can be made.

SCORPIO

The "M"-like glyph of Scorpio, with an arrowlike tail, is said to represent the scorpion and its deadly sting. Intense and brooding, Scorpios have a reputation for revenge and a sting in the tail. The eighth sign of the zodiac, this most secretive of water signs is also associated with erotic passion, sex, death, and other taboo subjects.

SAGITTARIUS

Sagittarius is represented by a centaur (half man, half horse) and is a sign renowned for being restless and eager to gallop off in search of new horizons. The arrow represents ambitions, dreams, and hopes being shot into the air toward some fanciful target. People born under this sign are usually philosophical about life and able to see life from a giant perspective.

CANCER

The crab symbol reveals the sidelong approach and incredible tenacity associated with this sign. Traditionally, people born under Cancer have a hard outer shell to protect their inner vulnerable side. Cancerians are usually very emotional, and often clingy, but they are completely loyal when they find their soul mate.

LEO

With its obvious symbol of a lion, Leo is a feisty fire sign that is also as soft as a kitten. Leos are usually proud, graceful, sensual, and pleasure loving. However, like the king or queen of the cats, Leo people demand to be the best and the center of attention, otherwise they may roar loudly to get their own way.

VIRGO

The Virgin symbol is the only female figure in the zodiac. Earth sign Virgo is traditionally linked with health, hygiene, and all forms of service and healing. People born under the sign are often obsessed with their health, but they also have an incredible ability for unearthing the truth, and sifting through details and information.

CAPRICORN

Earth sign Capricorn is ruled by Saturn and the symbol is a goat. Traditionally, Capricorns are thought to act like domestic goats—forever tied to a rope, never venturing out of their field—or mountain goats that see opportunities and climb ever higher. Those born under the sign can be ruthlessly ambitious or fearful of change.

AQUARIUS

Aquarians think, talk, and analyze everything. They can be emotionally detached, but have strong feelings about justice and human rights. Aquarius is an airy, intellectual sign, and the water pouring from the jar symbolizes communication: the endless pouring out of mental energy and original ideas from the Aquarian personality.

PISCES

The symbol of two fish swimming in opposite directions represents the inner battle of the Pisces personality. One side longs for spiritual redemption, the other in need of personal achievement. The last sign of the zodiac, Pisces is often thought to contain all the other signs, itself an ocean filled with the identities of everyone else.

ELEUSINIAN MYSTERIES
GREECE *c.* 1500 BCE

A cycle of well-known sacred religious rites and ceremonies

This French engraving (1819), in the style of ancient Greek vases, depicts scenes and rituals from the secret initiation ceremonies of the Eleusinian Mysteries.

Among the secret religious rites of ancient Greece, one of the best known is the Eleusinian Mysteries. These were initiation ceremonies held every year for the cult of Demeter and Persephone, based at Eleusis. They were probably rooted in an old agrarian cult surrounding Demeter, which began in the Mycenaean period between 1600 and 1100 BCE.

The later dated mysteries were symbolic of the myth of Persephone's abduction by Hades, and her mother Demeter's search for her daughter and their subsequent reunion. They are made up of a three-phase cycle: the descent (the loss), the search, and the ascent of Persephone from the underworld and the reunion with her mother. One of the main symbols is the three-eared sheaf of wheat; it is not only a symbol of fertility, growth, and harvest, but also of descent, search, and ascent.

The rites, ceremonies, and beliefs of the Eleusinian Mysteries were kept secret, and the initiated believed that they would receive a reward in the afterlife, similar to the Orphic Mysteries. The mysteries involved trance states or altered states of consciousness. Priestesses would have visions, and initiates were required to be involved in the conjuring of spirits from the afterlife. Some scholars believe that the power and longevity of the Eleusinian Mysteries were based on the use of psychedelic and other hallucinogenic substances. The mysteries were intended to elevate man above the human sphere: to become a god or divine himself and thus be rewarded with immortality.

The relationship between Demeter and Persephone held the key to the whole Hellenic Greek philosophy of death and rebirth and the changing cycle of life and the seasons. In her grief for the loss of her daughter, Demeter ensured that all fertility was withheld on Earth, and all must suffer with her. It was only when the gods stepped in and decided that Persephone could stay six months with Hades in the underworld and then return to Earth for six months that she relented. In this sense, Demeter symbolized the power of passive aggression.

The myth was first recounted in the Homeric Hymns of around 650 BCE. According to the hymn, Demeter's daughter Persephone was gathering flowers with friends when she was seized by Hades, who took her to his underworld kingdom. Distraught, Demeter searched high and low for her daughter, and overcome with grief she stopped tending to the plants, which led to mass starvation. The gods were deprived of worship and sacrifice, and so Zeus allowed Persephone to return to Earth for the allotted time.

LESSER AND GREATER

The Lesser Eleusinian Mysteries were held once a year in the early spring during the month of flowers, known as the Anthesterion. Four categories of people participated in the Lesser Eleusinian Mysteries: priests, priestesses, hierophants (interpreters of sacred mysteries and usually high priests), and initiates. Only those initiated into the mystery knew what the *kiste*, a sacred chest, and the *kalathos*, a lidded basket, contained. The contents, like so many elements of the Eleusinian Mysteries, remain unknown. However, one researcher wrote that the *kiste* held a golden mystical serpent, an egg, and a phallus, as well as seeds that were sacred to Demeter.

In order to qualify for initiation, participants would sacrifice a piglet to Demeter and Persephone, and then ritually purify themselves in the River Illissos. Upon completion of the Lesser Eleusinian Mysteries, participants were deemed worthy of witnessing the Greater Eleusinian Mysteries. These were also held once a year, but every fourth year they were celebrated with greater pomp and splendor.

In 170 CE the Temple of Demeter in Eleusis was destroyed by the Sarmatians but it was rebuilt by Marcus Aurelius, who was then allowed to become the only lay person to enter the temple. As Christianity gained in popularity in the fourth and fifth centuries, the Eleusinian Mysteries' prestige began to fade. The last pagan emperor of Rome, Julian, attempted to restore the mysteries after he became the last emperor to be initiated into them. However, they were finally closed by Emperor Theodosius I in 392 CE, and the remaining secret participants and their temples were destroyed in 396 CE, when Alaric, king of the Goths, invaded Greece and desecrated the sacred sites. The mysteries later became a powerful source of inspiration to nineteenth-century Romantic artists, such as Evelyn de Morgan, who was drawn to the plight of Persephone and her mother, Demeter.

In *Return of Persephone* (1891) by Frederick Leighton, Persephone is taken to the upper world by Hermes to be reunited with her mother.

The sheaf was symbolic not only of fertility, growth, and harvest, but also of descent, search, and ascent.

EVIL EYE

GREECE c. seventh century BCE

A malevolent motif that causes harm and misfortune

This Roman mosaic, from the House of the Evil Eye, Antioch, shows an evil eye being attacked by powerful talismanic charms, such as a penis, snake, scorpion, dog, trident, and sword.

The evil eye is a malevolent glance or look from someone, and in many cultures it is believed to cause injury, bad luck, and misfortune for the person at whom it is directed. Throughout the world, talismans have been created to protect against the evil eye, and these are confusingly called evil eyes, too. The term also refers to the power attributed to certain individuals whose intention is to harm or curse another human being.

Belief in the evil eye dates back to the seventh century BCE in ancient Greece, and can be found in references among such authors as Hesiod, Plato, Plutarch, and Pliny the Elder. A cross-eyed or squinting person was almost universally feared, and anyone with eye defects was considered suspicious among Greek fishermen. Many Mediterranean and Asian tribes and cultures also believed in the evil eye, and charms and decorations featuring the eye are still a common sight across most of the Middle East, as well as in parts of the Aegean and Egypt, where they have become a popular choice of souvenir with tourists.

In the Roman period it was not only individuals who were considered to possess the power of the evil eye. Whole tribes, especially those of Pontus and Scythia, were believed to be transmitters, too. In an extraordinary second-century mosaic found in Antioch, the eye is pierced by a trident and sword, pecked by a raven, barked at by a dog, and attacked by a centipede, scorpion, cat, and a snake. A horned dwarf with a gigantic phallus crosses two sticks. The Greek letters "KAI SU," meaning "and you (too)," suggest this was a mosaic that was used to prevent a curse from the evil eye.

PHALLIC CHARMS

Phallic charms, often winged, were ubiquitous in Roman culture, from jewelry to bells and wind chimes to lamps. Known as fascinums, from the Latin word *fascinare*, meaning "to cast a spell," they were used against the evil eye. A graphic representation of the power of the fascinum to ward off the evil eye is found on a Roman mosaic depicting a phallus ejaculating into a disembodied eye. The motif also appears on multiple relief sculptures from Leptis Magna, now in present-day Libya, and a first-century BCE terra-cotta figure shows two small phallus-shaped men sawing an eyeball in half. The fascinum was thought to ward off evil particularly from children, mainly boys. Pliny notes the custom of hanging a phallic charm on a baby's neck, and examples have been found of phallus-bearing rings that are so small they must have been worn by children.

Disks or balls consisting of concentric blue and white circles (usually, from inside to outside, dark blue, light blue, white, dark blue) represent an evil eye and are common apotropaic talismans in the Middle East. They are also found on the prows of Mediterranean boats. In most traditions the talismanic evil eye supposedly reflects or redirects the malicious gaze back to the person who is intending to do harm. It is almost exclusively in the Near East that the talismanic power of a nazar, a form of reverse evil eye, is used to defend against envious looks containing destructive power. In North India, the evil eye is called buri nazar, and a charm bracelet, tattoo, or other object may be used to ward off the evil eye.

In Mexico and Central America, infants are considered to be at particular risk from the evil eye due to the envy of others, and they are often given an amulet bracelet as protection, typically with an eyelike spot painted on it. Another preventive measure is to allow admirers to touch the infant or child and thus reduce the envious intent. In a similar manner, a person wearing an item of clothing that might induce envy may suggest to others that they touch it in order to dispel envy.

One traditional cure in rural Mexico involves a healer who sweeps a raw chicken egg over the body of a victim to absorb the power of the person with the evil eye. The egg is later broken into a glass of water and placed under the bed of the afflicted. It is then checked, and if it seems as if the egg has been cooked, it means that the victim was cursed. Thanks to the supernatural powers of the healer, the evil eye has transferred to the egg and the victim immediately gets well.

In the Near East, a protective and deflective talisman eye, known as a nazar, is often worn as a pendant.

The evil eye symbol is well recognized across the world as a talisman to ward off evil.

PROTECTIVE AMULETS

HAND OF FATIMA

Commonly known as a hamsa, this palm-shaped amulet is popular throughout the Middle East and Africa. In Islam, it is named after Muhammad's daughter Fatima Zahra. A universal sign of protection, the image of the open right hand was first found as an amulet among Mesopotamian artifacts in the temples of Ishtar.

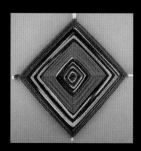

EYE OF GOD

In Mexico this protective amulet is weaved from colored yarn and wound around two sticks crossed at right angles. The eye of God is a magical object symbolic of the power to see and understand things unknown to the physical eye. It is also used to ward off the curse or apparent menace from anyone who casts the evil eye.

CIMARUTA

Commonly worn around the neck, this Italian folk amulet consists of a collection of charms attached to what is supposed to represent a sprig of rue, thought to have magical properties. The magic symbols often include a rose; a hand holding either a wand or a sword; a flaming heart; a fish; and a crescent moon.

CORNICELLO

An Italian amulet of good luck, the cornicello is also used to protect the wearer from the evil eye. The twisted horn-shaped charm is often made of gold, silver, or bone, and resembles the horn of an antelope. In some southern Italian regions, the amulet resembles a chilli pepper, which is indigenous to those regions.

OMAMORI

A traditional Shinto amulet, the omamori is a small brocade bag that usually contains a selection of papers or pieces of wood inscribed with prayers or religious invocations. The bag should never be opened in order to avoid losing its protective benefits. Amulets are replaced once a year to ward off bad luck from the previous year.

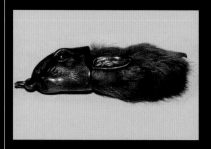

RABBIT'S FOOT

Popular in cultures worldwide, a rabbit's foot is worn or carried as an amulet for protection and good luck. It has been used in Europe since the seventh century BCE, and the Celtic people believed that for the charm to work, the rabbit must be killed in a particular place by a man with strange attributes, such as cross eyes or one leg.

MEZUZAH

The mezuzah is a small case containing a piece of paper with two verses from the Torah, and it must be attached to the entrances of all Jewish buildings. A powerful symbol of protection, it is customary for Jewish people to kiss or touch the container as they pass by. On the reverse side of the paper is the word "Shaddai," a coded name of God.

HANUMAN

Throughout Southeast Asia, Hanuman, the Hindu monkey-faced god, is worn as a protective amulet, usually in the form of a pendant. Hanuman temples are believed to keep the surrounding area free of evil beings and spirits, and his statues are often found on dangerous mountain roads to protect people from accidents.

HEI TIKI

This Maori decorative pendant is worn around the neck and is usually carved from pounamu, or sometimes from other green stones such as jade. The pendants are usually depictions and symbols of Tiki, the first man in Maori legend. Used as protective amulets, the hei tiki draw on the power of their first ancestors.

RED STRING

Associated with the mystical Kabbalah, Jewish people often wear a thin scarlet or crimson string to ward off misfortune and the evil eye. The red string is usually a simple wool thread, worn as a bracelet or band on the left wrist of the wearer. It is secured by knotting it seven times, and then sanctified with Hebrew blessings.

FASCINUM

In ancient Roman magic, the fascinum represented the divine phallus, and it was often used with spells to invoke the divine protection of the god Fascinus. It was also a remedy for envy and a protection from the evil eye. Phallic charms, often winged, were ubiquitous in Roman culture, and include jewelry, wind chimes, and lamps.

DEVIL-CHASING MEDAL

Also known as the Saint Benedict medal, this decoration is worn by Catholics as a protective amulet, and it is believed to have immense power against evil. Since the fifteenth century, the reverse side of the medal carries the Latin words *Vade retro santana*—"Step back satan"—and other magical formulae used to ward off evil.

BARESMAN

TADJIKISTAN fifth–fourth century BCE

Wand used for rituals, interpreting omens, and spell making

This gold votive plaque from fifth- or fourth-century BCE Persia depicts a magus holding his baresman.

The baresman is often made of a varying number of twigs, which represent different attributes needed in formal celebrations in Zoroastrian religion.

The baresman, also known as the barsom, is a sacred bundle of twigs that has been used as a ritual implement in Zoroastrian religious practices since ancient times. The baresman is thought to establish a connecting link between the physical world and the spiritual realms. When used as a magical wand, it is a conduit through which the archetypal principles manifest their presence, a receptor for spiritual power, and a conduit for channeling the power outward. It is considered to be one of the first magic wands and was later used for interpreting omens and making spells against curses.

In ancient Persia, the sticks or twigs in the baresman wand had a practical use and a deeper symbolic function, too. It is closely associated with ancient Zoroastrian healing practices, and many classical texts, rock carvings, and artifacts across all the known Zoroastrian regions depict magi carrying baresman bundles. Because of this iconography, the baresman became the principal identifying symbol of both the magi and the Zoroastrian faith, from Central Asia to the Pamirs.

Originally the twigs were taken from important healing plants, such as the pomegranate, myrtle, laurel, tamarisk, willow, and juniper. In religious ceremonies, the baresman bundle was placed on the Mah-rui (meaning moon-faced), a pair of metallic stands about 9 inches (23 cm) in height that resemble crescent moons.

In Zoroastrianism, the number of twigs used in the bundle varies according to the ceremony. The celebration of Yasna requires twenty-three twigs, of which twenty-one form a bundle. One twig is placed on the foot of the Mah-rui. This twig is called zorno tae, the twig of the saucer containing the zohr, or water. The twenty-third twig is placed on the saucer containing the jivam, a mixture of water and milk. The Vendidad ceremony requires thirty-five twigs, of which thirty-three form a bundle and the other two are used as described above. The celebration of the baj, in honor of the departed souls, uses five twigs. In the ceremony for the initiation into priesthood, the recital of the Mino Navarbaj requires seven twigs.

Today, the baresman comprises metal rods instead of twigs and it represents the vegetable creation and the Amesha Spena Amertat—

eternal life and an undying spirit—in Zoroastrian religious ceremonies and rituals. The qualities symbolized by the baresman include strength, good health, and overcoming disease.

In medieval magic texts, enhancing the wand's magic powers was achieved by using reinforcements that corresponded to the spell being cast. Semiprecious stones or herbal plants were employed to invoke the power of the planet associated with the wood used to make the wand. The trees believed to be infused with the most magical powers were the hazel, oak, laurel, poplar, and willow. For example, according to Renaissance occultist Cornelius Agrippa, the poplar tree was sacred to the planet Jupiter and by extension to the gemstones sapphire, emerald, and green jasper, whereas Jupiter's plants included basil, mint, and henbane. Originally, the baresman

In this bas-relief from Taq-e Bostan, Iran, the investiture of third-century Sassanid emperor Ardashir is accompanied by a priest with a baresman to sanctify the ritual.

MAGIC TOOLS

BANKISHI
The bankishi was used by shamans of the Luba people from the Democratic Republic of Congo. It has six heads to help the diviner see in all directions at once. An object with special powers, such as human bones or the hair of twins, was placed inside the bankishi.

ATHAME
An athame is a ceremonial dagger with a double-edged blade and usually a black handle. It is the main ritual implement among those used in the religion of Wicca and various other neopagan witchcraft traditions. It is often used to cast a magic circle and represents fire, one of the four elements invoked in spell casting.

CHALICE
The chalice is a symbol of universal creativity. In Wicca it is used as a feminine principle, usually in combination with the athame as the male principle. Combining the two evokes the act of procreation.

had been held ceremoniously in the right hand, and so similarly in medieval magic the wand was held in the right hand to invoke the spirits. It was grasped in the left hand when dismissing them.

Magic wands are also used in Wicca, in which it usually represents the element air, and by esoteric groups such as the Golden Dawn as well as in Kabbalistic traditions whose practice involves ceremonial magic. Wands are used for the channeling of cosmic or spiritual energy. They serve a similar purpose to the athame (ceremonial dagger) but the two have distinct uses. Although an athame is generally used to command, a wand is seen as an implement to invite or invoke. Traditionally made of wood, such as oak or hazel, they can also be made of metal or crystal.

The wand is most often used by modern pagans, witches, shamans, and others in rituals, healing, and spell casting. Some scholars believe that the magic wand may have originated as a phallic symbol or as the drumming stick of central Asian shamans, who used it to point on drums during healing and magical ceremonies.

The Mah-rui was a sacred stand on which the baresman was placed during and after ceremonies.

PETELIA TABLET

ITALY third–second century BCE

Small gold tablet that serves as a protective amulet

The gold Orphic Petelia tablet in the British Museum, London, guides the soul safely through the underworld to discover a secret spring where it would achieve immortality among the gods.

This tiny exquisite gold tablet was found near the ancient city of Petelia in southern Italy in the nineteenth century. Such tablets were regarded as a kind passport to the afterlife, similar to the Book of the Dead of ancient Egypt, and were placed on or near the body of the deceased. Sometimes they were rolled and inserted into a capsule and placed around the neck as a protective and guiding amulet. The Petelia tablet bears a mysterious Orphic inscription, which instructs the initiate on how to navigate the Greek underworld, ensuring the much promised rewards of a blissful afterlife in the Elysian Fields. The inscription reads:

"*Thou shalt find to the left of the house of Hades a well-spring, and by the side thereof standing a white cypress. To this well-spring approach not near. But thou shalt find another by the lake of memory, cold water flowing forth, and there are guardians before it. Say: 'I am a child of earth and of starry heaven; But my race is of Ouranos. This ye know yourselves. And lo, I am parched with thirst and I perish. Give me quickly the cold water flowing forth from the lake of memory.' And of themselves they will give thee to drink from the holy well-spring, And thereafter among the other heroes thou shalt have lordship.*"

Orphism was a Greek mystery religion based on literature ascribed to the mythical poet Orpheus, who descended to the underworld to save his lover Eurydice. The legendary musician was renowned for his ability to charm all living things, even stones, with his music. Orpheus was credited with the composition of the Orphic

Hymns, and shrines containing purported relics of Orpheus were regarded as oracles. A seer who practiced magical arts, Orpheus was even credited as being the harpist and companion of Jason and the Argonauts.

In Orphic cosmology, Time, who was also known as Aion, created the silver egg of the universe. Out of this egg burst Phanes, who gave birth to the universe. Some legends relate that Zeus later devoured Phanes to assume his primal cosmic power and redistribute it among a new generation of gods, the Olympians. Phanes was portrayed as a beautiful golden-winged hermaphroditic deity wrapped in a serpent's coils, and poets describe him as an incorporeal being, invisible even through the eyes of the gods.

ORPHEUS'S RETURN

The story of Orpheus's return from the underworld is at the core of the Orphic mysteries. When his lover, Eurydice, fell into a nest of vipers, she suffered a fatal bite on her heel. Orpheus, overcome with grief, played such sad and mournful songs that all the nymphs and gods wept. So Orpheus traveled to the underworld, and with his music persuaded Hades to agree to allow Eurydice to return with him to Earth. However, there was one condition. He must walk in front of her and not look back until they both had reached the upper world; if he looked back, Eurydice would disappear forever. Orpheus set off with Eurydice following him, but in his uncertainty that she was still behind him, he turned to look at her and she vanished forever.

From then on, Orpheus disdained the worship of all gods except Apollo. One early morning he went to the oracle of Dionysus to worship the sun, but was ripped to shreds by the frenzied female maenads for not honoring Dionysus. Orpheus's head floated down the river to the Mediterranean shore. There, the winds and waves carried it on to the island of Lesbos, where the inhabitants buried his head and a shrine was built in his honor.

It is speculated that the Orphic mystery cult regarded Orpheus as a parallel figure to or even an incarnation of Dionysus himself, due to their many similarities, such as their journeys into Hades and identical deaths. Orphics believed that human souls were divine and immortal but doomed to live in a cycle of reincarnation. By following an ascetic way of life, and performing secret initiation rites, there was a guarantee of not only eventual release from the "grievous circle" but also communion with the gods.

The Orpheus motif has permeated Western culture and has been used in most art forms, particularly in music by composers such as Joseph Haydn, Franz Liszt, and Igor Stravinsky, and in art by Pre-Raphaelite painter John William Waterhouse and Symbolist Gustave Moreau.

The Tears of Orpheus (c.1887) is one of several Orphic paintings by Symbolist Gustave Moreau.

Phanes burst from a cosmic egg to create the universe and wrapped himself in serpent coils.

SRI YANTRA
INDIA first century CE

Gives spiritual or magical benefit in the Tantra of Indian religions

First referred to in an Indonesian inscription in the seventh century, the sri yantra may have existed in India long before the time of its introduction to Indonesia.

Four isosceles triangles with the points upward represent Shiva, or the masculine. Five isosceles triangles with the apexes downward symbolize Shakti, or the feminine. In this way the sri yantra also represents the union of divine masculine and feminine. The triangles are enclosed by two rows of eight and sixteen petals, representing the lotus of creation and reproductive vital force. The broken lines of the outer frame denote the figure to be a sanctuary, with four openings to the regions of the universe. Together the nine triangles are interlaced in such a way as to form forty-three smaller triangles, in a web that is symbolic of the entire cosmos or a womb symbolic of creation. Together they express Advaita, or nonduality.

The term "sri" is used to denote the reverence to be given to this holy design. The prefix indicates that the yantra is auspicious, beneficent, salutary, benign, and conducive to prosperity. The sri yantra is often referred to as the chakra raja, which means "king of all chakra." This makes it a supreme instrument in the path of spiritual advancement, conceived as the perfect place for spiritual pilgrimage.

Wearing, depicting, or concentrating on the sri yantra gives spiritual or magical benefit in Hindu Tantric traditions. There is also a three-dimensional form, the meru chakra. This is made of rock crystal or metal, the latter of which is sometimes a traditional alloy of silver, antimony, copper, zinc, and pewter. This enhances the flow of its beneficial energies and is often covered in gold.

In the Shakta-based religion of Shri Vidya the goddess is supreme, transcending the cosmos that is her manifestation. She is worshipped in the form of the mystic sri yantra, which represents the goddess in her form as

The sri yantra (sacred instrument), also known as a sri chakra (sacred wheel), is a design formed by interlocking triangles that surround and radiate out from the central point, or bhindu, which represents the intersection between the physical universe and its numinous source. This beautiful and complex sacred design has been used for thousands of years as a mystical object of worship and meditation.

The geometric figure is composed of nine triangles, and every triangle is connected to the others by common points. The sri yantra is known to be difficult to draw correctly because changing the size or position of one triangle often requires changing the position of many other triangles.

HINDU NUMEROLOGY

Hindu numerology is called yantra, and it uses a combination of an individual's date of birth and their name to discover their destiny. Favorable omens, suspect traits to be avoided, and other aspects of the individual's personality can also be divined. The meaning of the numbers one to nine of this system correspond to the changing seasons, as well as to the progress of an individual's life. Zero represents bhindu, the central point of the sri yantra, and as such is not used.

1. Seed
2. Germination
3. Sprouting
4. Testing
5. Growth
6. Budding
7. Blossom
8. Fruit
9. Harvest

gradually increasing in size as they move outward toward the perimeter from the central point also symbolize the process of evolution and the growth of a human being's individual consciousness. As they move inward, they represent the process of growing toward the spiritual center.

In Tantric philosophy, once the complete state of evolution has been attained, the process must reverse and return to unity. Yantras are therefore symbols of this process of evolution and its opposite, involution, or the return to the source. The ancient mystical belief that the microcosm is reflected in the macrocosm is part of Tantric belief, too. This implies that the cosmos can be found within each individual, and, similarly, the principles that apply to the universe also apply to an individual.

In Tantra, the body is considered to be the most perfect and powerful of all yantras and it is seen as a tool for inner awareness. This means that every yantra contains not only a symbol of our spiritual pathway but also a universal one of outward growth and inward union with the divine. Most yantras are now also considered to be psychological symbols corresponding to inner states of human consciousness.

Yantras can take on many different evolving and geometrical forms, including triangles and lotus leaves, to create the sacred wheel.

Tripurasundari (beautiful goddess of the three cities). Tripursundari is also known as Shodashi, (sixteen), Rajarajesvari (queen of queens), and Lalita (she who plays).

YOGIC TANTRA

Many different types of yantras are used in yogic Tantra, and they are considered to be the equivalent of Buddhist mandalas. In Tantric philosophy, the universe is a manifestation of pure consciousness. The primary aspect of this is the masculine principle, Shiva, who has the power to be but not the power to change. The second aspect, Shakti, is feminine, dynamic, and energetic. Shakti is the great mother of the universe, and from her all form is created. Shiva is pure unity, and from this the explosive Shakti energy creates all that is the universe, seen as a continuous unfolding and shaped by the power of the female principle.

The central point of the yantra, known as the bhindu, represents the core of all manifestation—Shiva—from which everything emanates—Shakti. The shapes that are depicted

The Goddess Tripurasundari (nineteenth century) depicts the Indian "goddess of the three cities," worshipped in the form of the sri yantra.

MITHRAIC MYSTERIES
ITALY first century CE

A mystery religion that features seven grades of initiation

One of the most iconic images central to the Mithraic Mysteries is that of Mithras slaughtering a bull, depicted here in a fresco from Marino, Italy.

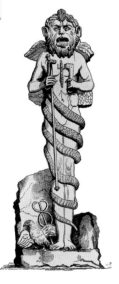

The leontocephaline is thought to be the keeper of the keys of the cosmos.

The Greeks were not the only ones to practice mystery religions, such as the Eleusinian Mysteries; the Romans had their own known as the Mithraic Mysteries, which were at their height between the first and fourth centuries CE. Originally an ancient Persian god, Mithra was known as Mithras among the Romans and was linked to a new and distinctive imagery.

The Romans regarded the mysteries as having Persian sources. However, contemporary scholarship has found no evidence of similarities between Persian Mithra worship and the Roman Mithraic Mysteries. The mysteries of Mithras are now generally seen as a distinct product of the Roman imperial religious world, and a rival to early Christianity.

Based in Rome, worshippers of Mithras had a complex system of seven grades of initiation. This included ritual meals, secret greetings,

and meetings in underground temples called mithraea. These still survive in large numbers across Europe, wherever the Roman Empire spread its wings. Numerous archaeological finds, including monuments and artifacts, have contributed to modern knowledge about Mithraism throughout the Roman Empire. Well-known scenes depicting Mithras include him being born from a rock, killing a bull, and attending a banquet with the god Sol.

One of the most characteristic features of the Mithraic Mysteries is the naked lion-headed (leontocephaline) figure often found in Mithraic temples. He is entwined by a serpent (or sometimes two) whose jaws often rest on the lion's head. It is believed that the serpents represent the cycles of life, planetary and solar cycles. The lion's expression is somewhat ghastly as his mouth is left open. The leontocephaline is commonly represented with four wings and holds two keys (sometimes a single key) and a scepter in his hands. The keys are the keys to the zodiac gates through which souls ascend and descend from boundless time. It seems that this curious and menacing beast is actually the keeper of the keys to the gates of cosmic eternity.

Sometimes the figure is standing on a globe inscribed with a diagonal cross; occasionally the four wings feature the symbols of the four seasons and a thunderbolt is engraved on the breast. Strange objects, such as the hammer and tongs of Vulcan, a cock, and the wand of Mercury, encircle the base of the statue.

Some scholars have suggested that the leontocephaline is a symbol of the initiate's baptism by "fire." This was in fact a baptism that used libations of honey, rather than water, and incense was burned nearby to symbolize fire. The statue was seen to preside over the temple, the lion representing the sun and therefore the source of all life.

GRADES OF INITIATION

St. Jerome listed the seven grades of initiation into the Mithraic Mysteries. A mosaic in the Mithraeum of Felicissimus in the Ostia district of Rome depicts these grades, with symbolic emblems connected to the grades or symbols of the planets. The grades also have an inscription besides them commending each grade into the protection of the different planetary gods.

In ascending order of importance the initiatory grades are Corax (raven or crow), whose symbol is a caduceus or beaker, protected by the planet and god Mercury. Next is the Bridesman; the symbol is a lamp, bell, or veil, and it is under the protection of Venus. The third is Miles (soldier), whose emblems are the helmet, lance, and breastplate, protected by Mars. Next is Leo, who is protected by Jupiter and whose symbols are the wreath, laurel, and thunderbolts.

The fifth grade is Perses (Persian) who is guarded by the moon and whose emblems

are the sling pouch, sickle, moon, stars, and Phyrigian cap. The sixth grade is known as Heliodromus (sun runner) and the emblems are the Helios whip, torch, and images of the sun, under the protection of the sun. The last grade is that of Pater, or father, who wears elaborate robes jewel-encrusted with metallic threads. The emblems include the cape, garnet or ruby ring, miter, and shepherd's staff.

The initiate into each grade was required to undertake a specific ordeal or test, perhaps involving exposure to heat, cold, or threatened danger. An "ordeal pit," dating to the early third century, has been identified in the mithraeum at Carrawburgh, Northumberland, England.

Around 400 mithraea have been found so far, and within the archaeological sites there is evidence of rituals associated with feasting. Eating utensils and food residues include animal bones, while cherry stones confirm mid summer (late June, early July) as a season associated with the festivities. The temples of Mithras were always built below ground, either excavated beneath Roman villas and then vaulted over, or converted from a natural cave. Mithraic temples were common throughout the Roman Empire, with considerable numbers found in Rome, Istria, Dalmatia, and Britain, as well as along the Rhine/Danube frontier.

The floor mosaic found in the Felicissimus Mithraeum near Rome depicts the various stages of initiation and associated symbols as the adept progresses toward the top grade.

Mithras was often depicted in sculpture as being born from a rock. In this version he is a fully grown man holding a dagger and torch.

MARY MAGDALENE

JERUSALEM, ISRAEL first century CE

Biblical figure who has become a complex symbol of femininity

The Penitent Magdalene (1635) by Guido Reni in the Walters Art Museum, Baltimore, USA, represents Mary in her more saintly guise.

The biblical story of Mary Magdalene is not only confusing and fragmented, but also very ambiguous, which is why it was so easy for the Church Fathers to portray her as a repentant sinner. Yet Mary Magdalene's mystique has become undeniably more than just a cultish following, because it seems probable that she was far more responsible for the teachings and following of Jesus than many believe. Indeed, many scholars have attempted to prove that

Mary was Jesus's wife or lover and also the power behind his own particular throne.

One document, believed to be written by Ermengaud of Beziers—undated and anonymous, but attached to his "Treatise against Heretics"—comments on the Cathars, who religiously endorsed Mary's involvement with Christ. "They teach in their secret meetings that Mary Magdalene was the wife of Christ. She was the Samaritan woman to whom He said, 'Call thy husband.' She was the woman taken into adultery, whom Christ set free lest the Jews stone her, and she was with Him in three places, in the temple, at the well, and in the garden. After the Resurrection, He appeared first to her." Recently, many conspiracy theories have developed about her real relationship to Jesus and whether in fact they had children. There is currently a belief that there is a Jesus and Mary Magdalene bloodline, and their descendants are in existence today.

The small town of Saint-Maximin-la-Sainte-Baume became a center for pilgrims in the late thirteenth century when it was claimed that Mary Magdalene's sarcophagus had been found in the basilica's crypt. Her apparent relics are still preserved there, most notably her skull, which is on display. The basilica attracts thousands of pilgrims each year, many of whom also visit the caves, high in the mountains, where Mary Magdalene is said to have retired.

A late medieval sculpture in lime wood by early sixteenth-century German sculptor Gregor Erhart depicts Mary as sensual, mystical, and striking. Not only does it reveal her spiritual grace and mysticism, but this late Gothic work is also leaning toward an Early Renaissance ideal of the sensual female body. This is particularly noteworthy in the portrayal of Mary's hair: its length, fullness, and golden color, as well as the way in which it covers just enough of the figure to guard her full nakedness. The sculpture represents Mary as the self-denying mystic who went to live in a lonely cave high in the Sainte-Baume mountain range. According to legend, while there she was clothed only by her hair.

The legend also relates that after being persecuted in the Holy Lands, along with her brother, Lazarus, and some other of Jesus's disciples, Mary led the group across the Mediterranean Sea in a tiny boat. Miraculously, they arrived at the tiny fishing village of Saintes-Maries-de-la-Mer, on the French coast, and made their way to Massilia (Marseilles) where they continued their evangelical work, converting most of Provence to Christianity. For the last thirty years of her life, according to Christian legend, Mary lived a secluded life like a hermit, repenting for her sins. Every day in her cave, she would be raised up to the sky by angels to hear the heavenly chorus.

Erhart's statue can be seen in the Louvre Museum in Paris, but originally it was held up by angels inside a metal structure and suspended from the ceiling of the Dominican Convent in Augsburg, Germany, where the artist lived. It is an exquisite symbol of all that Mary Magdalene, as a woman, could be: the archetypal female as lover, mother, whore, and virgin. It is this complex symbol of femininity that artists have attempted to capture throughout history.

Indeed, humankind has projected many qualities, both good and bad, onto female figures such as Mary Magdalene, goddesses

This sixteenth-century wooden statue of Mary by Gregor Erhart in the Louvre, Paris, combines her naked piety with the sensual beauty of woman.

such as Aphrodite and Lilith, and more recently icons of the modern world, such as Mata Hari and Marilyn Monroe. They have embodied ambivalent qualities: positive one moment and negative the next; sometimes virgin, sometimes lover, sometimes mother. This archetypal feminine was called the "anima" by Swiss psychologist Carl Jung, while the archetypal masculine he dubbed the "animus." Jung saw through history and mythology how a woman could be a saint or a whore, or both. This femme fatale has permeated art, literature, cinema, and human relationships to such an extent that, even today, the feminine can be considered both nurturing and destructive in our collective unconscious.

Mary Magdalene's relics are thought to lie in this fourth–fifth-century sarcophagus in the Basilica of Mary Magdalene, Saint-Maximin-la-Sainte-Baume, France.

ISTABY RUNESTONE
BLEKINGE, SWEDEN 550–790

Early runic inscriptions used for divination purposes

The Istaby Runestone, one of the finest examples of a standing stone in Sweden, is covered with runic inscriptions, probably in honor of a certain warrior and his descendants.

Runes are secret codes. In fact the word "rune" is rooted in an old Gothic word "runa," which means mystery. The earliest Germanic tribes first used runes to enhance their magical powers or to invoke the gods. They were later adopted by the Vikings, and the fierce Norse warriors, or "berserkers," carved runes on their swords before going into battle. They believed that the language of the gods would make them invincible. Runes were also often carved on large pillar stones, called standing stones, to warn travelers of the power of that particular place. Many people carved runes on their personal items, such as combs, boxes, and jewelry as well as on their homes as protective talismans. Many large standing stones found in Northern Europe have magical runic riddles, love spells, and incantations engraved on them to ward off evil or to help travelers on their way.

The oldest surviving Danish rune stone is known as the Istaby Runestone. It was found at Blekinge, now part of Sweden, and the inscription reads: "In memory of Hariwolfafr. Hathuwolafr, son of Haeruwulfafr, cut these runes." Blekinge is an important runic site and contains four stones that make reference to rune magic and the use of charms. One stone is inscribed with runes that reveal "He who breaks these stones will suffer by the hidden forces of rune magic."

Roman historian Tacitus wrote that the Germanic races attached the highest importance to casting lots and divining the future. He reported how they cut off branches from nut-bearing trees, slicing them into strips. The strips were marked with different signs and were thrown at random onto a white cloth. The priest or diviner then offered prayer to the gods, looked up to heaven, and picked up three strips one at a time. According to the signs they were marked with, the diviner then made his interpretation. The fact that the runes were each given meaningful names confirms that they had some magical significance long before they emerged as an alphabet for records and messages.

The twenty-four symbolic runes are divided into three groups, each credited with special powers. Each group was named after a Norse god: Freyr, Heimdall, and Tyr. Freyr was the goddess of fertility, Heimdall the guardian of the gods, and Tyr the god of war. In Norse legend, the warrior god Odin, seeking wisdom and understanding of life and death, fasted with neither food nor water. Hanging for nine days and nights upside down on Yggdrasil, the tree of knowledge, his experience gave him knowledge of the runes. From that time on, aided by Viking travels, the understanding of runes spread throughout the world.

The runes in general use today are from the Elder Futhark. This runic alphabet was made up from the symbols most commonly used in Northern Europe. The names of the runes are believed to be rooted in the Proto-Indo-European language, which developed among the tribes who lived in the steppes of

Eastern Europe, on the borders of the Indian subcontinent. These days runes are still used as a popular form of divination. Often, they are placed in a small pouch or bag and cast into the middle of a circle, or sometimes a certain number are simply taken from the pouch, one at a time, and placed in a specific layout as an oracle for self-development.

This twelfth-century tapestry from Skog Church, Halsingland, Sweden, depicts the three important Norse gods— Odin, Thor, and Freyr— symbolized in the runes.

SYMBOLIC MEANING OF RUNIC GLYPHS

ᚠ Fehu – Abundance	✳ Hagall – Delay	↑ Tir – Competition
ᚢ Uruz – Strength	ᛏ Nied – Need	ᗷ Beorc – New beginnings
ᚦ Thurisaz – Challenge	ᛁ Isa – Standstill	ᛗ Ehwaz – Progress
ᚨ Ansuz – Messages	◇ Jera – Harvest	ᛘ Mannaz – Self-acceptance
ᚱ Raidho – Journey	ᛇ Eihwaz – Decisive action	ᚴ Lagaz – Intuition
ᚲ Kenaz – Clarity	ᛕ Perth – Secret	ᛝ Ing – Accomplishment
✕ Gebo – Relationship	ᛉ Elhaz – Self-control	ᛞ Daeg – Light
ᚹ Wunjo – Success	ᛋ Sigel – Vitality	ᛟ Othel – Possession

This Norse symbol for the triad of Odin, Thor, and Freyr is surrounded by a circle of runes.

EMERALD TABLET

EASTERN MEDITERRANEAN sixth–eighth century

Thought to reveal the key to immortality

TABULA SMARAGDINA HERMETIS.

VERBA SECRETORUM HERMETIS.

The Emerald Tablet has been one of the key texts influencing most of Western esoteric magic, astrology, and mysticism.

According to Hermes Trismegistus, a legendary prophet whose name is a combination of the Greek god, Hermes, and Thoth, the Egyptian god of writing, magic, and knowledge, the Emerald Tablet revealed not only the secret of transforming lead into gold, but also, on a deeper level, the transmigration of the soul and the key to immortality. The cryptic work is also known as the Smaragdine Table, or Tabula Smaragdina, and influential physicians such as Isaac Newton and Robert Fludd, as well as Hermetic magi, astrologers, and Rosicrucians, followed its central philosophy of "as above, so below." The Emerald Tablet was highly regarded by European alchemists as the foundation of their art and as a bible for the Hermetic tradition.

Despite the claims that the Emerald Tablet dates back to before antiquity, it is now believed to be an Arabic work written between the sixth and eighth centuries CE. The oldest documentable source of the text is the *Kitab Sirr al-Khaliqa* (*Book of the Secret of Creation and the Art of Nature*), itself a composite of earlier works. It is attributed to the eighth-century CE mystic Balinas, also known as Apollonius of Tyana, who describes the Emerald Tablet as a wondrous piece of ancient Hermetic wisdom. Balinas also describes how he discovered the text in a vault below a statue of Hermes in Tyana. Inside the vault, an old corpse on a golden throne held the Emerald Tablet.

The tablet was first translated into Latin in the twelfth century by Hugo von Santalla. The text also appears in an enlarged thirteenth-century edition of *Secretum Secretorum* (*Book of the Secret of Secrets*), known as *Kitab Sirr al-Asrar*. A well-known translation by Isaac Newton was discovered among his alchemical documents, and this is currently kept in King's College Library, Cambridge, England. Numerous translations, interpretations, and commentaries have followed since, but the location and source of the original tablet or document are unknown.

The layers of meaning symbolized in the words of the Emerald Tablet have been associated with the creation of the philosopher's stone, the alchemical *magnum opus* (great work) and the correspondence between microcosm and macrocosm. Indeed, the tablet became a mainstay of medieval and Renaissance alchemy. Commentaries or translations were published not only by Newton but also by Trithemius, Roger Bacon, and Albertus Magnus among others. Trithemius equated Hermes's "one thing" with the world soul. This interpretation of the Hermetic text was adopted by alchemists

NEWTON'S TRANSLATION

Tis true without lying, certain & most true.

That which is below is like that which is above & that which is above is like that which is below to do the miracles of one only thing

And as all things have been & arose from one by the mediation of one: so all things have their birth from this one thing by adaptation.

The Sun is its father, the moon its mother, the wind hath carried it in its belly, the earth is its nurse.

The father of all perfection in the whole world is here.

Its force or power is entire if it be converted into earth.

Separate thou the earth from the fire, the subtle from the gross sweetly with great industry.

It ascends from the earth to the heaven & again it descends to the earth & receives the force of things superior & inferior.

By this means you shall have the glory of the whole world

& thereby all obscurity shall fly from you.

Its force is above all force. For it vanquishes every subtle thing & penetrates every solid thing.

So was the world created.

From this are & do come admirable adaptations whereof the means (or process) is here in this. Hence I am called Hermes Trismegist, having the three parts of the philosophy of the whole world

That which I have said of the operation of the Sun is accomplished & ended.

texts of Hermetic writings, which include the *Corpus Hermetica*, a collection of mysterious texts that reveal the secret wisdom of Hermes Trismegistus, the "thrice great." The *Corpus Hermetica* reveals the secret techniques, usually magical spells and invocations, for controlling and manipulating nature and the stars. The works are presented in a form in which Hermes Trismegistus teaches a puzzled initiate secret wisdom. The three parts of this wisdom or philosophy, which are alluded to at the end of the Emerald Tablet's text, are alchemy, astrology, and theurgy, the last being a ritual to invoke the power of the gods.

Although Hermeticism was driven underground by the Inquisition, most Western esoteric traditions are rooted in its philosophy. In the nineteenth century, Hermetic magic was revived in the light of a new interest in spiritualism and it was practiced by groups such as the Hermetic Order of the Golden Dawn. It was also hugely influential on Rosicrucianism and Freemasonry.

This floor mosaic at Siena Cathedral, Italy, depicts Hermes Trismegistus dressed in magician's robes, revealing to students the secrets of his thrice great wisdom.

such as John Dee, Agrippa, and Gerhard Dorn. The popularity of the Emerald Tablet is long-standing, making it the only real piece of non-Greek Hermetica, or wisdom texts, to attract widespread attention in the West.

The original text, which many believe will remain hidden until "mankind is ready" to discover its true location, is thought to have been inscribed on a large flat emerald or on green jasper stone. It is one of the major

ANTIMONY

Antimony resembles metal in its appearance and physical properties, but does not chemically react as such. By extension, this alchemy symbol represents animal tendencies found in humankind, or the wild nature in all of us. Traditionally, alchemists used this symbol to remind them of the instinctive animal power that dwells within.

ARSENIC

Arsenic is a chemical, poisonous metalloid, and its compounds are used as pesticides, herbicides, insecticides, and various alloys. The symbol for arsenic was used for medicinal and magical cures. A compound of arsenic and sulfur was said to induce trances of enlightenment and philosophical brain power.

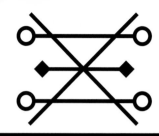

COPPER

Copper is a reddish colored metal, seen in artifacts dating back to 8700 BCE. The metal was associated with the goddess Aphrodite in Cyprus, where it was found in huge quantities, and its symbol is also the planetary symbol for Venus. Alchemical copper invokes love, balance, feminine beauty, and artistic creativity.

MAGNESIUM

Magnesium is a strong, silvery-white, lightweight element (one-third lighter than aluminum) that slightly tarnishes when exposed to air. Once ignited, magnesium is very difficult to extinguish. It is this property that associates this alchemy symbol with eternity, the infinity of the soul, and spiritual ascension.

PHOSPHORUS

This nonmetal substance, which glows in the dark from a source of light within itself, ignites spontaneously upon exposure to air and caught the imagination of seventeenth-century alchemists when it was first discovered. It seemed mysterious, magical, and filled with wondrous possibilities, and it was seen to be "the vital flame of life."

SILVER

In alchemy silver, along with lead, is often used as *prima materia* at the inception of a work. The alchemy symbol of silver is associated with the moon, and it also represents femininity, intuition, inner wisdom, and contemplation. It is believed that profound artistic expression can be harnessed by using the symbol as a talisman.

GOLD

Shiny, heavy, malleable, and very soft, gold is one of the most prized elements in the world. It represents perfection in all matter and on every level. It also symbolizes humankind's goal to obtain perfection in mind and spirit. For the medieval alchemist, transmuting "lead" into "gold" was not only a physical act, but also a spiritual one.

IRON

Iron is believed to be the tenth most abundant element in the universe. It represents the planet Mars in astrology. As such, iron rules physical strength and symbolizes predominantly male energy. In occult circles, iron represents a need to temper animal urges while at the same embracing the fire within.

LEAD

Lead is a dense, soft, highly malleable, bluish-white metal and it is highly resistant to corrosion. As an alchemy symbol, lead is the ruler of the dark *prima materia*, the first or base matter in the alchemical opus. It is associated with the planet Saturn and with the challenge of transforming this base material into gold.

SULFUR

Sulfur is an essential element for life. Also considered a transcendent alchemy symbol, it represents the multiplicity of human nature and the eternal aspiration to reach enlightenment. It also represents the triad of the sacred trinity. Sulfur is considered one of the three heavenly substances, along with salt and mercury.

TIN

Tin is ruled by Jupiter and is symbolic of the breath of life. When used alone as a symbol, it is weaker than if it is combined with another alchemy symbol. This reveals how the individual alchemist needs to call on many different powers to help him reach the goal of enlightenment, because he cannot do it alone.

AQUA VITAE

The "water of life," usually made from an alcoholic distillation of wine, can also be said to be the water "with life" or "with spirit" inside it. This is an allusion to the individual human being, who is mostly made up of water but is imbued with spirit. It represents the dweller in the innermost who we need to find.

DAKINI
INDIA c. ninth century

A female spirit whose positive aspect brings pleasure and spirituality

This nineteenth-century temple banner shows the dakini dancing, adorned with her skull necklace.

Dakini is a Sanskrit word meaning "sky dancer," and originally a dakini was a female spirit of ancient India who carried the souls of the dead to the sky. According to legend, a dakini also had the power to instantly seduce a mortal with her gaze. With her volatile temperament, a dakini can be likened to spirits, psychopomps, and angels who test a practitioner's awareness and adherence to Buddhist Tantric belief, either through temptation or seduction.

Dakini temples flourished in India from the ninth to the twelfth centuries. Erected in remote places, especially on hilltops, the temples were circular enclosures open to the sky. Around the inner circumference were sixty-four niches that housed exquisite stone carvings representing various aspects of Mother Goddess energy. They created a circular mandala around a central image of Shiva, who was the symbol of cosmic consciousness and the focus of yogic discipline.

Most depictions of dakinis show a young, naked figure in a dancing posture, holding a skull cup filled with menstrual blood, or the elixir of life in one hand and a curved knife in the other. She often wears a garland of human skulls, with a trident staff leaning against her shoulder. Her hair is usually wild and hanging down her back. Dancing on top of a corpse, she symbolizes her complete mastery over ego and ignorance. Practitioners often claim to hear the clacking of bone adornments as the dakini dances.

The dakini's dark aspect is depicted by her necklace of skulls; her peaceful aspect is depicted by the lotus frond. Dakinis are not only objects of desire but also carriers of the cosmic energies, bringing both pleasure and spirituality. As inspirational messengers, they were sent to tempt the Tantric initiate away from an ego-centered life and to aspire to a pathway of spirituality. If the apprentice proved his worth against the dakini, he would become a Tantric master, and be elevated into the paradise of the dakinis, a place of enlightened bliss. The depiction of dakinis as beautiful and naked tested the yoga master's control over his sexual desires. The practice of Tantric sex involved a symbolic, imagined, or real-life dakini; the last was usually a woman trained in Tantric yoga.

In Tantra, sex has three distinct purposes: procreation, pleasure, and liberation. Those seeking liberation overcome orgasm in favor of a higher form of ecstasy. Sexual rituals are recommended and practiced, involving elaborate preparatory and purification rites. The sexual act balances cosmic energy in the bodies of both participants, culminating in each individual's personality and identity being dissolved in the divine. Tantrics understand these acts on multiple levels. The male and female participants are conjoined physically, representing the merger of Shiva and Shakti (the male and female principles). This fusion results in a unified energy field; on an individual level, each participant experiences a fusion of their Shiva and Shakti energies, too.

BEDROOM ARTS

The ancient Taoists were proficient in what they called the bedroom arts. These practices, known as "Joining Energy" or "The Joining of the Essence," were used by practitioners for good health, and in an attempt to attain longevity.

A Taoist text titled "Health Benefits of the Bedchamber" indicates that certain times were better for intercourse than others. A person had to avoid intercourse on quarter or full moons and on days when there were great winds, rain, fog, cold or heat, thunder, lightning, darkness over heaven and earth, solar and lunar eclipses, rainbows, and earthquakes. Having intercourse at these times would harm a man's spirit and would cause women to become ill. Children conceived at these times would be mad, stupid, perverse, mute, deaf, crippled, or violent.

The location for having sex was also important. People had to avoid the glare of the sun, moon, or stars; the interior of shrines; proximity to temples, wells, stoves, and privies; and the vicinity of graves and coffins.

Taoist practitioners were encouraged to not limit themselves to one woman, and were advised to have sex only with the woman who was beautiful. While the man had to please the woman sexually, she was still considered an object. In ancient texts, the woman is often referred to as the "enemy." This was because the woman could cause the practitioner to spill semen and lose vitality.

A terrifying clay figurine at the British Museum, London, known as the "dakini of all the Buddhas," holds a dagger and a skull cup filled with blood, symbols of her power to destroy evil and ignorance.

POINT ZERO
PARIS, FRANCE twelfth century

Spot where the mysterious statue of Monsieur Legris once stood

The **Point Zero** plaque beside the Louvre in Paris is considered a lucky place to stand and make a wish. It is the exact spot where a mystifying statue once stood.

On the ground of the Place du Parvis in Paris, in front of Notre-Dame Cathedral, 16 feet (5 m) or so directly west from the cathedral's left-hand portal, is a brass plaque titled "Point zero des routes de France": the point zero of French routes. Laid into the paving stone in 1924, by the Commission du Vieux Paris, it marks the point from which all distances in France are measured from this exact center of the country's capital city.

The point zero plaque is considered a lucky place to make a wish. Couples stand here to kiss; others dance under the full moon or bless every destination measured from this spot. There is also a belief that if you stand on this spot as a tourist, it means you are going to return to Paris. Yet there is more to this simple marker than meets the eye.

Until the eighteenth century, a mysterious statue stood at this very spot. No one knows when it first appeared in the square, but it dated from the pre-Roman period. During the twelfth and thirteenth centuries, as the construction of Notre-Dame Cathedral mounted stone by stone, people called the statue Monsieur Legris. The origin of the name is not clear, but *le gris* means "the gray." Most scholars believe this name was used because erosion and pollution had given the stone a gray appearance.

In medieval days, the cathedral was surrounded by narrow courtyards, wooden houses, and gabled buildings dotted with chimneys and weather vanes. There were tiny shops among the medieval tangle of timber-frame cottages packed together tightly like a deck of cards. The timber-frame houses had carved beams and niches on each corner of the street where religious statues were placed.

The statue of Monsieur Legris was placed upon a stone column attached to the end of a block of shops. It was of a man or god holding a book and accompanied by a serpent. Over the years, the stone was so weathered that the figure was barely recognizable. The local people would tell pilgrims who were trying to find their way out of the web of streets that Monsieur Legris would show them the way, and then point to the disfigured statue.

Historians and scholars have suggested various identifications for the statue. Some say it was Hercules or Aesclepius, the Greek god of medicine. Others proffered Jesus Christ, the Danish Catholic saint Guillaume de Paris, the patron saint of Paris St. Genevieve, and the Roman god of boundary stones and journey endings Terminus. Another contender was Mercury, the god of travel and trade.

The Hermeticists believed the statue to be of philosopher Hermes Trismegistus, who was thought to have knowledge of everything in the universe. The Hermeticists created a secret way of transferring this divine knowledge through a rich imagery of symbols and alchemical metaphors. For alchemists, gray signified fire, one of the five elements and part of the alchemical process for achieving divine knowledge. The statue was also known as Maitre Pierre, a term that to the alchemists referred to the philosopher's stone, the key to divine union.

In 1625, a Roman inscription found on the statue was re-etched in Latin into the fountain, "Approach those of you who are altered, and if by chance my waters are not enough, go to the temple, and the goddess you invoke will prepare eternal waters for you." During the seventeenth century, Monsieur Legris was also known as the "Vendeur des Jeunes," which means a seller of fasts. This inscription may be a simple Christian reminder of the need to fast and to pray, or to go into the cathedral and devote yourself to the Virgin Mary.

A politically satirical pamphlet published in 1649 by the anti-Royalists, when the young Louis XIV was under the wing of the corrupt Cardinal Mazarin, was titled "An oracle given by the Faster of Notre-Dame," and it listed all the remedies needed to "cure" the country of its cardinals and kings. Maybe this statue was once an oracle for messages from the gods, too?

The statue was destroyed in 1748, when it was decided to enlarge the square and demolish many of the houses. It was replaced by a triangular marker with the emblem of Notre-Dame at its center. At the time, during the ongoing War of Austrian Succession (1740–1748), it became the "zero point" for measuring distances to the network of military outposts and camps along a series of milestones (approximately every 1.2 miles/2 km) from this central point in Paris.

Monsieur Legris was identified as an oracle, messenger, and alchemist, as well as the hero Hercules and the Roman god Terminus.

CELESTIAL ASTROLABE
IRAN 1144

Used by astrologers to calculate horoscopes

This celestial globe, believed to be from Isfahan, Iran, and dated 1144, is the third oldest surviving one in the world.

In the medieval period, Islamic astrologers were also astronomers, and two-dimensional, or flattened astrolabes became highly popular devices for calculating a horoscope, saving the astrologer many hours' calculation of the celestial positions.

The fashion for astrology in the Middle East began in the Sasanian city of Harran, in northwest Mesopotamia. Harran was an important center for mysticism, Hermetic philosophy, astrology, and magic, and continued to influence Western magic traditions right through the Renaissance. The scholars of

Harran were also the last custodians of the Mandaean cult, a pre-Islamic religion of the Middle East that involved star worship. They resisted both Christianity and Islam until the eleventh century, and adopted Hermes as their prophet, identifying him with Idris in the Koran.

Islam embraced astrology quite fervently, mostly because of the Islamic doctrine of Tawhid, which equates the oneness of God with the wholeness of wisdom. By the thirteenth century, Islamic scholars had merged pagan astrology with philosophical foundation, and the astrolabe became the visible symbol of the astrologer's or astronomer's skill. Much of the information was derived from ancient Greco-Egyptian mathematician and astrologer Ptolemy, but Islamic astrologers built up their own corpus of techniques and observations.

Among medieval Islamic astrologers, a myth grew that Ptolemy had discovered the astrolabe by accident. When out riding one day on his horse, he carried with him a small celestial globe made of brass, which he dropped. His horse trampled it flat, and this became the first two-dimensional astrolabe. The attribution to Ptolemy is probably correct, although the details may be flawed. Although the theory for projecting a celestial sphere onto a plane surface was well known to Ptolemy, there is no evidence of any instruments of this kind being made during this period in Hellenic Egypt.

EARLY ASTROLABE

Engraved in bronze and inlaid with silver, this rare spherical astrolabe (opposite) is a three-dimensional model of the universe, used for observation and measurement by astrologers, navigators, and astronomers. It shows the forty-eight constellations as identified by Ptolemy in Alexandria in the first century. The 1,025 stars are represented by silver dots that vary in size according to the observed brightness of each one. It is signed "Yunus b.al-Husayn al-Asturlabi," and the inscription states that Yunus recalculated the coordinates taking into account the lapse of time between Ptolemy's work and his own. Scientifically based in mathematical astronomy, beautifully crafted in metal, and a superb model of the heavens, the spherical astrolabe was not only a symbol of the known universe, but also a visible symbol of the process by which classical science and astrology were developed by Islamic scholars and eventually transmitted to the West.

Islamic philosopher al-Kindi merged Hellenistic concepts with Islamic thought. His work *On Rays* supported the principles of magic and how the rays of cosmic energy could effect other things, for example the astrological

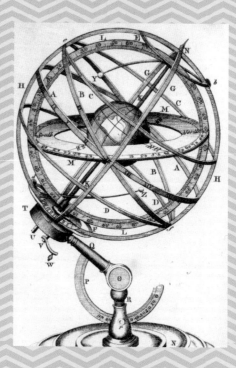

Armillary spheres consist of a framework of rings surrounding the Earth, representing astronomical features such as lines of celestial longitude.

power of the planets. He believed that if anyone acquired the knowledge of celestial harmony, they would know the past, present, and future. So it was hardly surprising that Islamic astrologers were devoted to learning everything about the heavens, and astrolabes were the means by which the sky could be mapped.

Before long, astrologers began to be employed by military leaders because the old star catalogues and documents needed to calculate the likely outcome of a battle were time-consuming and fragile in the midst of battle. However, the astrolabe was a masterly device, which could be taken onto the field and observed on horseback by the astrologer to determine the outcome of the conflict.

Western knowledge of the astrolabe entered Europe via Spain in the eleventh century. In the fifteenth century, French instrument maker Jean Fusoris started selling astrolabes in his shop in Paris, along with portable sundials and other scientific gadgets of the day. In fact the astrolabe was the probable precursor of the astronomical clock, a well-known example of which can be seen in Old Town Square in Prague, Czech Republic.

The planisphere, or flat astrolabe, eventually replaced the celestial globe because it could be transported easily.

ZODIAC CIRCLE
FLORENCE, ITALY 1207

A marble floor zodiac that is a symbol of the dawn of a new age

Not just a decorative embellishment of monthly associations and zodiac signs, San Miniato's floor zodiac has a deeper secret encoded in its setting.

The sign of Taurus is aligned directly with the rising sun, revealing the start of a new age.

The floor zodiac, marble pavement, pulpit, and decorative carvings at San Miniato Basilica, Florence, were all constructed by a team of mysterious stonemasons, including one who left the inscription "Joseph." Pagan and Christian symbols also adorn the stone doorways, facades, and walls of the basilica. However, the apparent jumble of unusual motifs is centered around the marble zodiac and its accompanying inscription, which states the time, date, and names of the planets involved with the stellium. However, it also contains a coded message with many layers of hidden meanings: for example, one interpretation is that the symbolic nature of the basilica acts as a doorway between the divine world and the mundane world.

Most medieval churches were built on an east–west orientation, complying with the image of a solar Christ who took over the role of pagan sun deities and their daily east to west journey through the heavens. Unlike other medieval churches, San Miniato is on a peculiar northwest–southeast axis. Although the church is not aligned to the rising sun, the zodiac circle, and specifically the sign of Taurus, is in perfect alignment. Moreover, it is the Taurean symbol of permanence and endurance that is alluded to in the coded text.

More than 10 feet (3 m) in length, the inscription is a complex system of medieval codes. On May 28, 1207, according to medieval astronomers, a group of planets was seen to be clustered together in the constellation known as Taurus, rising in the dawn sky. This particular stellium in Taurus was predicted not to appear again for thousands of years. In fact, the date recorded in the inscription by the stonemason refers not only to the date of the completion of his masterpiece, but also to the exact date of this unusual astronomical event. More importantly, it reveals that the Taurus astrological alignment of that day marks the beginning of a new age, and the marble zodiac is in fact a symbol of this new cycle.

In the early thirteenth century, belief in Italian theologian Joachim di Fiore's, prediction of the coming of the Antichrist and the end of the world was widespread, causing much fear and misery. The Taurus alignment in the heavens was a sign that, far from being the end of the world, it was the beginning of something enduring and eternal. In addition, the new cycle would reveal a secret truth to those initiated into the esoteric world that it was time to venerate the healing power of the sun. It is this secret that is yet to be deciphered in the marble inlays and walls of the San Miniato Basilica.

Some accounts say that Joseph and the other stonemasons were part of an esoteric group, who knew of the Christian Kabbalah and the mysteries of ancient Egyptian wisdom. One legend tells of how one morning in 1207—at the height of the belief in the coming of the Antichrist and the end of the world—as the sun rose over Florence, Joseph rubbed away the dust from the Latin inscription he had been carving in the marble floor of the basilica. As the stonemason stood up, pleased that his work was finished, the sun streamed diagonally across the nave from the east window. The brilliant rays shone directly into the center of the exquisite marble zodiac circle he had sculpted some months before. The new dawn heralded not the end of the world, but a new beginning.

OTHER ZODIAC EXAMPLES

In many Christian churches and cathedrals across Europe can be found the curious addition of zodiac symbols, whether as facade reliefs, mosaics, or floor medallions, or even in stained glass windows. Before astrology was considered heretical and therefore banned by the Church, it was absorbed as part of everyday life. The twelve zodiac signs and constellations represented not so much the esoteric qualities associated with astral magic, but simply the months of the year and the typical activities that were identified with each zodiac month.

In France, great examples can be found in Chartres Cathedral, which has a magnificent zodiac rose window dating to 1217 and other zodiac associated statues in the west and north sections of the building. Similarly, Notre-Dame in Paris has a complete collection of zodiac signs, with accompanying monthly activities and associated sins, in its west rose window, as well as in the sculptures on the portals of the west facade. Small numbers of surviving zodiac signs and their associated labors can be found in several French churches: one of the finest examples is in the town of Avallon in Burgundy.

The pulpit at San Miniato Basilica, Florence, was constructed by the same team of stonemasons as the floor zodiac.

Meanwhile, in Italy, the cathedral at Otranto is well known for its eastern nave section of zodiac mosaics, and in Canterbury Cathedral, England, an inset in the floor on either side of where Thomas à Becket's shrine used to stand, is a set of thirteenth-century floor medallions depicting months, labors, vices, and virtues among the stunning bronze zodiac signs.

Although not embraced as part of Orthodox Jewish religion, the astral culture of the Greco-Roman period appealed to the non-Rabbinic mystical Jews. For example, at the Beth Alpha sixth-century synagogue at the foot of the Gilboa mountains, near Beit She'an, Israel, is a fine example of a Jewish adaptation of the Greco-Roman zodiac. The twelve signs appear in the outer circle, whereas the sun god, Helios, features in all his glory in the inner circle. The outer circle consists of twelve panels, each of which corresponds to one of the twelve months of the year and contains the appropriate symbol for each zodiac sign. Four female figures, symbolizing the four seasons, appear in the four corners immediately outside the zodiac. It seems that for all the attempts of organized religions to stamp out pagan beliefs, the zodiac continued to remain entrenched in religious art and architecture, just as it remains so perfectly set in the sky.

This fresco (1573) at the cathedral of Santa Severina, Italy, depicts the thirteenth-century Italian prophet, Joachim di Fiore.

BOOK OF RAZIEL THE ANGEL
SINAI PENINSULA thirteenth century

A medieval practical grimoire of Kabbalistic magic

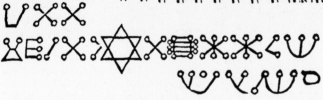

The **Book of Raziel the Angel** includes a complete collection of magical talismans and sigils for performing protective spells and for creating healing amulets.

Legends surrounding the Book of Raziel the Angel recount how it was originally a work of the secrets of all knowledge revealed to Adam by the angel Raziel. The archangel Raziel stood close by God's throne and therefore heard and wrote down everything that was spoken. Raziel purportedly gave the book to Adam, after Adam and Eve ate from the forbidden tree, so he could better understand God. Raziel's fellow archangels were angry that he had given away the knowledge to humanity, and stole the book from Adam and threw it into the ocean. God decided not to punish Raziel, but instead retrieved the book by sending another angel down to the ocean to find it and returned it to Adam and Eve.

According to some sources, the book was eventually passed on to Enoch, who later became the angel Metatron—guardian of celestial treasures—and who may have incorporated his own writings into the work. After Enoch, the archangel Raphael gave the book to Noah, who used the wisdom within it to build the ark. Later, the Book of Raziel the Angel was said to have come into the possession of King Solomon, and a number of texts attributed to Solomon's specific volume have appeared recently.

Most historians consider that the Book of Raziel the Angel originated in the thirteenth century, but had drawn on older texts. The likely compiler of the medieval version is the Jewish mystic Eleazer of Worms, who combined several Kabbalistic mystical works. The complete tome was subsequently divided into five books. Some of it is in the form of a mystical story of creation, but it mostly features an elaborate angelology, magical uses of the zodiac, gematria, names of God, protective spells, and a method of writing magical healing amulets. According to the work by Eleazer of Worms, it was Raziel who taught Adam the power of speech and the power of the soul within the confines of the physical body and physical world. Raziel taught Adam that by using "magic"—whether gematria or by invoking planetary forces via talismans—one could shape one's life, rather than accept that it was fated. Gematria was an Assyro-Babylonian system of numerology, adopted by Jewish mystics, that assigned numerical value to a word or phrase, and thus gave the word and the number magical properties. Each letter of the Hebrew alphabet is deeply symbolic, both in the sound it makes and its position in a word.

KABBALAH

Raziel's book was notoriously popular in German Renaissance magic, and together with the *Picatrix*—another handbook of talismanic magic—it was considered heretical by the Church. It was during the Renaissance that many occult practitioners combined heretic thought, Christian belief, and mystical Kabbalah into their esoteric exploration. Kabbalah is an ancient Judaic wisdom that reveals how the universe and life work. On a literal level, the word "Kabbalah" means "to receive." It teaches how to receive fulfillment in one's life.

Medieval Kabbalists believed that all things are linked to God through the sephirot, known as the ten emanations of God. These emanations make all levels of creation part of one great, gradually descending, chain of being. According to Lurianic Kabbalah's cosmology, the sephirot correspond to various levels of creation in each of the four worlds, and four worlds within each of the larger four worlds, each containing ten sephirot, which themselves contain ten sephirot, and so on, to infinity. These emanated from the creator, when creating the universe. Today, the Kabbalah is a popular form of mysticism and flourishes both as part of a new wave of Jewish liberal traditions and as part of esoteric Western non-Jewish spirituality.

KABBALAH SYMBOLS

EIN SOF
This represents God's light and the infinite nature of God that existed before creation. It is an unknowable nothingness that manifested as the God of creation and is worshipped via the sephirot.

SEPHIROT
The Kabbalah tree of life is often inverted, and rooted in heaven. Each of the ten stages, known as sephirot, are symbolic of the different aspects of an individual's deepening relationship with God. They are connected to others by channels and groups of emanations.

SEVENTY-TWO NAMES OF GOD
This symbol is used in Kabbalah meditation and is said to have enabled prophets to perform miracles. The seventy-two names derive from three verses of Exodus, each of which contains seventy-two Hebrew letters. By taking a letter from each verse, working from left to right for the first verse, then right to left for the second, and so on, the seventy-two names of God are formed.

TETRAKTYS
A symbol of the cosmos, based on Pythagoras's original pyramid of creation symbol, this version uses the letters of the Hebrew alphabet that spell out the four-lettered name of God: Y. H. W. H.

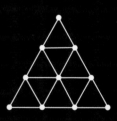

HEBREW TRIAD
The Hebrew triad is a graphic depiction or sign for the first three sephirot. It symbolizes the father on the left, the mother on the right, and the crown in the center.

SIGILLUM DEI

LONDON, ENGLAND fourteenth century

A magical sigil created by astrologer John Dee

The Sigillum Dei was first described in a fourteenth-century grimoire and later utilized by sixteenth-century astrologer John Dee.

The Sigillum Dei, or Seal of God, was a sigil used by Elizabethan mathematician, astrologer, and magician John Dee in his angel conjuring. It was developed by Dee from a fourteenth-century magical diagram composed of two circles, a pentagram, and three heptagons labeled with the name of God and his angels. Dee created it as a multi-faceted symbolic map, believed to be capable of invoking the power of the angels.

Sigils were amulets that, according to ancient texts, allowed the initiated magician to have power over all creatures except Archangels. The word "sigil" originates from the Latin word for "seal." However, a Hebrew word, which

may be associated with the Latin version *segulah*, describes very accurately what a sigil is. *Segulah* means a "word, action, or item of spiritual effect," similar to a talisman. Sigils usually appear as drawn symbols, but they can be created as three-dimensional objects. Whether complex or simple, in either case their design and creation will have an intricate and secret series of meanings attached to them. Sigils are usually made up of many different elements, and astrological signs and corresponding planets all have their own sigils.

Dee was a true Renaissance man, embodying everything about the Renaissance, from its esoteric and literary revival, its art, and its search for the truth and divine knowledge, to the scientific revolution that seemed to oppose all that the Renaissance truly represented: the rebirth of the golden age. For Dee, the development of science was simply a discovery of all that was already stored in the cosmic mind waiting to be revealed by man, and the secrets of the universe were being discovered in a variety of ways. Some of those who are considered the founders of modern science, such as Copernicus, Tycho Brahe, Johannes Kepler, and Isaac Newton also had a deep interest in the mystical world.

Although Dee dabbled in magic, like many other scientists and philosophers of his day, he was particularly interested in a book called the *Steganographia*, ostensibly a work on angelic magic created by the monk Johannes Trithemius. Dee had already used skryers (mediums or channelers) to contact spirits. But with the arrival into his personal life of Edward Kelly in 1582, the angels appeared to be more easily invoked. It seems that Kelly had a powerful influence over Dee to such an extent that by the time of their split, in 1587, Kelly had not only become a prominent alchemist in his own right, but he had also persuaded Dee to a wife swap.

Among Dee's collection of reflective objects that he used as tools for his occult work was an obsidian mirror. Aztec priests used highly polished mirrors in a variety of rituals: for divination, accessing the underworld, and communicating with the spirits of the dead. These mirrors were associated with Tezcatlipoca, the Aztec god of rulers, warriors, and sorcerers, whose name can be translated as "Smoking Mirror." Dee's obsidian mirror, made of highly polished volcanic glass, was one of many treasures brought to Europe after the conquest of Mexico by Hernán Cortés between 1527 and 1530.

Medieval magicians used sigils to call up angels, demons, and other spirits. Each entity had its own sigil, which represented its essential nature, a sort of spiritual signature or blueprint of that entity. Sigils were powerful magical tools in the right, and even the wrong, hands. Throughout medieval grimoires (spell books)

This mask is of the Aztec sorcerer god Tezcatlipoca, whose name means "Smoking Mirror." Dee's obsidian mirror was associated with Tezcatlipoca.

and magic texts are pages and pages of sigils, most notably in the work titled the "Lesser Key of Solomon." This anonymous seventeenth-century text contains a complete reference guide to the personal sigils of seventy-two demons of hell.

Also known as the "Clavicula Salomonis Regis," the work is divided into five books. One book instructs the magician on how to create a wax tablet with specific designs intended to contact angels via scrying, or using a crystal ball or other reflective material to "view" the spirit world. Another book contains a series of prayers intended to grant instantaneous learning to the magician.

Once the adept had learned how to use a sigil, and gave correct attention to the ritual and outcome, he would quickly have power over the very thing or entity he was conjuring up. More recently, self-professed adepts, such as occultist Aleister Crowley, have used sigils in their mystical and magical explorations. In Wiccan practice, sigil magic is still used to cast a spell to attract the object of your desire, as an alternative to cosmic ordering.

This hieroglyph, made up of symbols of the sun, moon, and stars, is used to represent John Dee.

SANDPAINTING

NORTH AMERICA *c.* 1400

Magical designs made on the floor in healing and ritual ceremonial magic

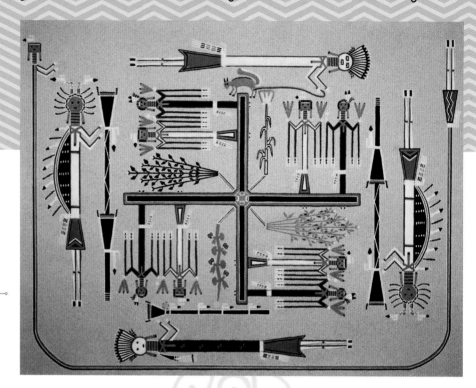

This Navajo sandpainting depicts the Whirling Logs narrative, often identified with the curing ceremony known as the Nightway chant.

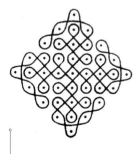

The sikku kolam is usually symmetrical when viewed from any direction. Sikku means "knot."

The Navajo peoples of southwestern United States are renowned for their sandpainting and its use in healing and ritual ceremonial magic. Sandpainting is the art of pouring colored sands or powdered pigments from minerals or crystals onto a surface to make a fixed, or unfixed, sandpainting. Unfixed sandpaintings have a long established cultural history in numerous social groupings around the globe, and are often temporary, ritual paintings prepared for religious or healing ceremonies. For example, this kind of sandpainting is used by Tibetan and Buddhist monks and Australian indigenous peoples, as well as by Latin Americans on certain Christian holy days.

In the sandpainting of the Navajo, the medicine man paints on the ground of the "hogan"—a traditional Navajo dwelling—or wherever the ceremony is taking place. With great control and skill, he lets the colored sand flow loosely through his fingers to create the sandpainting, which can also be performed on a buckskin or cloth tarpaulin. According to experts, there are about 600 to 1,000 different traditional designs for sandpaintings. The Navajo people do not regard the paintings as static objects, but as spiritual, living beings to be treated with great respect. More than thirty different sandpaintings may be associated with one ceremony.

The colors for the painting are usually made with naturally colored sand: crushed gypsum for white, yellow ocher, red sandstone, charcoal, and a mixture of charcoal and gypsum to make blue. Other coloring agents include cornmeal, flower pollen, and powdered roots and bark.

The paintings are usually made for healing or other ritual purposes. Many of them contain images of yeibichai: supernatural beings who created the Navajo people and taught them how to live in harmony with the universe. While creating the painting, the medicine man will chant, asking the yeibichai to come into the painting and help heal the patient.

Similarly, dating back to the fifteenth century in Japan, Buddhist artists practiced the craft of bonseki. This was a way of sprinkling dry colored sand and pebbles onto the surface of plain black lacquered trays. They used bird feathers as brushes to move the sandy surface into seascapes and landscapes. These Japanese Buddhist tray paintings probably evolved from the more intricate brightly colored Buddhist sand mandalas created by Tibetan Buddhist monks and also from the kolams of India.

Kolam designs are derived from ancient magical motifs and abstract designs blended with later philosophic and religious motifs. Symbols may include fish, birds, and other animal images to represent the unity of man and beast. Also used are designs for the sun, moon, and other zodiac symbols, representing the

Sandpainting appears in many cultures worldwide, as seen in this Australian Aboriginal Yuendumu design and its striking wave pattern.

cosmos and the power of the planets. The ritual kolam patterns created for special occasions such as weddings often stretch all the way down the street. Many of these created patterns have been passed on generation to generation, from mothers to daughters.

KOLAM

A kolam is a form of sacred painting performed in various regions of India, as well as in Indonesia, Malaysia, and Thailand. Kolams are drawn by using rice, chalk, or rock powder as well as naturally pigmented colored powders. They are usually geometrical line drawings composed of curved loops, drawn around a grid pattern of dots. In South India, Hindu female family members practice this art outside the front of their homes. More complex kolams are drawn and colors are often added during holiday occasions and for special events.

Traditionally, kolams are a sign of invitation or welcome into the home, mostly to Lakshmi, goddess of prosperity and wealth. The patterns range from mathematical line drawings around a matrix of dots to free-form artwork and closed shapes. The lines must be completed to symbolically prevent evil spirits from entering the inside of the shapes, and therefore the inside of the home.

LADY AND THE UNICORN TAPESTRY
FLANDERS fifteenth century

Series of tapestries that presents the idea of a mystical sixth sense

The mysterious sixth tapestry in the Cluny Museum, Paris, is thought to represent the sixth sense or to be a mystic symbol of how the soul is connected to the stars.

This beautiful series of fifteenth-century tapestries was woven in Flanders, an area that is now part of Holland and Belgium. Discovered by writer and archaeologist Prosper Merimée at the Château de Boussac in the Limousin region of France, the tapestries soon became known as important works of medieval art history, and were eventually bought by the Cluny Museum in Paris in 1882.

There are six tapestries: five of them represent the well-known five senses—*La gout* (taste); *L'ouie* (sound); *La vue* (sight); *L'odorat* (smell); and *Le toucher* (touch). In each of the five tapestries depicting the temptation of the sensual world, an unknown lady is accompanied by a lion and a unicorn, as well as by a collection of other familiar animals such as rabbits, dogs, monkeys, and birds. However, the sixth tapestry, the meaning of which has been subject to much debate, represents the mysterious sixth sense.

There are some accounts that the sixth tapestry, on the wall opposite the other five, represents an unknown mystical essence: either the soul itself or perhaps an esoteric riddle or secret known only to the owner. It has a strange statement written across the top of a tournament tent—*A mon seul desir*. This is often translated as "my only desire" or "to my heart's desire," but it could also be a play on the word *seul*. In French *seul* means "only," but early Saxon, Germanic, and Flemish words for "soul" have spellings such as *seola* and *seula*. The woven inscription could be referring to the soul and not to the ego's desire.

The word *desir* in fourteenth-century France meant "lust," but the term "desire" is rooted in an early Latin word meaning "of the stars." In other words, the phrase could have been a secret or mystical lure, and a way of revealing that the soul is connected to the stars.

Whether the lady is putting the necklace into the casket or taking it out has been hotly debated, too. Some historians believe that she does not want to be led astray by her senses or her desires, and has decided to remain pure and virtuous and put back the tempting jewels. Others argue that she is open to seduction and to being led astray.

Many historians now believe that the series of tapestries is an allegory of courtly love. In the Middle Ages, ladies of the court were idolized by heroic knights, while minstrels, poets, and troubadours roamed the courts of Europe singing and telling love stories. Knights sent tokens and secret messages and spent hours romanticizing their chosen lady, who was often married to a noble and unavailable. Unrequited love was fashionable, and a lady's sexual power, considered evil by the Catholic Church, was idealized by the chivalrous knight or lover. The more the desire for her, the less she was available, and the more erotic the experience.

The unicorn is rich in magical symbolism. In the earliest myths of ancient Greece, the unicorn had supernatural powers. By the Middle Ages, in Christian myth, the unicorn had become known as a mystical wild beast, only tameable by a virgin. It also became a mythic symbol of the "lady" as being as pure as the Virgin Mary and

the unicorn a symbol of the resurrected Christ. However, in the popular imagination and in the courts of Europe, the ancient threads of the myth carried on in the allegories of courtly love. Here the unicorn represented the lover, or the knight in shining armor, who placed his head in the lady's lap: a symbol of surrender to her power. In one tapestry, the unicorn places his paws in the lady's lap and looks in the mirror to see his own lust reflected there.

The tapestries were apparently made for Jean Le Viste, a wealthy aristocrat who was promoted to the French court in 1489. His family coat of arms can be seen throughout. Le Viste's family had bought their way into nobility, and it is believed that the tapestries were made to show off Jean's rise to great wealth, or that he had them made as a secret demonstration of his love for a woman other than his wife. Whatever the story, this set of tapestries reveals not only how the symbols of romance and love can be woven into Christian mysticism but also how several allegories can be mirrored in each other.

This fifteenth-century manuscript illumination of troubadours is from Alphonse Le Sage's Cantigas de Santa Maria.

The unicorn, with its supernatural powers, was adopted by Christianity as a symbol of the Resurrection.

TAROT
ITALY fifteenth century

A universal language of archetypal symbols

Ladies and Gentlemen Playing Tarot is an Early Renaissance painting from the Lombard School, Italy, showing a group possibly using the tarot to determine their future.

The tarot may have originated several thousand years before the Common Era in ancient Egypt, when places such as Giza and Abydos were centers for mystical practice and the worship of gods. Certain symbols were created to produce a secret language known only to initiates of these mysteries. However, the earliest known decks of tarot cards appeared in Italy in the fifteenth century. The Renaissance heralded a renewed interest in ancient esoteric mysteries, and a significant number of tarot decks were developed in Italy, such as the exquisite Visconti-Sforza deck, painted for the fifteenth-century duke of Milan.

The tarot is usually made up of a deck of seventy-eight cards rich in symbolism and imagery, although some early decks have a different amount of cards. Each card has a name, number, and specific image, and these work together to create the card's meaning. The tarot is quite simply a universal language spoken through the use of archetypal symbols.

The structure of the tarot deck is made up of twenty-two main cards, known as the Major Arcana, and four suits of fourteen cards, called the Minor Arcana. The twenty-two cards represent universal archetypes, whereas the Minor Arcana represents the way these manifest in daily life. The term *arcana* is the Latin plural of *arcanum*, meaning "secret," so the Major and Minor Arcana refer to big secrets and little secrets.

An archetype is a quality, essence, blueprint, or original model of behavior, personality, feelings, experience, or idea. Throughout history, certain words, symbols, and codes have been used to describe these archetypes. According to psychoanalyst Carl Jung, we all resonate to these symbols because they are carried in both our personal and collective unconscious.

Antoine Court de Gébelin, an eighteenth-century French linguist and Freemason, believed the word "tarot" was derived from the name of the Egyptian god of wisdom, Thoth. He went on to suggest that the twenty-two main cards were based on an ancient set of tablets of mystical wisdom, saved from the ruins of a burning temple. This Book of Thoth outlined a secret language in which all gods could be contacted through hieroglyphs and numbers.

He also discovered that the hieroglyph "tar" meant "way" or "road," and "ro" meant "king," so together they meant the "royal road of life." From stone carvings, there is evidence of sets of Thoth tablets used by pharaohs to discover their future. Many scholars agree that after the Greeks conquered Alexandria, mystics and seers from Egypt probably translated these hieroglyphs into images that could be understood in Europe. Some nineteenth-century scholars prefer to believe the word "tarot" is partly formed from an anagram of the Latin word *rota* meaning "wheel." In occult circles, "rota" means the eternal ending and beginning of cycles of change, as revealed through tarot card readings.

SYMBOLIC MEANINGS OF THE MAJOR ARCANA CARDS

THE FOOL
Astrology key: Uranus
Keyword: Adventure

THE MAGICIAN
Astrology key: Mercury
Keyword: Manifestation

THE HIGH PRIESTESS
Astrology key:
the Moon
Keyword: Secrets

THE EMPRESS
Astrology key: Venus
Keyword: Abundance

THE EMPEROR
Astrology key: Aries
Keyword: Authority

THE HIEROPHANT
Astrology key: Taurus
Keyword: Knowledge

THE LOVERS
Astrology key: Gemini
Keyword: Love

THE CHARIOT
Astrology key: Cancer
Keyword: Willpower

STRENGTH
Astrology key: Leo
Keyword: Courage

THE HERMIT
Astrology key: Virgo
Keyword: Soul-searching

THE WHEEL OF FORTUNE
Astrology key: Jupiter
Keyword: Beginning

JUSTICE
Astrology key: Libra
Keyword: Balance

THE HANGED MAN
Astrology key: Neptune
Keyword: Sacrifice

DEATH
Astrology key: Scorpio
Keyword: Change

TEMPERANCE
Astrology key:
Sagittarius
Keyword: Compromise

THE DEVIL
Astrology key:
Capricorn
Keyword: Illusion

THE TOWER
Astrology key: Mars
Keyword: Disruption

THE STAR
Astrology key:
Aquarius
Keyword: Realization

THE MOON
Astrology key: Pisces
Keyword: Confusion

THE SUN
Astrology key: the Sun
Keyword: Joy

JUDGMENT
Astrology key: Pluto
Keyword: Liberation

THE WORLD
Astrology key: Saturn
Keyword: Fulfillment

The Major Arcana cards in the tarot deck depict a range of simple images, such as Death, The Magician, and The Hanged Man, easily interpreted by adepts.

TAROT CARDS

THE FOOL

Associated with the planet Uranus and the number zero, this card indicates the querent is ready to take a risk. The fool is an eternal optimist. He represents new beginnings, unconventional life quests, and the urge to leap in at the deep end. He reminds us that resistance is sometimes more foolish than risk.

THE MAGICIAN

A magician stands before a table; he holds a wand in one hand pointing to the sky and points to the earth with the other. Linked to Mercury and the number one, this card symbolizes putting ideas into action and manifesting dreams. It indicates it is time to juggle with ideas, adapt to changing circumstances, and be ready to persuade others of plans.

THE HIGH PRIESTESS

Associated with the Moon, the number two, hidden things, and secrets, the high priestess card usually indicates that a secret is about to be revealed, either one of the querent's own or one from someone close to them. Alternatively, it may mean that a wise woman or a healer will be of beneficial influence in the future.

THE HANGED MAN

This strange card is about seeing the truth from a new angle. It represents doing something we had not anticipated doing that will bring benefits. In fact, like the upside down man, seeing things from a very different angle is the answer to success. It means that we may have to give up an old belief, idea, or feeling to be happy.

DEATH

Although often seen as a portent of doom, death is simply about closing one door and opening another. It represents the parting of ways, the closing of doors, and the dumping of emotional baggage. Inevitable change means that other doors will open and that new emotions will bring happiness, as will new encounters.

THE TOWER

The tower itself represents structure in our personal world. But the lightning symbolizes unexpected or external events that happen to change our life or force us to rethink our lives. This card indicates that it is time to adjust quickly to change; it will be for the better, but we must accept the challenge and chaos around us.

THE HIEROPHANT

This card represents being influenced by a religious figure or someone from a traditional establishment. When this card is drawn, the querent needs to conform to and trust what others are saying, or to listen to advice from a guru or trustworthy friend. It can also represent that doing what is expected is the right pathway.

THE LOVERS

Two naked lovers are watched over by an angel. In some tarot decks a third person appears in the scene, as if a choice must be made. Associated with Gemini and couples, this card suggests that a love relationship will be hugely influential, and that in the future an important choice or a commitment must be made.

WHEEL OF FORTUNE

This card represents a turning point, the changing cycles in our lives, and how we are both influenced by apparent fate and our own free will. There will be choices to be made, new journeys to begin, and the chance to jump on the bandwagon. It also indicates that luck can be both good and bad, depending on our perspective.

THE STAR

The ancients used the stars as a method of navigation, and when the querent draws the star card we know that we can trust in the universe to help us manifest our goals. Associated with Aquarius, the star card always implies progress, renewed self-confidence, and a time for inspiration and "seeing the light."

JUDGMENT

This card means that it is time to wake up and liberate oneself from the past, to re-evaluate what one has and has not got, and to accept the truth. It always indicates that we can drop old values and accept new ones. Very soon, the weight of guilt, self-sabotage, or blame will be lifted from our shoulders, bringing a time to start afresh.

THE WORLD

Accomplishing our dreams is what the world is all about. When we draw the world card, we know that this is going to be a time when the world is our oyster. It is time to complete a project or be rewarded for something. What we can do now is to feel good about our plans for the future and be at one with the universe.

DIVINATION CALENDARS
MEXICO *c.* 1520

Aztec codices depicting sacred divination calendars

Page 13 of the Codex Borbonicus reveals a period of thirteen days, starting with 1 Earthquake, 2 Flint/Knife, and 3 Rain on the bottom row.

In Aztec culture, the goddess Tlazolteotl was the "eater of filth," who absorbed sins and redeemed the guilty.

The Codex Borbonicus was commissioned by the Spanish authorities in *c.* 1520, and it comprises a single 46-foot-long (14 m) sheet of amate paper. The paper was made from the ficus tree, which was considered to have magical properties. The codex can be divided into three sections, and the first section is one of the most intricate surviving sacred divination calendars. Most of the page features a painting of the ruling deity or deities, with the remainder taken up by the thirteen day signs of the trecena (period of thirteen days) and thirteen other glyphs and deities. With these twenty-six symbols, the priests were able to create horoscopes and divine the future.

Although there were originally forty accordion-folded pages, the first two and the last two are missing. Like all pre-Columbian codices, it was entirely pictorial in nature, although some Spanish descriptions were added at a later date. The first eighteen pages of the codex (all that remains of the original twenty) show considerably more wear than the later sections, which very likely indicates that these pages were consulted more often. The original page thirteen of the Codex Borbonicus shows the thirteenth trecena of the Aztec's 260-day calendar, which was divided into twenty trecenas. This thirteenth trecena was under the auspices of the goddess Tlazolteotl, who is shown on the upper left wearing a flayed skin and giving birth to Cinteotl, the maize god.

The second section of the codex documents the Mesoamerican fifty-two-year cycle, showing in order the dates of the first days of each of these fifty-two solar years. These days are correlated with the nine lords of the night. The third section is focused on rituals and ceremonies, particularly those that end the fifty-two-year cycle. The sequence apparently finishes with a New Fire ceremony, marking the end of one cycle and the start of another.

CODEX BORGIA

The Mesoamerican Codex Borgia is considered to be one of the finest Aztec ritual and divinatory manuscripts discovered. It is generally believed to have been written before the Spanish conquest of Mexico and is named after its first known owner in the late eighteenth century, Cardinal Stefano Borgia. The codex is made of animal skins folded into thirty-nine sheets, making a total length of almost 35 feet (11 m). All but the end sheets are painted on both sides, providing seventy-six pages, and the codex is read from right to left.

The first eight pages list the 260 day signs of the tonalpohualli (day sign), while each trecena of thirteen signs forms a horizontal row spanning two pages. Certain days are marked with a footprint symbol, while divinatory symbols are placed above and below the day signs. Pages nine to thirteen are divided into four quarters. Each quarter contains one of the twenty day signs, its patron deity, and associated symbols.

Page fourteen is divided into nine sections for each of the nine lords of the night. They are accompanied by a day sign and symbols indicating positive or negative associations.

Pages twenty-nine through forty-six apparently show a journey, but the complex iconography and the lack of any comparable document have led to a variety of interpretations. These range from an account of actual astronomical and historical events, to the passage of Quetzalcoatl in the form of the planet Venus, a journey through the underworld, or a narrative of the creation of the cosmos.

Page seventy-one depicts Tonatiuh, the sun god, receiving blood from a decapitated bird. Surrounding the scene are the thirteen birds of the day, which correspond to each of the thirteen days of a trecena.

The pre-Columbian codices are considered to be a superb documentation of early Aztec culture. Most of them included divinatory calendars and specific dates and cycles when rituals were meant to be performed. Later codices, such as the Boturini Codex that depicts a legendary Aztec journey, are valuable social records of Aztec rulers and their history.

In the Codex Borgia, the sun god Tonatiuh is surrounded by the thirteen birds of each day, used to divine the future by Aztec priests.

PORTA ALCHEMICA
ROME, ITALY 1678–1680

The only surviving gate to an ancient villa with alchemical inscriptions

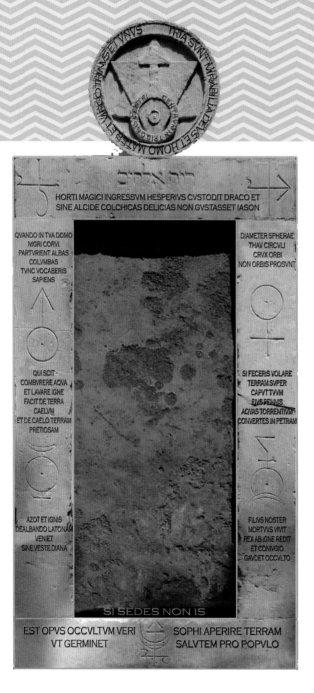

Surrounding the Porta Alchemica are symbols, sigils, and Latin inscriptions, said to be clues to discovering the secret formula for making gold.

To the east of the historic center of Rome on Esquiline Hill is a strange blocked-up gateway, an entrance to where the Villa Palombara once stood. The doorway, known as the Porta Alchemica, or Alchemical Doorway, is the only survivor of the villa's five gateways.

During the mid seventeenth century, the villa belonged to Massimiliano Palombara, marquis of Pietraforte. A Rosicrucian and member of the elite circles of Rome, the marquis was fascinated by the esoteric arts, and his wealth and social position enabled him to act as a patron to a number of alchemists. In his villa, he often held meetings attended by important people who shared his interests, such as the eccentric Swedish queen, Christina, who lived in Rome after her abdication. Other adepts included distinguished astronomer Gian Domenico Cassini, renowned scholar Athanasius Kircher, and a young doctor and alchemist from Milan named Giuseppe Borri. Borri had been expelled from the Jesuit college where he studied medicine due to his dabbling in alchemy.

There are a number of legends concerning Borri and the Porta Alchemica. One tells that Borri, sponsored by the marquis, carried out several experiments to discover the mythical philosopher's stone and to turn lead into gold. However, one night he disappeared suddenly after being told that he was being followed by the Inquisition. He left behind a number of papers inscribed with mysterious symbols that nobody was able to interpret. The marquis had them inscribed on the doorway of his laboratory, and they were transferred to the outer gateway.

According to another legend from a historical record dated 1802, Borri stayed for a night in the gardens of the villa in search of a mysterious herb capable of producing gold. The next morning he was seen fleeing in haste through the doorway, but left behind a few flakes of gold, the result of his successful alchemical transmutation. He also left a mysterious document full of puzzles and magic symbols that were believed to contain the secret formula. Vexed by the symbols and riddles, the marquis had them engraved on all five gates of the villa and on the walls of the mansion, in the hope that one day someone would be able to decipher them.

MURDEROUS PLOT

There is another more sinister tale. The enigmatic Queen Christina had a secret alchemical laboratory built for herself at Riario Palace, where she lived while in Rome. It is believed that, with the help of Borri, she discovered the secret formula for producing gold. To celebrate the discovery, at some time between 1678 and 1680, Borri collaborated with Athanasius Kircher to construct the Porta Alchemica. The doorway was designed by an architect friend of Kircher, the well-known Baroque painter and sculptor Gian Lorenzo Bernini, who engraved the secrets of the alchemical experiment on the door. It is suggested that Borri, fearful that the marquis, Bernini, and Kircher would work out the formula from the symbols, had the three men murdered by poison on November 28, 1680. It seems that Borri wanted to keep the secret for himself and fled with the knowledge, assured that no one would be able to decipher the secret.

Six sigils around the doorway have curious phrases attached to them. For example, the sigil for Saturn/lead is accompanied by "When in your house black crows give birth to white doves, then will you be called wise." The phrase next to the Mars/iron sigil reads: "He who can burn with water and wash with fire makes a heaven of earth and a precious earth of heaven." For the Venus/bronze sigil is the inscription, "If you make the earth fly upside down, with its wings you may convert torrential waters to stone," and on the base, for Vitriol/sulfuric acid, is the phrase, "It is an occult work of true wisdom to open the earth, so that it may generate salvation for the people."

There is a palindrome—SI SEDES NON IS—on the doorstep, which, when read from left to right, means "If you sit, you do not proceed." However, from right to left—SI NON SEDES IS—the meaning is "If you do not sit, you proceed." In either direction, this alludes to the idea that if you persist in your progress, you may find the philosopher's stone. The inscription also suggests that the door may have represented a Rosicrucian-based threshold, across which adepts symbolically crossed. This was in order to reach the highest degree of purity of their souls. According to Rosicrucian principles, this was an absolute requirement in order to fathom the alchemic secrets.

The figures on both sides of the door were not originally from the villa. They were found near Quirinal Hill, where a large temple dedicated to the Egyptian gods Isis and Serapis once stood. During works for the opening of Piazza Vittorio in 1888, the statues were moved to stand beside the Porta Alchemica. Perhaps they make a fitting pair of guardians for the doorway's undeciphered secrets.

This portrait (left) from 1675 shows ex-Jesuit doctor Giuseppe Borri, who dabbled in alchemy but fled after being tracked down by the Inquisition.

Anselm van Hulle's portrait (right) depicts Queen Christina of Sweden, who abdicated to Rome and built herself a secret laboratory where she practiced the magical arts and alchemy.

This symbol can be seen in a prominent position at the top of the Porta Alchemica.

FREEMASON'S TRACING BOARD
ENGLAND c. 1700

Depicts the symbolic emblems of Freemasonry

This tracing board cloth from c. 1800 reveals the numerous symbols used to teach initiates about the secrets of Freemasonry.

The set and compass has layers of meaning, one of which is of God drawing up plans for the universe.

In the early eighteenth century, practicing Freemasons brought their tools, including objects such as ladders and even beehives, to the Masonic Lodge, where they were arranged and used to illustrate the mystery of Freemasonry. Due to the difficulty of filling lodges (usually privately hired rooms in taverns) with equipment, the more artistic Freemasons began to draw the objects on a tracing board as symbols. To begin with they were drawn on the floor in chalk and charcoal; later they were painted on small squares of marble and larger canvases. The painted cloth—sometimes more than 6 feet (1.8 m) in length—was either hung on the wall or laid flat on the floor. This way it became a functional part of initiation rituals.

Evidence suggests that a simple boundary in the shape of a square, rectangle (or double square), or cross was created first, with various Masonic symbols drawn later. Symbols of objects were added, and sometimes drawings were interchangeable with physical objects. At the end of the work, a new member was often required to erase the drawing with a mop, as a demonstration of his obligation to secrecy.

The time-consuming business of redrawing the symbols at every meeting was gradually replaced by keeping a removable "floor cloth" on which to display the symbols, and of which different portions could be revealed. By the mid nineteenth century tracing boards had become fairly common, and a variety of different forms and designs survive, some to be displayed on the floor and others vertically. If the tracing board was painted on canvas it could be displayed on an easel. As part of an initiate's degree, a Master Mason would give a standard lecture, during which he could point to the symbols illustrated as necessary.

Sets of three boards, corresponding to the three degrees, are now an accepted, though unofficial, part of Craft Freemasonry, and there are sometimes tracing boards in other degrees. Since different Masonic traditions have now established standard degree rituals, the creation of new tracing boards by Freemasons has disappeared in favor of standard designs. However, the tracing board is still presented during the three Craft Masonic degrees, and it is also found in a few so-called higher degrees.

Freemasonry never set out to teach the art of stonemasonry, or any other mason's work, but to use work as a symbol or metaphor for moral development. These symbols include the set square, which puts initiates and members on the correct path to duty and moral obedience. The set of compasses is an important Masonic emblem, signifying God drawing his plans for the world. When merged with the set square—in other words, two triangular symbols—the combination of energies indicates the power of solar and lunar energy, or the opposites as one, such as the yin and yang symbol of Taoism. Similarly, the level symbolizes equality and justice, and it is always united in ritual work with the plumb rule. The latter is also an emblem of the junior warden of the lodge.

Handshakes and secret grips are part of symbolic gestures, too. It is believed that during a handshake, a true Freemason will press the thumb against the top of the first knuckle joint of their fellow Mason. Gripping another's hand with spread middle and fourth finger in a "V" shape like a lion's paw is said to be the sign of a Master Mason.

Although Freemasonry is shrouded in mystery and is often thought of as an elitist society deliberately masking its true intentions, its origins seem to have two paths. The first stems from the Middle Ages, at a time when across Europe many stonemasons were employed by royalty and by the Church to construct churches, cathedrals, and castles. There were two types of masons: the "rough" masons, who worked with crude stone; and the "freestone" masons, who worked with softer stone, carving, shaping, and producing stonework to architectural design. Eventually, the freestone masons formed their own guilds and created their own legislation concerning payment, craftsmanship, and morality, and its from these guilds that the lodges developed.

By contrast, one legend that is told to initiate Freemasons connects their roots to biblical times and the building of King Solomon's Temple in Jerusalem in 967 BCE. The temple was adopted as one of the Freemason's most potent symbols, because according to some Masonic scholars it was the most perfect, magnificent structure ever built. The legend tells that the builders of the temple were the forefathers of today's Freemasons. Solomon hired a great stonemason, Hiram Abiff, to oversee the work and he claimed that he had discovered all the

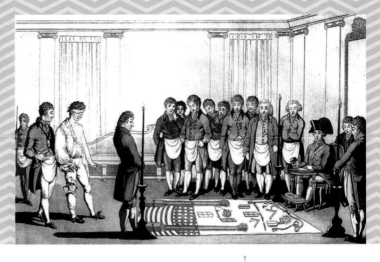

mystical secrets of the temple. After he refused to give away his secrets, he was murdered by three "rough" masons, and Solomon realized that with the loss of his architect, the secrets were lost, too. According to the myth, Solomon established a new secret, and this was the word "mahabone," meaning "the grand lodge door is open." This is now believed to be the password used to enter the third degree of Masonry.

This engraving (c. 1805) is based on one by Freemason Gabanon in 1745 and portrays an initiation ceremony.

PIGPEN CIPHER

The pigpen cipher used frequently among Freemasons to record secrets exchanges letters for specific symbols made up of various parts of a grid.

X MARKS THE SPOT

LOA

HAITI eighteenth century

Voodoo spirits that signify different aspects of the natural world

In *Voodoo Ceremony around a Holy Tree* (1963) by Gerard Valcin, the spirits of everything in nature are worshipped and invoked for the celebration.

The spirits, or loas, of voodoo culture manifest in various ways. Beneath the supreme divine being known as the Gran Met (or Great Master), there is a multitude of loas. They are usually ancestral spirits, who signify different aspects of the natural world. Whether rivers, oceans, love, birth, trees, hunger, or abstract concepts, these spirits have the power to influence whatever they represent, for better or worse. Most voodoo believers invoke a loa at the start of a ritual by drawing the spirit's veve (symbol) on the ground. This is usually performed by sprinkling a powderlike substance—commonly cornmeal, wheat flour, bark, or some kind of powder—in one continuous line or a series of lines. In Haitian voodoo, a mixture of cornmeal and wood ash is used.

There are two types of loa. These are the rada, or kind spirits, who are thought to be of African origin, and the petro, or bitter spirits, who are vengeful and thought to be of Caribbean origin. Practitioners of rada are believed to provide beneficial white magic, and to create charms and talismans known as wanga for protection; they also make love potions and healing balms. A darker form of voodoo is associated with sorcery and black magic, where the petro spirits are invoked, and it is this form that has led to voodoo's association with all things evil.

Each loa has a different symbol made up of a unique combination of motifs, signifying different aspects of their power. In return for food, usually given by the worshippers in the form of bread, candies, or a symbolic animal sacrifice, the loa provides good fortune and protection from evil spirits.

Veves are believed to derive from the beliefs of either the indigenous Caribbean peoples or of the Kongo peoples of West Africa. Other theories suggest that the symbols may also have originated from the Nsibidi system of writing, practiced in southern Nigeria and transported to Haiti through the Atlantic slave trade, thus evolving into the veve. Every loa has his or her own unique veve, although regional differences have led to different veves for the same loa. Veves can also be made into screen prints, paintings, patchwork, wall hangings, artworks, and banners.

HAITIAN VOODOO

Originating from the West African word *vodun*, meaning "spirit," voodoo is essentially a Haitian religion that began in the slave era of the eighteenth century. It combines elements from a number of different African beliefs that

were kept alive by the slaves when combined with Christian rituals. They also gave Christian names to the old spirits but retained the original symbolism. Often associated with black magic and evil spirits, voodoo was and still is regarded with great suspicion by outsiders.

In Haitian voodoo, Papa Legba is the spirit or loa who serves as the intermediary between all the spirits and humanity. He stands at a spiritual crossroads and gives (or denies) permission to speak with the loa. His veve acts as a beacon for other spirits, and a symbol of his presence during practical rituals and healings. Papa Legba is always the first and last spirit invoked in any ceremony, because his permission is needed for any communication between mortals and loa. He is likened to a spiritual doorman, who opens and closes the door between the mundane and spiritual worlds.

In Haiti, he is considered the god of communication, and his invocation also helps in the healing of speech or thought processes. In the Yoruba tradition of West Africa, Cuba, and Brazil, a spirit known as Elegua is also associated with Papa Legba since both share the role of being god of the crossroads. In contrast to Papa Legba, however, Elegua is a trickster spirit. Legba is often associated with Orunmila, the god of prophecy who taught humankind how to use the Ifa oracle, a system of divination practiced by the Yoruba peoples. In Benin and Nigeria, Legba is depicted as young and virile, and is often horned and phallic. His shrine is usually located at the gate of the village in the countryside.

Another important loa in Haitian voodoo is Baron Samedi, the deity of sex and death. Possessed by Baron Samedi, followers would sweep along in a trancelike dance behind a chief adept who would act out the part of the Baron. Originally a phallic ritual, this later became a dance of death when the Baron's orgies would end at the boundary of the afterlife. Although traditionally depicted dressed in black and with a top hat, in more recent times the Baron has been portrayed wearing sunglasses and twirling a cigarette holder between his fingers.

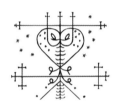

Veves (symbols) for voodoo loa (from top to bottom): Ogoun, the warrior spirit; Brigitte, who protects graveyards; and Legba, the spiritual doorman.

Among some African peoples, Legba is depicted as a youthful horned man with an erect phallus, as seen in this statue in the Tropenmuseum, Amsterdam.

INDEX

INDEX

PICTURE CREDITS